THE TEXT AND BEYOND

THE
TEXT & BEYOND

ESSAYS IN LITERARY LINGUISTICS

Edited by

Cynthia Goldin Bernstein

THE UNIVERSITY OF ALABAMA PRESS
Tuscaloosa and London

Library of Congress Cataloging-in-Publication Data

The Text and beyond : essays in literary linguistics / edited Cynthia
Goldin Bernstein.
    p.   cm.
   ISBN 0-8173-0699-4
   1. Discourse analysis, Literary. 2. Criticism. I. Bernstein,
Cynthia Goldin, 1947–
   P302.5.T49   1994
   808'.0014—dc20   93-29447

British Library Cataloguing-in-Publication Data available

In loving memory of
Bryan and Laura Bernstein

Contents

Preface

This book provides a collection of suggestive models for the student or scholar who is interested in using the tools of linguistics to meet the aims of literary criticism and theory. The idea for a book on literary linguistics grew out of a special issue I edited for *South Central Review* (Summer 1990). My purpose there, as here, was to show that linguistic approaches to literature could extend beyond the text to all those things outside it that contribute to our understanding of language: history, culture, politics, social context. The quantity and range of papers I received made it clear that a book would be needed even to begin to explore how linguistics might inform the study of literature.

The variety of approaches and kinds of texts included here are intended to encourage both the linguist and the literary critic to find value in what the other might offer. If the linguist comes to see the literary text as an authentic source of linguistic data and the literary critic finds in linguistics a means of accessing the literary text, then the aims of this book will have been met.

Acknowledgments

I gratefully acknowledge permission to publish the following material:

"I know a man," from *Collected Poems of Robert Creeley, 1945–1975*. Copyright © 1983 by The Regents of the University of California. Reprinted by permission of University of California Press.

From *The Glass Menagerie* by Tennessee Williams, copyright © 1945 by Tennessee Williams and Edwina D. Williams. Reprinted by permission of New Directions Pub. Corp.

"Logic and 'The Magic Flute,'" copyright © 1956 by Marianne Moore, from *The Complete Poems of Marianne Moore* by Marianne Moore. Used by permission of Viking Penguin, a division of Penguin Books USA Inc.

"The Monkey Puzzle," "The Jerboa," "Virginia Brittania," "Sea Unicorns and Land Unicorns," "The Frigate Pelican," "His Shield," and "Smooth Gnarled Crape Myrtle." Reprinted with permission of Macmillan Publishing Company from *Collected Poems of Marianne Moore*, copyright © 1935, 1941, 1951 by Marianne Moore. Copyrights renewed 1963 by Marianne Moore and T. S. Eliot, 1969 by Marianne Moore, and 1979 by Lawrence E. Brinn and Louise Crane.

From *Eight Corners of the World,* copyright © 1988 by Gordon Weaver. Used with permission from Chelsea Green Publishing Company, Post Mills, Vermont.

From *Who's Afraid of Virginia Woolf?* by Edward Albee. Reprinted with permission of Macmillan Publishing Company. Copyright © 1962 and renewed 1990 by Edward Albee.

From *American Buffalo* by David Mamet, copyright © 1981. Used with permission of Grove Press, Inc.

From *Endgame* by Samuel Beckett, copyright © 1958. Used with permission of Grove Press, Inc.

From *The Birthday Party* by Harold Pinter, copyright © 1976. Used with permission of Grove Press, Inc.

From *The Caretaker* by Harold Pinter, copyright © 1977. Used with permission of Grove Press, Inc.

Excerpts from *Save Me the Waltz* are reprinted with permission of Charles Scribner's Sons, an imprint of Macmillan Publishing Company, from *Zelda Fitzgerald: The Collected Writings,* edited by Matthew J. Bruccoli. Copyright © 1932 by Charles Scribner's Sons; renewal copyright © 1960 by Frances Scott Fitzgerald Lanahan.

From *Tender Is the Night* by F. Scott Fitzgerald. Copyright © 1931, 1934 by Charles Scribner's Sons. Copyrights renewed. Used by permission of Charles Scribner's Sons, an imprint of Macmillan Publishing Company.

From "Aufstiege" by Franco Biondi, in *Zu Hause in der Fremde,* edited by C. Schaffernicht, copyright © 1981. Used with permission of Verlag Atelier im Bauernhaus.

From "Verstehen" by Pasquale Marino, in *Dies ist nicht die Welt, die wir suchen,* edited by Suleman Taufiq, copyright © 1983. Used with permission of Klartext/PRO.

ACKNOWLEDGMENTS / xv

From "Nicht nur Gastarbeiterdeutsch" by Franco Biondi. Used with permission of the author.

From *Body* by Harry Crews. Copyright © 1990 by Harry Crews. Reprinted by permission of Poseidon Press, a division of Simon & Shuster, Inc.

Although I am fully responsible for the flaws in this volume, there would undoubtedly have been more of them without the patience and perseverance of the contributors; the invaluable advice of Timothy Austin, Suzanne Fleishman, and Boyd Davis; the helpfulness of The University of Alabama Press, particularly of Nicole Mitchell, Suzette Griffith, and Paula Dennis; the good work of Anne Gibbons and Jane Powers Weldon; the assistance and inspiration of my son Robin Bernstein; and the unfailing support and optimism of my husband Robert Bernstein.

THE TEXT AND BEYOND

PART 1

Text and Context

In the years of New Criticism, the study of literature focused on the text as artifact, for the most part disregarding contexts of production and reception. Broadly speaking, meaning was presumed to reside within the text, and the language of the text was regarded as a static object, steadily poised awaiting interpretation.

Such perception of language and literature gave way to a systemic approach. Structuralist linguistics, beginning with Ferdinand de Saussure in the early part of the twentieth century, regarded every word as part of a system of language. Structuralist poetics, emerging in the 1970s in the United States but evident a decade earlier in the writings of Russian, Czech, and French theorists, regarded every literary work as part of a system of literature. Structuralism, as applied both to language and literature, saw elements fitting together in an orderly way like pieces of a puzzle so that the whole picture could be seen, the whole truth be known. Structuralism stressed ideal speakers (authors) and ideal hearers (readers), whose knowledge of the system made possible unaltered transmission of the text.

Today literary theorists ask whether a reader can, in fact, perceive unchanged a writer's message. If a text cannot be regarded as transmitting meaning, if words are not the arbitrary conveyers of that meaning, then Saussurian linguistics would seem irrelevant to the study of literature. But other areas of linguistics do address the same questions asked by literary theorists. Discourse analysis, pragmatics, sociolinguistics, and psycholinguistics all are concerned with meaning as it derives from the context of language. Applied to literature, those disciplines can help explain the contribution of context to the understanding of text. The first essay of this volume explores how linguistic criticism, in seeking meaning outside the text, complements the aims of literary theory.

The Contextualization of Linguistic Criticism

Until very recently linguists have been reluctant to admit literary studies to their discipline, and literary theorists have been even less welcoming of linguistic criticism. These attitudes derive from two presumptions that have long separated literary and linguistic studies. First, linguists have presumed literary language to be unnatural language and thus to lie outside the domain of linguistics. The discipline restricted its field of study to natural language, that is, speech. Only recently have linguists come to recognize that literature, too, is a natural use of language and that the study of literature lies properly within the bounds of linguistics.

The second presumption, held by literary theorists, has been that linguistics lacks the tools needed to examine anything but features contained within the text. As literary theory moved further from text-centered New Criticism, linguistics was presumed to have even less to contribute toward its aims. In actuality, though, linguists have been developing the tools to study precisely those cultural and psychological features of language that concern literary theorists today.[1] Without the contributions of linguistics, the postmodern study of literature is incomplete.[2]

The presumption that excluded literature from linguistic study can be traced to the beginnings of modern linguistics. It is inherent in Ferdinand de Saussure's *Course in General Linguistics*, first published in 1916; to the extent that the *Course* accounted for writing at all, it was as the representation of oral language. Sound, according to Saussure, is "the natural bond, the only true bond" between signifier and signified (46). He argues that speech alone is the province of linguistics: "The linguistic object is not defined by the combination of the written word and the spoken word: the spoken form alone constitutes the object" (45).

Written language is similarly excluded from the development of speech-act theory in the 1960s. J. L. Austin (1962) and John Searle (1969) argue that utterances in literature cannot be said to have the same relation to the world that ordinary utterances do. *Illocutionary force* — stating, requesting, thanking, blessing — can be named as an expression of the speaker's intent vis-à-vis the listener; but what can be the relevance of such force to literary language? Richard Ohmann (1971) addresses this question by defining literature in relation to its illocutionary force: "*A literary work is a discourse whose sentences lack the illocutionary forces that would normally attach to them. Its illocutionary force is mimetic*" (14, italics in original). This definition, with its notion that written language imitates spoken, contains echoes of Saussure. It gives primacy to the spoken as the origin of illocutionary force and takes no account of the potential force of the text vis-à-vis the reader.

The presumption excluding literature from linguistic study has not gone unchallenged. Roman Jakobson argues for inviting literature into the linguistic fold in his "Closing Statement: Linguistics and Poetics," delivered to the Conference on Style at Indiana University in 1958 and published two years later. Calling it the "right and duty of linguistics" to take charge of the "investigation of verbal art in all its compass and extent," he blames prior reluctance to do so on the "poetic incompetence of some bigoted linguists" (377).

Saussure's exclusion of written language from linguistic study is refuted by Jacques Derrida. In *Of Grammatology*, Derrida disputes Saussure's premise that "the spoken form alone constitutes the object" of linguistics (quoted in Derrida 1974, 30). Contending that "there is no linguistic sign before writing" (14) and that "language is a possibility founded on the general possibility of writing" (52), Derrida refuses to accept the notion that written language is simply the representation of oral language.

Written language, others have argued, is not merely "mimetic" in its illocutionary force. Wolfgang Iser (1978) contradicts Austin's and Searle's exclusion of literature from speech-act theory on the basis that literary language "takes on an *illocutionary force*," which "not only arouses attention but also guides the reader's approach to the text and elicits responses to it" (61–62). Mary Louise Pratt (1977), posits the term "display texts" to refer to speech acts — such as stories, poems, or jokes — characterized by their tellability. Using Searle's (1976) taxonomy, she classifies these as *representative*. A good case can be made, though, for considering them as a separate category. Display texts are not subject to the truth conditions of ordinary assertions; they are judged or described, instead, by their success or failure in entertaining, grabbing attention, and so on. The notion of a "display text" category is important in giving literature a place within the larger context of language use. Literature has the power not only to represent the speech acts of everyday life but also to be a channel of expression for the concerns of the social context in which it is produced.

Modern linguists have begun to appreciate the value of the literary text in supplying linguistic data. Historical linguists have always done so, for the diachronic study of language prior to the twentieth century had no alternative to written data. From written texts one could, to a certain extent, infer the spoken language. Texts can do more than that, though. Even when spoken alternatives are available, there is no need to limit the understanding of language only to its oral representation. B. A. Fennell, in this volume, illustrates how the study of *Gastarbeiterliteratur* (German Immigrant Worker literature) can contribute to pidgin and creole theory. Her argument: literature is linguistic data.

At the same time linguists have come to accept literature as part of their domain, many literary theorists have come to realize that linguistic approaches have much to offer. The supposition mentioned earlier, that linguistic criticism seemed limited to textual studies, harks back to Jakobson. Jakobson's discussion gives the *impression* of discourse-centered criticism, of criticism aimed at context as well as text, when he writes, "Insistence on keeping poetics apart from linguistics is warranted only when the field of linguistics appears to be illicitly restricted, for example, when the sentence is viewed by some linguists as the highest analyzable construction . . ." (352). However, Jakobson's own application of linguistics to literature is neither so broad nor so bold as his argument would suggest. His definitions of *poetics* and *linguistics* are structuralist ones: "Poetics deals with problems of verbal structure, just as the analysis of painting is concerned with pictorial structure. Since linguistics is the global science of verbal structure, poetics may be regarded as an integral part of linguistics" (350). "Verbal structure," then, is what Jakobson supposes to be the common ground of poetics and linguistics. "The message for its own sake" (356) is the poetic function of language. The approach is reminiscent of New Criticism. Indeed, in "Closing Statement," Jakobson's linguistic approach to poetry stresses meter, rhyme, syntax, semantics, phonology, and figurative language.

These topics still represent a substantial contribution of linguistics to literary criticism — William Chisholm, in this volume, affirms his approach to be "unabashedly Jakobsonian" — but they are not the only ones that linguistics has to offer. Other approaches, ones that may be more compatible with recent developments in literary theory, have broadened the scope of linguistic criticism.

The archetypal application of Jakobson's methods may be found in Jakobson and Lévi-Strauss's (1962) analysis of Baudelaire's "Les Chats." What Michael Riffaterre (1966) objects to in that application is the omission of the reader's response as a determinant of meaning. Riffaterre's analysis addresses the communication model introduced by Jakobson (1960):

	CONTEXT (REFERENTIAL)	
ADDRESSER	MESSAGE (POETIC)	ADDRESSEE
(EMOTIVE)	CONTACT (PHATIC)	(CONATIVE)
	CODE (METALINGUAL)	

Jakobson's model associates six "factors" with a corresponding set of "functions" (indicated, above, in parentheses). Jakobson defines the POETIC function as centering on the message: *"The poetic function projects the principle of equivalence from the axis of selection into the axis of combination"* (358). In other words, the POETIC function focuses not on the poet's selection of words from among possible ones (i.e., paradigmatic choices), but on the organization of those words into sequences within the text (i.e., syntagmatic choices). The sense of Jakobson's assertion is well illustrated by Melissa Monroe (in this volume): it is Marianne Moore's "combinations" of words — in odd and intriguing compounds — that call attention to the MESSAGE of her poetry. Riffaterre, however, argues that the poetic function is not only the message but "the whole act of communication." He claims, in fact, that MESSAGE and ADDRESSEE are the only required factors in communication: the ADDRESSER in a poem is absent; and CONTEXT, CONTACT, and CODE are all part of the message or of the interaction between MESSAGE and ADDRESSEE. For the poetic text, then, according to Riffaterre's analysis, what matters is the reader's response.

The usefulness of reader-response criticism has been established through a profusion of works appearing in the 1970s and 1980s, which I shall not retrace here.[3] Consideration of the reader, though, has led to a broader understanding of context. Derek Attridge (1987) asks, "[H]ow might we follow through the implication, suppressed in Jakobson, that readers are active in determining what is poetry and what is not?" (23). The answer: "We would need some account of the role of ideology, of gender, of institutional practices, perhaps of the unconscious; and we would need to take account of our own position as culturally and ideologically situated readers" (23). The direction of linguistic criticism during the 1980s and its course for the 1990s lie in the relation between the language of a text and its social and discursive contexts.

Linguists have come to approach the literary text not so much as "the message for its own sake," but, to use the definition of Robert Scholes (1982), as "the product of a person or persons, at a given point in human history, in a given form of discourse, taking its meanings from the interpretive gestures of individual readers using the grammatical, semantic, and cultural codes available to them." "A text," Scholes adds, "always echoes other texts, and it is the result of choices that have displaced still other possibilities" (16). The relation of the codes of the literary text to the codes of culture or to the codes of other texts has been the business of semiotic criticism—as elaborated, for example, by Barthes (1974) or Riffaterre (1978, 1987). Like reader-response criticism, semiotic criticism sees a work of literature as no more isolated than any other form of communication from the circumstances that surround its production or reception.

Linguists today, like their counterparts in literary theory, see meaning as contextual. Colin MacCabe (1985) puts it this way:

> [T]he relations of the meanings of a text to its socio-historical conditions (of both production and reception) are not secondary but constitutive. . . . [T]here is no such thing as meaning in so far as the term assumes an entity independent of the different ideological, political or theoretical positions which inform language and the different institutional conditions of utterance. It is not that a word has different meanings for different speakers but that the same lexical item appears in different discourses. (124)

Similarly, Roger Fowler (1986) considers it "fundamental" to linguistic criticism to see the text in relation to "the social, institutional, and ideological conditions of its production and reception" (12). The point is that many linguists do not consider language to exclude context; on the contrary, meaning itself depends upon what Fowler calls the "*pragmatic* dimensions of language" (11). To incorporate pragmatics, in its broadest sense, into a model of linguistic criticism is to relate language to the social, historical, cultural, political, and psychological contexts of writer and reader.

The trend toward contextualization has not been met with approval in all quarters. Seymour Chatman (1990)—in an article appearing in the first of three issues of *Poetics Today* devoted to "Narratology Revisited"—argues that narratologists should oppose the "Contextualists" (e.g., Pratt 1977). He objects, in particular, to

Pratt's use of the Labovian model of narrative (Pratt 1977, 38–78). Derived from interviews with inner-city teenagers, the model posits six components of narrative structure: abstract, orientation, complicating action, result or resolution, evaluation, and coda (Labov and Waletzky 1967; Labov 1972). Chatman disputes Pratt's claim that the abstract, which Labov defines as a brief summary introducing most natural narratives, can be supplied by the title of the work; *Tom Jones*, after all, is the main character's name, not the theme of the work. Furthermore, the title is outside the narrative proper, and Labov's model cannot account for the multiple voices of a literary text. In response to Chatman's criticism, it must be noted that Labov and Waletzky did not intend their model to apply to such complex structures as "myths, folk tales, legends, histories, epics, toasts and sagas" (12). Their original work was based on six hundred interviews, and they were looking for the most basic common elements within them. Nevertheless, their model can account for multiple voices in the context of everyday narratives. Context often supplies the abstract and even the evaluation: a question is asked; other stories on the same theme are being told; indications of approval or disagreement are made by listeners. In that way, other voices are often accounted for in the Labovian model.

In general, narratology has moved away from its strictly structuralist position. Gérard Genette (1990) and Dorrit Cohn (1990), writing in the second volume of the *Poetics Today* series, apply the methods of narratology to nonfictional texts, investigating signs that distinguish fact and fiction. Gerald Prince (1991), in volume three of the same series, points out that the "classical" narratologist "practically never ponders . . . the relations of the narrative text with truth or falsehood, the nature of the fictional as opposed to the real" (543). Yet he, like Riffaterre (1990) in *Fictional Truth*, argues that narratology today must ask such questions in order to "fit into a general semiotics" (551).

Like narratology, stylistics has evolved to account also for the contextualization of the literary act. Nils Erik Enkvist (1991) captures this contextualization of linguistic criticism in his definition of style: "Style is an impression triggered off by textual features governed by a situation-based strategy." Style, according to this definition, is a "parallel distribution process," penetrating simultaneously the syntax, semantics, and pragmatics of the text. Earlier, Enkvist (1964) had defined style as "an aggregate of the contextual probabilities of linguistic [phonological, grammatical, and lexical] items" (28). The earlier definition centers on quantitatively determined norms and variations from those norms.[4] The change from an aggregate-based process to a parallel distribution process represents a new emphasis on discourse-centered stylistics (see also Enkvist 1990).

The shift in emphasis from primarily phonological, grammatical, and lexical structures to discourse structures is a recent one. In general, essays in collections of the 1970s and early 1980s — such as Freeman (1970, 1981); Fowler (1975); and Leech and Short (1981) — were not centered on discourse. The shift might be represented best by the titles of two collections of essays: Ronald Carter's *Language and Literature: An Introductory Reader in Stylistics* (1982), and Carter and Paul Simpson's *Language, Discourse and Literature: An Introductory Reader in Discourse Stylistics* (1989). The addition of the word *discourse* to the title and subtitle of the later work suggests a shift in emphasis represented also by Leo Hickey's *Pragmatics of Style* (1989) and Timothy Austin's *Poetic Voices: Discourse Linguistics and the Poetic Text* (1994). Other collections reflect continuing interest in the concerns of discourse-based criticism: *Literary Pragmatics* (1991), edited by Roger Sell; *Language, Text and Context* (1992), edited by Michael Toolan; and *Dialogue and Critical Discourse* (1993), edited by Michael Macovski. Toolan's (1992) volume is published as part of Routledge's Interface Series, edited by Ron Carter, whose stated purpose is "to examine topics at the 'interface' of language studies and literary criticism and in so doing build bridges between these traditionally divided disciplines."

A new tradition is bringing the disciplines together. The Poetics and Linguistics Association, chaired by Ron Carter, is one of several organizations promoting a dialogue between linguistics and literature. Others include the Literary Pragmatics Research Group, established by Roger Sell at Åbo Akadami in Helsinki; the Programme in Literary Linguistics, established by Colin MacCabe in 1983 at the University of Strathclyde, which sponsored the 1986 conference "The Linguistics of Writing," the proceedings of which were published a year later (Fabb et al. 1987); and the International Association of Literary Semantics, which sponsored a 1992 conference on the topic. The Modern Language Association, too, has its Division on Linguistic Approaches to Literature, which sponsors several sessions at the national meetings each year. Journals such as the *Journal of Literary Semantics, Style*, and *Language and Style* provide continuing outlets for linguistic criticism. Nationally and internationally, then, linguistics and literary theory are no longer divided disciplines but interdependent fields of study that require each other's insights for meaningful access to literary texts.

Notes

1. Beaugrande (1992) provides a cogent analysis of how trends in linguistic studies emphasizing text linguistics and discourse analysis parallel trends in literary studies. The object of study is perceived not as a "written (and presumably closed) *artifact*" but as an "open-ended *transaction*."

2. Brief portions of this essay appeared in Bernstein (1990).

3. On reader-response criticism, see Bleich (1978), Chatman (1978), Genette (1980, 1988), Fish (1980), Mailloux (1982), Ong (1975), Prince (1980), Rabinowitz (1977), Wilson (1981). Jane P. Tompkins (1980) offers a useful collection of reader-response approaches. See Robert M. Fowler (1985) for descriptions of *implied reader, narratee*, and *ideal reader*. See T. Austin (1984) on *native reader* and Bernstein (1987) on *internal audience*.

4. An updated approach to the study of norms in various discourse genres is the focus of Biber (1988).

References

Attridge, Derek. 1987. "Closing Statement: Linguistics and Poetics in Retrospect." In *The Linguistics of Writing: Arguments Between Language and*

Literature, ed. Nigel Fabb, Derek Attridge, Alan Durant, and Colin MacCabe, 15–32. New York: Methuen.

Austin, J. L. 1962. *How to Do Things with Words*. New York: Oxford UP.

Austin, Timothy R. 1984. *Language Crafted: A Linguistic Theory of Poetic Syntax*. Bloomington: Indiana UP.

———. 1994. *Poetic Voices: Discourse Linguistics and the Poetic Text*. Tuscaloosa: U of Alabama P.

Barthes, Roland. 1974. *S/Z*. Trans. Richard Miller. New York: Hill and Wang. Translation of *S/Z*. Editions du Seuil, 1970.

Beaugrande, Robert. 1992. "Discourse Analysis and Literary Theory: The Rapprochement of Linguistics and Literary Studies." Paper presented at the Southeastern Conference on Linguistics, Gainesville, Fla., April 4, 1992.

Bernstein, Cynthia. 1987. "The Internal Audience in Literary and Rhetorical Discourse." Ph.D. diss., Texas A&M U.

———. 1990. "Linguistic Approaches to Literature: Beyond the Text." Introduction to Special Issue of *South Central Review* 7 (Summer): 1–4.

Biber, Douglas. 1988. *Variation Across Speech and Writing*. Cambridge: Cambridge UP.

Bleich, David. 1978. *Subjective Criticism*. Baltimore: Johns Hopkins UP.

Carter, Ronald. 1982. *Language and Literature: An Introductory Reader in Stylistics*. London: Allen & Unwin.

Carter, Ronald, and Paul Simpson, eds. 1989. *Language, Discourse and Literature: An Introductory Reader in Discourse Stylistics*. London: Unwin Hyman.

Chatman, Seymour. 1978. *Story and Discourse: Narrative Structure in Fiction and Film*. Ithaca: Cornell UP.

———. 1990. "What Can We Learn from Contextualist Narratology?" *Narratology Revisited I. Poetics Today* 11 (Summer): 309–28.

Cohn, Dorrit. 1990. "Signposts of Fictionality: A Narratological Perspective." *Narratology Revisited II. Poetics Today* 11 (Winter): 775–804.

Derrida, Jacques. 1974. *Of Grammatology*. Trans. Gayatri Chakravorty Spivak. Baltimore: Johns Hopkins UP. Translation of *De la Grammatologie*. Les Editions de Minuit, 1967.

Enkvist, Nils Erik. 1964. "On Defining Style." In *Linguistics and Style*, ed. John Spencer, 1–56. London: Oxford UP.

———. 1990. "Stylistics, Text Linguistics, and Text Strategies." *Hebrew Linguistics* 28–30:7–22.

———. 1991. "On Re-Defining Style." Paper presented at the Southeastern Conference on Linguistics. Knoxville, Tenn., April 5, 1991.

Fabb, Nigel, Derek Attridge, Alan Durant, and Colin MacCabe, eds. 1987. *The Linguistics of Writing: Arguments Between Language and Literature.* New York: Methuen.

Fish, Stanley. 1980. *Is There a Text in This Class? The Authority of Interpretive Communities.* Cambridge, Mass.: Harvard UP.

Fowler, Robert M. 1985. "Who Is 'The Reader' in Reader Response Criticism?" *Semeia* 31 (1985): 5–23.

Fowler, Roger, ed. 1975. *Style and Structure in Literature: Essays in the New Stylistics.* Ithaca: Cornell UP.

———. 1986. *Linguistic Criticism.* Oxford: Oxford UP.

Freeman, Donald C., ed. 1970. *Linguistics and Literary Style.* New York: Holt.

———. 1981. *Essays in Modern Stylistics.* London: Methuen.

Genette, Gérard. 1980. *Narrative Discourse: An Essay in Method.* Trans. Jane E. Lewin. Ithaca: Cornell UP. Translation of *Discours du récit.* Editions du Seuil, 1972.

———. 1988. *Narrative Discourse Revisited.* Trans. Jane E. Lewin. Ithaca: Cornell UP. Translation of *Nouveau discours du récit.* Editions du Seuil, 1983.

———. 1990. "Fictional Narrative, Factual Narrative." *Narratology Revisited II. Poetics Today* 11 (Winter): 755–74.

Hickey, Leo, ed. 1989. *The Pragmatics of Style.* New York: Routledge.

Iser, Wolfgang. 1978. *The Act of Reading: A Theory of Aesthetic Response.* Baltimore: Johns Hopkins UP. Translation of *Der Akt des Lesens: Theorie ästhetischer Wirkung.* Munich: Wilhelm Fink, 1976.

Jakobson, Roman. 1960. "Closing Statement: Linguistics and Poetics." In *Style in Language,* ed. Thomas A. Sebeok, 350–77. Cambridge: MIT P.

Jakobson, Roman, and Claude Lévi-Strauss. 1962. "'Les Chats' de Charles Baudelaire." *L'Homme* 2 (jan.–avril): 5–21. Reprinted in *The Structuralists: From Marx to Lévi-Strauss,* ed. and trans. Richard T. De George and Fernande M. De George. Garden City, N.Y.: Anchor Books, Doubleday, 1972.

Labov, William. 1972. *Language in the Inner City.* Philadelphia: U of Pennsylvania P.

Labov, William, and Joshua Waletzky. 1967. "Narrative Analysis." In *Essays on the Verbal and Visual Arts,* ed. June Helm, 12–44. Seattle: U of Washington P.

Leech, Geoffrey N., and Michael H. Short. 1981. *Style in Fiction: A Linguistic Introduction to English Fictional Prose.* London: Longman.

MacCabe, Colin. 1985. "Language, Linguistics and the Study of Literature." In *Theoretical Essays,* 113–30. Manchester, Eng.: Manchester UP.

Macovski, Michael S., ed. 1993. *Dialogue and Critical Discourse: Language, Culture, Critical Theory.* Oxford: Oxford UP.

Mailloux, Steven. 1982. *Interpretive Conventions: The Reader in the Study of American Fiction.* Ithaca: Cornell UP.

Ohmann, Richard. "Speech Acts and the Definition of Literature." *Philosophy and Rhetoric* 4 (1971): 1–19.

Ong, Walter J. 1975. "The Writer's Audience Is Always a Fiction." *PMLA* 90:9–21.

Pratt, Mary Louise. 1977. *Toward a Speech Act Theory of Literary Discourse.* Bloomington: Indiana UP.

Prince, Gerald. 1980. "Introduction to the Study of the Narratee." Tompkins 7–25.

———. 1991. "Narratology, Narrative, and Meaning." *Narratology Revisited III. Poetics Today* 12 (Fall): 543–52.

Rabinowitz, Peter. "Truth in Fiction: A Reexamination of Audience." *Critical Inquiry* 4:121–41.

Riffaterre, Michael. 1966. "Describing Poetic Structures: Two Approaches to Baudelaire's 'Les Chats.'" In *Structuralism*, ed. Jacques Ehrmann, 188–230. Garden City, N.Y.: Anchor Books, Doubleday.

———. 1978. *Semiotics of Poetry.* Bloomington: Indiana UP.

———. 1987. "The Intertextual Unconscious." *Critical Inquiry* 13 (Winter): 371–85.

———. 1990. *Fictional Truth.* Baltimore: Johns Hopkins UP.

Saussure, Ferdinand de. 1959. *A Course in General Linguistics.* Trans. Wade Baskin. New York: McGraw-Hill. Original French edition first published in 1916.

Scholes, Robert. 1982. *Semiotics and Interpretation.* New Haven: Yale UP.

Searle, John. 1969. *Speech Acts: An Essay in the Philosophy of Language.* London: Cambridge UP.

———. 1976. "A Classification of Illocutionary Acts." *Language in Society* 5:1–23.

Sell, Roger, ed. 1991. *Literary Pragmatics.* New York: Routledge.

Tompkins, Jane P., ed. 1980. *Reader-Response Criticism: From Formalism to Post-Structuralism.* Baltimore: Johns Hopkins UP.

Toolan, Michael, ed. 1992. *Language, Text and Context: Essays in Stylistics.* New York: Routledge.

Wilson, W. Daniel. 1981. "Readers in Texts." *PMLA* 96:848–63.

PART 2

Pattern

This section focuses on three related concepts: cohesion, or techniques used to bind together the parts of a text; foregrounding, the emphasis achieved by creating patterns and then breaking them; and reference, the relation between a word and what it represents.

More than any other topic in this collection, cohesion, as defined by Halliday and Hasan's classic work on the subject, centers on the text itself: on the phonological, morphological, and syntactic structures that link its parts together. Yet, as the chapters in this section illustrate, the effect of cohesion depends not only upon the structures themselves or even upon the relation of those structures to each other, but also upon the reader's perception of them and their relation to structures outside the text.

To the extent that cohesion involves close study of a text, it lends itself to the kind of analysis favored by Roman Jakobson (see the preceding chapter by Cynthia Bernstein). William S. Chisholm admits, in fact, that his analysis is "unabashedly Jakobsonian." Yet such study of linguistic patterns cannot ignore the reader's response to them. Chisholm points out that by establishing patterns of linguistic structures and by intentionally breaking those patterns, writers *foreground* the messages of their text. The reader thus becomes involved in distinguishing patterns and deviations from those patterns. Referring particularly to Jan Mukařovský's "Standard Language and Poetic Language," Chisholm shows how attention to foregrounding reveals layers of meaning quite different from the superficial content of a text. His study of the lexical and syntactic patterns of Robert Creeley's "I Know a Man" demonstrates that underneath its whimsical surface and colloquial language is a more somber poem — a prayer — with dread, death, and disorientation at its center.

Mary Jane Chilton Curry takes the subject of foregrounding a step further outside the text. She looks at two novels that foreground matters of epistemology and shows how different patterns of reference relate to realist and modernist traditions. Realism takes for granted that one can both define and find truth; modernism, in contrast, questions the nature of existence. Curry's study of anaphoric and cataphoric references in Dickens's *Our Mutual Friend* and James's *The Golden Bowl* reveals that both authors foreground questions about the nature of truth but that James is more modernist than Dickens in avoiding explicitness of reference and certainty of solutions.

In the final chapter in this section, Melissa Monroe shows that linguistic patterns are a means not only of describing the world but also of perceiving and organizing it. Her study of Marianne Moore's poetry challenges the general notion that there is a clear-cut relation between a word and its referent. New combinations of words correspond to new ways of seeing relationships between objects. Such relationships, which broaden the traditional concept of *cohesion*, are seen here to involve matters of morphology, syntax, and semantics. In her discussion of Moore's poetry, Monroe points out that the "objective" taxonomic classification of the scientist and the "subjective" description of the poet share a common goal: to propose a system of relations among the elements of the world. Moore's thematic concerns are reflected stylistically in her use of compound nouns. Moore uses compounding to link diverse elements of the natural world in a complex network of interrelations. Her most characteristic nominal structure is the noun + noun compound, a referring unit composed of two potentially autonomous elements. The nouns *pine-tiger* and *camel-sparrow* are not arbitrary labels but condensed statements of relation. Moore's compounds often link objects from different natural classes, and these nominal compounds are mirrored at higher syntactic levels in elaborate composite images. The reader is made constantly aware that any relation expressed in words is an illusion, a mental construct.

In a sense, it is language that holds the world together. Linguistic interpretation of literary texts cannot, then, be limited to the text. Any attention to language is also attention to how the world is perceived, organized, and represented.

Lexico-Syntactic Cohesion in Creeley's "I Know a Man"

Of the many structural components of language that may be artfully controlled to make writing expressive,[1] the phonology, the lexicon, and the syntax are certainly crucial. But it is patterns of these that authors devise, the cohesiveness, that strike through decisively.

Though my intention here is to describe the expressiveness in Robert Creeley's poetic language, some brief examples from other authors will illustrate how phonological, lexical, and syntactic patterns can control a reading of the text. Edward Taylor's famous poem, "Upon a Spider Catching a Fly," begins this way:

> Thou sorrow, venom elf:
>   Is this thy play,
> To spin a web out of thyself
>   To catch a fly?
> For why?
>
> I saw a pettish wasp
>   Fall foul therein,
> Whom yet the whorl-pins did not clasp
>   Lest he should fling
> His sting.

The tight rhymes in the last two iambic feet of each stanza are arresting: this metrical pattern repeats in all ten stanzas of the poem, and so it constitutes a cohesive stitching. Shelley, in his turn, uses a kindred metrical scheme in "Lines: When the Lamp Is Shattered," although the details of the pattern at the ends of each line in each couplet are much more complex than those in Taylor's poem. Here is the first stanza:

> When the lamp is shattered
> The light in the dust lies dead —
> When the cloud is scattered
> The rainbow's glory is shed.
> When the lute is broken,
> Sweet tones are remembered not;
> When the lips have spoken,
> Loved accents are soon forgot.

Each succeeding stanza manifests the same play of meter and rhyme. But Shelley's poem, four stanzas long, has a spondaic foot at the very end:

> From thy nest every rafter
> Will rot, and thine eagle home
> Leave thee naked to laughter,
> When leaves fall and cold winds come.

In fact, of the seven syllables in the last line here, five are strongly stressed (and each is a word), so that the poem slows to a metrical dirge, just as Keats's last line of "La Belle Dame sans Merci" does:

> Though the sedge is withered from the lake
> And no birds sing.

These latter points touch on the mechanism of foregrounding, which, as we have just seen, may be nothing more than the breaking of a pattern, or, in Jan Mukařovský's words "the violation of a scheme" (Mukařovský 1964, 19).[2] It is this sense of foregrounding, similar to the sense that Halliday and Hasan (1976) assign it, that accords well with this study of expressiveness. The reader's attention is riveted on the point of disruption with the consequence that the semantic import strikes through.

The effect can be achieved through disruption in patterns not only of phonology, as noted above, but also of lexicon and syntax. In Tennessee Williams's *The Glass Menagerie*, Tom's last speech concludes with these sentences:

> Oh, Laura, I tried to leave you behind me, but I am more faithful than I intended to be! I reach for a cigarette, I cross the street, I run into the movies or a bar, I buy a drink, I speak to the nearest stranger — anything that can blow your candles out!
> *(Laura bends over the candles.)*
> — for nowadays the world is lit by lightning! Blow out your candles, Laura — and so good-bye . . .
> *(She blows out the candles.)*

This is not a fade-out. This is a plummeting into darkness. Very dramatic. Very theatrical! But without these words and this syntax, there would be little expressiveness. Suppose Williams had chosen the less elegant "because" as his conjunction (instead of "for") and "these days" in place of "nowadays" (so that the line would read " — because these days the world is lit by lightning!"). Then we would have had flat, colloquial language, an unfortunate irony in the company of the word "lit," and we would have lost the paired alliterations "nowadays . . . world / lit . . . lightning." "Nowadays" is romantic and fine. It is foregrounded against the background of the humdrum world of a street, a cigarette, a drink, and a stranger; and Williams deploys an indefinite noun phrase with an embedded relative clause, "anything that can blow your candles out," against the background of simple clauses that express a litany of commonplaces. Also, the particle "out," shifted to the end of the clause from its normal position next to the verb, dramatically extinguishes the flames. Had Williams written, "I am looking for ways to blow out your candles" (or something like this), we would recognize the expression as idiomatic to a real and mundane world, not an imaginary one. The last stage direction (*She blows out the candles*) is *linguistically* anticlimactic and an expressive element in the text. For these reasons, all linguistic (and for more customary theatrical reasons), we return to new productions of Williams's play.

These isolated examples illustrate the impact of patterns of language and variations and disruptions of such patterns. They will serve, I trust, to focus attention on the contributions lexico-syntactic forms can make. A full-scale analysis of Robert Creeley's "I Know a Man" will show how such forms of expression can force a reading of the text.

Here is Creeley's twelve-line poem:

> I KNOW A MAN
> As I sd to my   1
> friend, because I am   2
> always talking, — John, I   3
>
> sd, which was not his   4
> name, the darkness sur-   5
> rounds us, what   6
>
> can we do against   7
> it, or else, shall we &   8
> why not, buy a goddamn big car,   9
>
> drive, he sd, for   10
> christ's sake, look   11
> out where yr going.   12

Though the poem can be read superficially as a trifle, an ingenious whimsy, close analysis makes it clear that the outer poem is a mask that the deeper poem wears. Leaving aside the question of how far linguistic and pragmatic competencies take readers into a poem, my intention is to unearth what is *in* this poem but below its surface, including even etymological information that informs interpretation. Though it is not common to expose etymological facts in the determination of meaning, there is no *a priori* reason to exclude them. After all, when we read in Thoreau's "The Battle of the Ants" (*Walden*, "Brute Neighbors," 474) that "legions of . . . Myrmidons covered all the hills and vales," we can recognize that etymological information (Gr. *myrmex*, 'an ant') figures in the meaning of the text and our appreciation of it.

If the words on the page constitute a poem, we must attend to them. Looking at the words in Creeley's poem, we see immediately that it is about talking and saying, about conversation. It's also about friends and cars. It's about God and Christ, too. But the poem is about disorientation and confusion as well; and it's about anger, aggression, and belligerence, about broken things, and about menace, dread, and death. The evidence for these latter perceptions of what is in the poem is not very pointed or straightforward. It is there, nevertheless. We can find the evidence by looking closely at the words and at the structures in which they fall.

Consider the verbs first. There are nine different ones: "say" (line 1), "talk" (line 2), "be" (line 4), "surround" (lines 5, 6), "do" (line 7), "buy" (line 9), "drive" (line 10), "look out" (lines 11, 12), and "go" (line 12). All of these, except "surround," are plain, basic, high-frequency, monosyllabic, Anglo-Saxon verbs — the common coin of conversation. All except "be" are action verbs, so they serve the purposes of the voice that recounts events. And they do so colloquially. Their forms express the action in mostly monosyllabic hammer strokes — go, drive, do (something), look out! (I'll return to the exceptional verb "surround.")

Now consider the pronouns and the nouns. Conspicuous by their absence are the third-person plural personal pronouns and the feminine pronouns.[3] Both are of worlds other than the world of the poem. But "I" and "my" are present, and so are "he" and "his," together with "we" and "us," "my" and "his," and "you" (hidden in "yr"). These are a symmetry, a three-way, conversational paradigm — the speaker, the one spoken of, and the one spoken to. The character deixis is intense, because in only three lines of the twelve is one or another of these pronouns not mentioned. The characters in the poem are central, because everything pronominal points directly and only at them. (You will notice that I have left out the "it" in line 8, the anaphor for "darkness." I'll return to this pronoun when I take up the verb "surround.")

As for the nouns, we can count seven: "friend" (line 2), "John" (line 3), "name" (line 4), "darkness" (line 5), "car" (line 9), "christ('s)" and "sake" (line 11). These nouns group themselves into two sets. First, "friend," "John," and "name" go together for the obvious reason that they are the sign and the significatum/designatum of the same entity. Second, "darkness," "christ," and "sake" go together, but not so obviously, "christ" and "sake" because they are glued together in the idiom, and "darkness" because it metaphorically names the Prince of Darkness, the antithesis of God; so these three are bound to each other as well. The name "John" derives from the contracted form of the Hebrew *Yĕhōḫānān*, an expression meaning "God is gracious." Now all six nouns are caught in a religious, semantic net. And let us not forget that the word "friend" derives from the West Germanic verb **frijon*, 'to love' (God is love).

What about the remaining noun, "car"? Originally designating a Celtic war chariot, this word derives from the Latin *carrus*, which is also the source for the word *chariot*. And most pertinently, the word *car* has been used to mean "chariot" in English poetry since the beginning of the sixteenth century. It is not hard to think of "Swing Low, Sweet Chariot" or of Andrew Marvell's "time's wingèd chariot":

> But at my back I always hear
> Time's wingèd chariot hurrying near;
> And yonder all before us lie
> Deserts of vast eternity.

Clearly, in Creeley's poem is the lexical substance of a religious motif — darkness and death, God and John. Further evidence for it comes from the "damn" (damnation) part of the oath, "goddamn," and from the etymological sources for both "God" and "Christ," "God" from **IE ghau-*, "to invoke," and "Christ" from **IE ghrei-*, "to spread over" (like oil).

This last connects to "surround." So I'll take that word up presently, along with "darkness." First, "darkness." This word is the focal point of the menace in the poem, the "it." Darkness, that is, evil and death, is expressed emphatically in the poem, first, because this ancient Old English word is the only disyllabic noun among the nouns; second, because deictic "the" isolates it as shared information; and third, because its meaning is abstract, insubstantial "darkness" (unlike John who is — or was — real, and unlike the substantial "car"). All of this deautomatizes the expression, to use Havránek's word. But the verb "surround" is foregrounded, too, against the background of common, monosyllabic verbs. It derives from the Latin *super-* + *undare*, meaning "to rise, move in waves, overflow" like the etymological oil of Christ "spreading over." Thus "surround" adjoins the godly and the ungodly, forming the good/evil ganglion of the eternal conflict. So "surround" is a powerful verbal stroke in the poem. Creeley highlights the word even further by breaking it apart, placing "sur-" at the end of line 5 and "-rounds" at the beginning of line 6, forcing us to read it as SUR-ROUNDS and forcing us, all told, to regard the entire expression, "the darkness surrounds us," as quite extraordinary. The author couldn't have called attention to it more decisively if he had stuck a pin in it.

We now come to the syntax. There are five sentences in the poem, but they are separated by commas, making them sentential "waves." There is a statement first (lines 1 through the middle of line 6), then two questions (lines 6 through 9), followed by two imperatives (10–12). These constitute three well-recognized dramatic units: the statement is the exposition; the two questions state the conflict; and the imperatives express the resolution (or denouement). The constituent structures of these are regular and unexceptional. "The darkness surrounds us," for instance, is simplicity itself, two words for the subject, then one for the verb and one for the objective complement. Its crispness is stunning, especially considering that it follows a tangle of premodifiers. Creeley has found a way to express his theme unmistakably.

Looking more closely, we see that the first interrogative following this simplex declarative is quite pristine, the two constructions being the only unelaborated sentence structures in the poem. Both of these clauses are bare bones. The others, broken to pieces, move in fits and starts. They are interrupted, confused, parenthetical, disjointed — reflecting the authentic patterns of speech — lurching, fragmented, and contradictory. "Because I am always talking" interrupts "as I said to my friend." Then "John" serves as a reorientation after "because I am always talking." But then "which was not his name" breaks the flow again. All together, we have reasons to think that the main argument of the poem is "the darkness surrounds us," considering that the surrounding syntactic landscape (the background) is a chaotic field that resonates disorder.

The interrogative construction beginning in line 6 is a *wh*-question, that is, a content question, but the question following, set as an alternative, is, in form, a yes/no question. More confusion and disorientation (strictly linguistic) envelop the thematic focal point. Then the double imperative at the end is broken by the oath "for christ's sake."

The poet also imitates the fragmented world of the poem by breaking the constituent structures at the ends of the lines. Such well-formed syntactic structures as there may be are sundered when the poet not only enjambs the lines but also divides the constituents as he goes:

> As I sd to [my
> friend], because I [am
> always talking] John, [I
>
> sd], which was not [his
> name], the darkness [sur-
> rounds us], what . . .

and so on. The only construction not split in these ways, "buy a goddamn big car," and foregrounded thereby, has the effect of making the proposed solution to the problem outrageous. The irregular syntax ("big" after "goddamn" instead of before it) makes an emphatic contribution, too.

A first reading of the poem leads us to smile and to take delight in the "goddamn big car," to appreciate the irony and the fun, the apparent frivolity. But even a preliminary analysis of a few salient lexico-syntactic facts leads to a deeper assessment.

The poem (published in 1957) dramatizes metaphysically the malaise and trauma of mid-century man. He rambles on. He contradicts himself. He can't remember his friend's name (= God is dead?). He worries about "time's wingèd chariot." He plots against it and proposes absurd defenses. ("What can we do AGAINST it?")[4] But he goes on in a chaotic world peopled merely by himself and his "friend." He drives. He looks out. He talks to himself in ancient, simple language — his anger spilling out in blasphemous colloquialisms. And he keeps talking to prove his own existence. (*Dico ergo sum.*)

The comic, ironic tone on the surface of the poem is a veil. Behind the veil is a prayer rendered in the modern idiom, a twentieth-century parable with the same pericope values that the parables of Christ served, the banishing of the Prince of the Earth (Satan) by the Light (Christ). And like Christ, Creeley conceals himself behind his lection.

In the end, "drive," either as John's (God's) admonition or as an expression of resolve by the persona, is prelude to "for christ's sake, look out where yr going." These, together, are a paraphrase of chapter 12, verse 35 of the gospel of John: "Go on your way while you have the light, so that the darkness may not overtake you" (The New English Bible).

It is not important that Creeley knew or did not know that he was managing the words or the syntax in the ways that I have described. The cohesiveness is *there* and so, as it turns out, is the "aktualisace" (Mukařovský's term). The poem means what its words and the syntactic structures that contain them impart. As language, the poem's lexico-syntax and the consequent expressive use of foregrounding/backgrounding are majestic achievements.

Notes

1. I do not suggest that speech and other modes of language use may not also be expressive. See Mary Louise Pratt (1977) for pertinent discussion of the *generality* of "poetic language."

2. The literature on foregrounding dates back to the formalists but in particular to Bohuslav Havránek (the "deautomatized" use of language) and Jan Mukařovský ("aktualisace" — backgrounding the communicative function of language in favor of emphasizing "the act of the speech itself"). (See Garvin 1964.) Mukařovský (1964, 19) says, "Objectively speaking: automatization schematizes an event; foregrounding means the violation of the scheme." My analysis is unabashedly Jakobsonian.

3. The gender of the persona is indeterminate.

4. The preposition "against," in place of the idiomatic "about," makes the darkness an enemy, not a topic.

References

Creeley, Robert. 1982. "I Know a Man." *Collected Poems of Robert Creeley, 1945–1975.* Berkeley: U of California P.

Garvin, Paul, ed. and trans. 1964. *A Prague School Reader on Esthetics, Literary Structure, and Style.* Washington, D.C.: Georgetown UP.

Halliday, M. A. K., and Ruqaiya Hasan. 1976. *Cohesion in English.* London: Longman.

Jakobson, Roman. 1960. "Closing Statement: Linguistics and Poetics." In *Style in Language,* ed. Thomas A. Sebeok, 350–77. Cambridge: MIT P.

Keats, John. 1982. "La Belle Dame sans Merci." In *Complete Poems,* ed. Jack Stillinger. Cambridge: Harvard UP.

Marvell, Andrew. 1927. "To His Coy Mistress." In *The Poems and Letters of Andrew Marvell,* ed. Herschel Margoliouth. Oxford: Clarendon.

Mukařovský, Jan. 1964. "Standard Language and Poetic Language." In *A Prague School Reader on Esthetics, Literary Structure, and Style,* ed. and trans. Paul L. Garvin, 17–30. Washington, D.C.: Georgetown UP.

The New English Bible. 1971. New York: Oxford UP.

Pratt, Mary Louise. 1977. *Toward a Speech Act Theory of Literary Discourse.* Bloomington: Indiana UP.

Shelley, Percy Bysshe. 1975. "Lines: When the Lamp Is Shattered." In *The Poetical Works of Shelley*, ed. Newell F. Ford. Boston: Houghton.

Taylor, Edward. 1960. "Upon a Spider Catching a Fly." In *The Poems of Edward Taylor*, ed. Donald E. Stanford. New Haven: Yale UP.

Thoreau, Henry David. [1854] 1975. *Walden.* In *The Portable Thoreau*, ed. Carl Bode, 258–572. New York: Viking Press, Penguin Books.

Williams, Tennessee. 1945. *The Glass Menagerie, A Play.* New York: Random.

Anaphoric and Cataphoric Reference in Dickens's *Our Mutual Friend* and James's *The Golden Bowl*

Despite over two decades of insightful critical analysis, no clear boundaries between the realistic, modernist, and postmodernist novel have been drawn. In *Postmodernist Fiction* (1987, 8–11) Brian Mc-Hale argues that the modernist text, beginning for him with Proust and James, foregrounds questions of epistemology.[1] That is, the novel asks such questions as "What is truth?" "What is the truth about a given situation?" "How will I find it?" "How will I know when I have found it?" McHale's distinctive feature of modernism, however, is R. F. Brissenden's (1974) defining characteristic of the first realistic novel, the eighteenth-century "novel of sentiment" (e.g., Richardson's *Clarissa Harlowe*), and it is also a key feature of the first novels for Michael McKeon (1987). For McKeon, this genre was born out of a climate of epistemological destabilization — political, social, and religious — in the late seventeenth and early eighteenth centuries (20–21, 27). Similarly, Brissenden (1974) shows how the novel of sentiment incorporates realistic characterization in order to subvert the early eighteenth-century sentimentalist's basic tenets: a belief in the truth of individual judgment and in benevolence as an innate human quality (33). That is, these early realistic novels have at their thematic cores "the problem of epistemological uncertainty" (176) — the same question McHale poses for the twentieth-century modernist novel. Like Brissenden and McKeon, George

Levine (1981), studying the Victorian novel, sees it as a product of a complex historical situation that fosters indeterminacy about truth and how to represent it.[2] To blur the distinction even more, McHale's modernist classification of the novels of Henry James, a founder of the psychological novel, runs counter to Levine's (1981), Percy Lubbock's (1921), E. M. Forster's (1927), Ian Watt's (1960), and Wayne Booth's (1961), all of which place him among the great realists. The scholarship of these men amounts to a bible of criticism on the novel, yet McHale's argument also deserves serious consideration.

In addition to its foundation of epistemological destabilization, the realistic novel has variously been defined as having four components. First, its characters are shown within complex sociohistorical contexts, and the problematic nature of the individual's responses to the outer world is emphasized (Forster 1927, 63; Auerbach 1953, 473–78; and Watt 1960, 17–19). Second, the development of a character's personality is shown to be a function of time and memory, so that, to Watt, novelists explain "personality as it is defined in its past and present self-awareness" (21–22). The third quality of realism, one that Watt mentions but does not develop, is "a preoccupation with the relationship between words and their referents, between meaning and object" (28). Levine (1981), too, speaks of the "multivalence" of realism, saying, "Whatever else it means, it always implies an attempt to use language to get beyond language, to discover some nonverbal truth out there" (6). I shall discuss this significant characteristic in detail later. A fourth component of the realistic novel is unresolved: the much-disputed question of the relationship between authorial intrusion and realism, the pivotal, extensive discussion of which is Booth's. Booth's sensible conclusion is that "what seems natural [realistic] in one period or to one school seems artificial in another period or to another school" (42). In other words, realism is probably not dependent upon whether or not a narrator or author interjects commentary about some aspect of the text, as Henry Fielding does as author in *Tom Jones* or as Dickens does, less obtrusively, as narrator in *Our Mutual Friend,* or remains as unobtrusive as Hemingway. Realism seems to be a function of the interaction between character and context. On the level of plot, realism centers on a character's response to circumstances; on the level of language, it centers on referentiality.

McHale argues that the postmodernist text, developed since World War II, foregrounds questions of ontology: it asks, "Which world is this? What is to be done with it? Which of my selves is to do it? . . . What is a world? . . . What happens when the different kinds of worlds are placed in confrontation, or when boundaries between worlds are violated?" (10). Postmodernist novels include Samuel Beckett's *The Unnamable* (1952), Robbe-Grillet's *La maison de rendez-vous* (1965), Carlos Fuentes's *Terra nostra* (1975), Vladimir Nabokov's *Ada* (1969), and Thomas Pynchon's *Gravity's Rainbow* (1973). McHale argues that these late works of each man are the result of a process in his career from a modernist emphasis upon epistemology to a postmodernist emphasis upon ontology (10–11).

Such definitions emphasize the effects of, and sometimes the processes at work in, the novel, but one necessary component is lacking: additional work is needed on its infrastructure — what Nils Erik Enkvist (1988) has called the linguistics of "text strategies."[3] That is, in order to explain what prompts us to identify a novel as belonging to the realistic, modernist, or postmodernist tradition, we also need explanations of the linguistic bases for identifying those traditions. Of course, pigeonholing a text is not the goal of definition; rather, the goal is, or should be, to clarify the ways in which a particular novel is related to other texts, including those that belong to other genres, in its techniques, forms, and ideologies. This understanding can then become a basis for delineating the larger distinctions between realism, modernism, and postmodernism.

My contention is that the degree and nature of textual cohesion — specifically, how the language in a novel creates degrees of explicitness or ambiguity, continuity or disruption — is in large part the basis for traditional distinctions. My purpose here is first to provide an analysis of two influential novels that in their forms of cohesion suggest certain attitudes toward epistemology, and second to relate those linguistic features to the emphasis upon epistemology that Brissenden (1974), McKeon (1987), and McHale (1987) find. That is, I am trying to construct another section of the bridge between literary theoretical and text linguistic approaches to the novel. Charles Dickens's *Our Mutual Friend* (1865) and Henry James's *The Golden Bowl* (1904) illustrate two paths the novel has taken in its epistemological focus. One path has been followed by Dickens and writers like him who adhere to explicitness of reference, the other by writers in the Jamesian tradition, who create ambiguous or elliptical connections, which may be classified as modernist and which, taken to their extremes, underlie the postmodernist novel. In particular, comparison of a basic and pervasive technique of textual cohesion, anaphoric reference, and its less-pervasive but significant counterpart, cataphoric reference, as they function in *Our Mutual Friend* and *The Golden Bowl*, reveals those two divergences. I contend that distinctions between realism and modernism are dependent upon types of referentiality and degrees of referential explicitness. While a study of two novels, however pivotal they may be, does not constitute adequate proof, I hope that it provides a new basis for redefinition.

Anaphora denotes a reference to some previously mentioned entity in the text. In the following example, the italicized phrases are anaphoric: "Mr. Boffin's face denoted Care and Complication. Many disordered papers were before *him*, and *he* looked at *them* about as hopefully as an innocent civilian might look at a crowd of troops *whom he* was required a five minutes' notice to manoeuvre and review" (*Our Mutual Friend*, 226, italics added). *Him* and *he* refer back to Mr. Boffin, *them* refers back to his papers, *whom* refers back to "a crowd of troops," and *he* refers back to "an innocent civilian."

Cataphora denotes a forward-pointing reference; its meaning is clarified by some other word, phrase, or longer discourse unit that comes later in the text (Halliday and Hasan 1976, 14, 17–19). In this example, the italicized clauses represent clarifications of cataphoric references: "It had been as strange as she could consent, afterwards, to think it; it had been essentially, *what had made the abrupt bend in her life: he had come back, had followed her from the other house, visibly uncertain —* this was written in the face he for the first minute showed her" (*The*

Golden Bowl, 308). The italicized clauses clarify the meaning of "it"; moreover, the second clarifying clause ("he had come back") is more specific than the first. Thus, the first clause becomes not only a clarifying clause but also a cataphoric reference for the second clause.

In comparing the functions of reference in the two novels, I am suggesting that referentiality helps to create a continuum from realism to modernism to postmodernism. James's work in *The Golden Bowl* is much farther along the continuum — from my findings, just outside of realism and within the boundary of modernism; it also evinces some postmodernist ontological concerns, but these are not foregrounded, as epistemological uncertainty is. *Our Mutual Friend* betrays some epistemological uncertainty, some discomfort about the possibility of finding the truth, but not nearly so much as *The Golden Bowl*. Even in surreal passages of *Our Mutual Friend*, the reader can easily distinguish tenor from vehicle and understand the metaphoric context. The novel is, therefore, by my defintion, realistic. Dickens's main characters are all empiricists who succeed: in one way or another, they are all detectives like Mr. Inspector. However, their success is also partly the result of fortuitous accidents. The very intricacy of the plot seems to assume no need to pose the ontological question "What is a world?" — while at the same time this intricacy undermines its own credibility. The coincidences are too neat; moreover, the plot has a flaw: the reader is no more prepared for Mr. Boffin's ruse than Bella is. I shall return to this point in the conclusion.

Both Dickens and James make prominent use of anaphoric and cataphoric reference in order to create thematic links between characters and discourse worlds — subplots in *Our Mutual Friend* and individuals' points of view in *The Golden Bowl*. In both novels the main vehicles of reference are metaphors and other noun phrases, including pronouns (for a discussion of the noun phrase, see Quirk and Greenbaum, 59). These cohesive phrases suggest that individual epistemological discovery is a recursive process: main characters, and we along with them, must frequently double back and revise our interpretations of previously acquired information, or must read on in order to find the referent for an as-yet-unclear entity. As a metaphor is repeated in a text, it adds discrete sets of referents, rather like pictures taken of one event, such as a vacation to a particular place, that are pasted into one's scrapbook; each image contributes to a viewer's understanding of the total experience.[4] The modes of discovery in the two novels differ, however, in one crucial way: Dickens puts the recursive thinking process in an explicitly interconnected social context; that is, his repetitions help us make links between subplots. In contrast, James takes us through mazes of frequently ambiguous contexts, sometimes so vague that they have no single lexical referent — they are what I am calling supralinguistic.

In the mystery plot of *Our Mutual Friend*, one prominent recursive process invites the reader (and some characters) to revise the referents for the "bird of prey" metaphor, in order to determine who is and is not a predator. Moreover, the reader's discoveries frequently coincide with characters' discoveries. In contrast to the discoveries in *Our Mutual Friend*, at the end of James's novel none of his characters' truths seem to coincide. In the course of *The Golden Bowl*, a central recursive process involves revision of the referents for the "pagoda" metaphor. Discovery of truth is a process of redefining the referents for the pagoda, a process that the reader shares with all six characters: Maggie; her father, Adam; Maggie's husband, Prince Amerigo; Charlotte, who is Maggie's school chum, the prince's lover, and, thanks to the naive Maggie's matchmaking, Adam's wife as well; and those two couples' friends Fanny and Bob.

I shall first examine some of Dickens's references to birds of prey. The bird of prey metaphor forms cohesive ties of the types that Halliday and Hasan (1976) describe as "reiterations" and "collocations." *Reiteration* refers to exact duplications of a phrase, or the use of "a synonym, near-synonym, or superordinate" (a class of which something mentioned is a member; e.g. the class predator and its member vulture). Reiterations function anaphorically, referring to previously named entities; for example, in the sequence "that elm . . . the tree . . . that old thing," the second and third noun phrases refer to the first, *that elm* (1976, 278).

Collocation refers to pairings of words with cultural or semantic links (1976, 284–85): we associate "green" with "envy," "bird" with "feathers." In *Our Mutual Friend*, the first three mentions of a bird of prey show a progression from a simile (the first two mentions) to a metaphor (third mention) that equates the riverman Gaffer, who has discovered a body, with predators: "He was a hook-nosed man, and with that and his bright eyes and his ruffled head, bore *a certain likeness to a roused bird of prey*" (45, italics added). "Hook-nosed" and "bright eyes" and "ruffled head" collocate with "roused bird of prey." In the next mention, "wulturs" (vultures) is a reiteration of "bird of prey": (Rogue Riderhood speaking) "I a'most think you're *like the wulturs*, pardner, and scent 'em [bodies in the river] out" (46, italics added). By the third mention, Gaffer is equated with a bird of prey; having given the facts of Gaffer's behavior, the narrator implies that the evidence warrants this label: "He had the special peculiarity of some *birds of prey*, that when he knitted his brow, *his ruffled crest* stood highest" (65, italics added).

In the description above, Gaffer is talking to two lawyers, Eugene and his friend Mortimer, the latter of whom has been hired to execute the estate of millionaire John Harmon. Later, however, Gaffer disappears and is suspected of having murdered a man he found in the river. At this point in the text, the referents for "bird of prey" multiply. Playing detectives — socially acceptable scavengers — Eugene and Mortimer go to a waterfront tavern and pretend to be lime merchants. Lime was used to cover the stench of the dead or to capture small birds; therefore, *lime* collocates in a subtle manner with *bird of prey* and other related phrases and so suggests the predatoriness of Mortimer and Eugene.

Mortimer falls asleep and has a dream, described in the passage below. In this dream oblique anaphoric references collocate to suggest the similarity between two sets of men belonging to two distinct subplots. One subplot is centered upon Eugene, who confides to Mortimer his boredom with the law and with his father, who has planned out every event of Eugene's life, including his marriage; the other concerns the rivermen Gaffer and his "pardner" Rogue, who are somehow involved in the death of the drowned man. Locations of anaphoric references are given in square brackets:

> As Mortimer Lightwood sat before the blazing fire, conscious of drinking brandy and water [previous paragraph this page] then and there in his sleep, and yet at one and the same time drinking burnt sherry at the Six Jolly Fellowships [the riverfront tavern, frequented by Gaffer and Rogue, where Mortimer now dreams, 209], and lying under the boat on the river shore [where Mortimer, Eugene, Mr. Inspector, and Rogue lay to watch for Gaffer, 214–15], and sitting in the boat that Riderhood rowed [something Mortimer only imagines, 218], and listening to the lecture recently concluded [by Mr. Inspector, reconstructing how Gaffer drowned, 222–23], and having to dine in the Temple with an unknown man [Rogue, who comes to see Eugene and Mortimer as they are dining, 194–95], who described himself as M. R. F. Eugene Gaffer Harmon ["M. R. F." is Eugene's facetious name for "My Respected Father," 193], and said he lived at Hailstorm [the weather on this night, 204] — as he passed through these curious vicissitudes of fatigue and slumber, arranged upon the scale of a dozen hours to the second, he became aware of answering aloud a communication of pressing importance that had never been made to him, and then turned it into a cough on beholding Mr. Inspector. For, he felt, with some natural indignation, that that functionary might otherwise suspect him of having closed his eyes, or wandered in his attention. (224)

In this surreal passage, the cohesive devices of reiterative verbs and syntactic parallelism reinforce the connection between past and present events and between characters from the two subplots. On an earlier visit to the tavern Mortimer was "drinking burnt sherry" (209); on this one he is "drinking brandy and water." The other parallel anaphoric references ("lying under the boat . . . and sitting in the boat . . . and listening . . . and having to dine . . .") seem unconnected when those events occur; now Dickens merges them. They collocate to give us reader-detectives the first clues that the predators and the prey may inhabit the same minds and bodies.

Mortimer's comic dream contains some serious and partly subliminal messages about birds of prey: he has merged Eugene with Gaffer with Harmon with "M. R. F." — all mystery men to us at this point in the text as well as to Mortimer. Gaffer's primary identity is as a predator, and John Harmon's is as the prey, so the syntactic link with Eugene implies that Eugene is either (1) a predator, or (2) prey; given Eugene's previous behavior, the former role seems more likely, but we cannot be certain — yet. This composite name ("M. R. F. Eugene Gaffer Harmon") is, then, a cataphoric reference to a passage that clarifies Eugene's nature: on the next page Eugene's connection with Gaffer is made explicit when he asks Mortimer, "Are *my feathers* so very much *rumpled?*" — a collocative reminder of Gaffer's "ruffled crest." Eugene has this night shown an interest in Gaffer's daughter Lizzie; his behavior appears predatory because their social stations are so far apart that an illicit relationship seems the only probable outcome.

The use of anaphoric and cataphoric reference in this passage is typical of Dickens's style throughout the novel: it adds information or clarifies with every concrete image. The parallel phrases, all objects of the preposition "of," move Mortimer to different scenes, but the referent for each phrase is unambiguous and easy to locate. This syntactic parallelism and lexical reiteration and collocation push us to make thematic connections, as we do here between Mortimer's subconscious links, and mentally to view them as a cinematic montage. Thus syntax and reference work together with metaphor to create thematic and structural cohesion among the subplots. Epistemology is problematic for us as it is for Mortimer (and later for a number of other characters), but the work that we have to do in order to reconcile the murder mystery and several other factual ambiguities eventually pays off.

Unlike the explicit or only temporarily ambiguous referents in *Our Mutual Friend*, a number of prominent referents in *The Golden Bowl* are not named by a single, unambiguous noun phrase; instead, an entire complex event, signified by metaphor, is the referent. The pivotal passage in this novel is the one I call the "pagoda passage"; it concerns Maggie's search to understand her feelings for her father and for the prince and her search for the truth about the prince's past and present affair with Charlotte, which Maggie will not acknowledge until much later, in that famous crisis when Fanny breaks the golden bowl. The pagoda passage is located at the physical and thematic center of the book. It shows Maggie worrying vaguely about "the difference" she has "made . . . in the situation" — the situation being the two couples' marriages and friendships. This situation is represented metaphorically either as an ivory tower or an "outlandish pagoda" that she walks around in the Edenic garden which she imagines her life to be:

> This situation had been occupying, for months and months, the very centre of the garden of her life, but it had reared itself there like some strange, tall tower of ivory, or perhaps rather some wonderful, beautiful, but outlandish pagoda, a structure plated with hard, bright porcelain, coloured and figured and adorned, at the overhanging eaves, with silver bells that tinkled, ever so charmingly, when stirred by chance airs. She had walked round and round it — that was what she felt; she had carried on her existence in the space left her for circulation, a space that sometimes seemed ample and sometimes narrow; looking up, all the while, at the fair structure that spread itself so amply and rose so high, but never quite making out, as yet, where she might have entered had she wished. She had not wished till now — such was the odd case; and what was equally odd . . . no door appeared to give access from her convenient garden level. (299)

Maggie is confused about the meaning of the pagoda — she cannot find a "door" through which to enter it — so for her the pagoda is a cataphoric reference. It appears to be clarified on the next page: "The pagoda in her blooming garden figured the arrangement — how otherwise was it to be named? — by which, so strikingly, she had been able to marry without breaking, as she liked to put it, with her past. She had surrendered herself to her husband without the shadow of a reserve or a condition, and yet she had not, all the while, given up her father by the least little inch" (300). In the first sentence of the first passage above (299), the narrator compares Maggie's "situation" to *either* a "tall tower of ivory" *or* an "outlandish pagoda," two different metaphors that both represent Maggie's uncertainty and create uncertainty in us — we visualize one metaphor, then must replace it with another. It is "rather" a pagoda — this is the image Maggie finally chooses. "The situation" (pagoda) is made animate: it "reared itself"; this animacy renders Maggie a passive onlooker, so passive and disconnected from her physical surroundings that she appears to be dreaming.[5]

The syntax in this passage is disruptive. Two clauses start with the same subject-verb construction "she had," but the first clause is interrupted by a "that" clause, the second interrupted by a long appositive phrase. There are also two parallel participles: "looking up" and "making out," but the parallelism stops with these two-word phrases, so, as is typical in reading this novel, our expectations of syntactic patterning, of parallelism, are thwarted, whereas, as we have seen in the passage from Dickens, our syntactic expectations are met.

This passage also contains contradictions: Maggie is "looking up . . . but never quite making out where she might have entered *had she wished.*" The next sentence negates that clause: "She *had not wished* till now. . . ." This switch from *had* as a conditional verb to an auxiliary marker of past tense disconcerts because it thwarts reader expectations of parallelism. One must compare a hypothetical state of mind posited by the narrator ("had she wished") to Maggie's "actual" state, as best one can recover it from the text; this foregrounded disparity between Maggie's not wishing "to enter" and the narrative implicature,[6] that she *should* have wished to, implies that Maggie has erred. The analeptic "she had not wished till now" reinforces the disparity.

This subversion of syntactic expectations, so characteristic of James, contributes to the mood of emotional and epistemological instability of which the shifting metaphor of ivory tower-to-pagoda is a symbol. Finally, the phrase "garden" appears at the beginning and at the end of this passage, so one circles back, as it were; the pagoda, or "situation," is enclosed in Maggie's garden, or life. Metaphor, then, *creates* its own referents ("situation," "life"): their meaning depends upon how we "see," or interpret the significance of the metaphor, which is always slippery because readers' perceptions differ.[7] Here, as throughout the novel, one is left with a sense of the redefining process as an infinite loop, forced into finitude arbitrarily, by the author's ending the novel.

For the reader, the referent for "pagoda" is both cataphoric and anaphoric and cannot be connected with any specific linguistic entity. Rather, it is supralinguistic: it comprises more than any segment or collection of segments of the text contains.[8] James's references to the pagoda and to its collocations — flowers and the garden associated with it — illustrate all four characters' shifting, elusive perceptions of their entangled feelings. This passage functions as a *mise en abyme* of the entire plot; it illuminates meanings within the larger narrative.[9] The pagoda metaphor refers anaphorically to the conversation in the previous chapter between Maggie's friends Fanny and Bob. Here, Fanny tells Bob there is "nothing" between Charlotte and the prince (269); however, twenty pages later she realizes that Maggie "did it originally — she began the vicious *circle* [italics mine]" (289). When we read of Maggie's walking "round and round the pagoda, in the space left her for circulation," we are led, by reiterative phrases, to compare her perception of her "situation" with Fanny's perception in the chapter that precedes the pagoda passage. Fanny realizes that the "vicious circle" began with Maggie's behaving as if she were mistress of her father's house and his wife, rather than his daughter. She tells Bob:

> "Maggie had in the first place to make up to her father for her having suffered herself to become — poor little dear, as she believed — so intensely married. Then she had to make up to her husband for taking so much of the time they might otherwise have spent together to make this reparation to Mr Verver

perfect. And her way to do this, precisely, was by allowing the Prince the use, the enjoyment, whatever you may call it, of Charlotte to cheer his path — by installments, as it were — in proportion as she herself, making sure her father was all right, might be missed from his side." (289)

Maggie, as we have seen, views her problem quite differently. Ten pages after the passage above, Maggie's revised interpretation of the pagoda makes it clear that she is deceiving herself, that she has misperceived "the situation" — that is, she has misread the signs of the pagoda. At this point the disparity between Fanny's and our understanding and Maggie's is greatest. We read on in order to discover whether Maggie will realize a meaning that more closely coincides with our own, which is also subject to revision. The cataphoric referent for the pagoda becomes, then, whatever we finally decide it symbolizes about the four people's relationships as well as what Maggie later admits to herself about the prince's affair with Charlotte and about her feelings for them and for her father.

The next reference to the garden/tower-or-pagoda metaphor comes twenty-seven pages later; here Maggie thinks naively of giving the prince her "flower of participation." Without her knowledge he has just returned from renewing his affair with Charlotte.

> . . . her plan had begun to work; she had been, when he brightly reappeared, in the act of *plucking it out of the heart of her earnestness — plucking it, in the garden of thought,* as if it had been *some full-blown flower* that she could present to him on the spot. Well, *it was the flower of participation,* and as that, then and there, she held it out to him, putting straightway into execution the idea, so needlessly, so obscurely absurd, of her *sharing* with him, whatever the enjoyment, the experience, might be — and sharing also, for that matter, with Charlotte. (316)

This passage refers us to others, but, again, the reference is supralinguistic and therefore more elusive than any in *Our Mutual Friend.* Getting the connection requires unusually close attention to the text. Anaphorically the reference to Maggie's "flower of participation" suggests the real flower of an illicit "participation" that Charlotte tosses down to Amerigo as a signal that she wishes to renew their affair: "She detached a white rosebud from its company in the front of her dress and flung it down to him" (262). Both flower descriptions occur in prepositional phrases ("out of the heart of her earnestness" and "in the front of her dress"). However, Maggie's flower is romantic and abstract; Charlotte's, sexual and physical. At another critical juncture earlier in the plot, Charlotte thinks of her "easy command" of her social standing and of her relationships with Adam, Maggie, and the prince. This "command" is likened to "the strong-scented flower of the total sweetness" (180). The effect of these anaphoric references is ironic: Maggie's vague, abstract flower is juxtaposed to Charlotte's real, sensual one, in the former passage, and to her own explicit (for James, that is) intellectual one in the latter passage. This juxtaposition emphasizes Maggie's emotional and intellectual isolation. Moreover, Charlotte's symbolic flower is "strong-scented," another contrast to Maggie's unscented one — Charlotte is participating in a real relationship with the prince, whereas Maggie's "participation" is an illusion. So the meaning of *flower* shifts; we expect that repetition will add information and clarify the meaning of the word; instead, we must revise our conception of it with every encounter.

Maggie intends to share "whatever the enjoyment, the experience might be." The second of these two parallel nouns, "experience," does not add information, as a Dickensian parallel phrase usually does; instead, its referent is an event even vaguer than the general "enjoyment." Maggie's thinking here is ironic: the "experience" that we anticipate her sharing with the prince is a confrontation about his and Charlotte's affair; so the effect of the passage is to increase our sense of Maggie's misreading of the two couples' problems. In contrast, the passage from Dickens in which Mortimer dreams of recent events and conflates Eugene, Eugene's father, Gaffer, and John Harmon sets Mortimer — and us — on the road to solving the mystery of the real nature of several individuals as well as of the supposed murder of John Harmon.

I have shown, above, that reiteration and syntactic parallelism serve as devices to foreground the bird of prey metaphor. In addition, these techniques are themselves foregrounded in other passages in order to serve the same cohesive purpose as metaphor: they refer backward and forward to connect characters from different subplots. In contrast to James's references, those in *Our Mutual Friend* form syntactic links that, in turn, create semantic, mystery-solving links. In the following passage, Mortimer has just asked the predatory Rogue Riderhood "on what grounds" he accuses Gaffer of the murder of John Harmon:

> "*On the grounds,*" answered Riderhood, wiping his face with his sleeve, "that I was Gaffer's pardner, and suspected of him many a long day and many a dark night. *On the grounds* that I broke the pardnership because I see the danger; which I warn you his daughter may tell you another story about that, for anythink I can say, but you know what it'll be worth, for she'd tell you lies . . . to save her father. *On the grounds* that it's well understood along the cause'ays and the stairs that he done it. *On the grounds* that he's fell off from, because he done it. *On the grounds* that I will swear he done it. *On the grounds* that you may take me where you will, and get me sworn to it. . . ." (198)

As in the Jamesian passages, the syntactic parallelism and reiteration in Rogue's speech involve prepositional phrases, but there the similarity ends. Dickens's syntax adds information (although Rogue's assertion is false) and the clauses beginning with "that" allude to specific events. The prominent reiteration makes us recall — or turn pages back to — the interview between Gaffer and Rogue in chapter 1; we may also ask ourselves if we have overlooked any intervening evidence about them. At any rate, in order to verify the accuracy of our referents, we undergo a process of anaphora, or backtracking.

Thematically, Rogue's use of "on the grounds" constitutes a misuse of legalese and reveals the comic deficiency of his logic. We realize the depth of his deficiency as we mentally (or physically) flip back to check our own recollections of the Gaffer-Rogue scenes against Riderhood's version. In so doing we are rewarded with epistemological certainty: when our readings of the truth conflict with a character's, we are able to retrace the referents that confirm our ability to interpret with accuracy.

Rogue gives "it" several syntactic functions and referents in this passage, but even though he mingles these, we do not become confused, as we might in a Jamesian narrative in which a pronoun shifts referents and syntactic uses. In the third sentence, "it" (in "what it'll be worth") refers to Lizzie's story, as Rogue interprets it, about the just-mentioned "that," which refers in turn to reason(s) why the Gaffer-Rogue "pardnership" broke up. In the sentence after "father," resuming the repetition of the phrase "on the grounds," the first "it" (in "It's well understood") functions as an anticipatory subject,[10] specified by "that he done it." This last "it" refers to Harmon's murder, which is mentioned explicitly two short paragraphs before. We know exactly what "it" means because the context of this speech, the conversation between Mortimer, Eugene, and Rogue, is confined to that one subject. "It" in the next-to-last sentence above also refers to the murder. The last clause, "get me sworn to it," alludes to Rogue's fingering Gaffer as the murderer.

This segment of *Our Mutual Friend* typifies Dickensian language, in which referents are easily recovered from a semantic context involving one topic; we shall see that in *The Golden Bowl* pronominal ambiguity is frequently used to foreground topic-switching, especially in dialogue.[11]

In *Our Mutual Friend*, even when a subplot is interrupted by many pages, the reader easily picks up the referents when the subplot resumes. On pages 363 to 364 of *Our Mutual Friend*, Rokesmith (really John Harmon) hints that Bella has neglected her family in not going home. Bella then pouts and tells him she plans to see them the next day — a plan she forms on the spot. It is not until page 431, sixty-seven pages later, that the topic of Rokesmith's implied criticism comes up again, when Bella petulantly says he had no right to think ill of her: "I wanted to say something when I could have the opportunity, as an explanation of why *I was rude to you the other day.* . . . Truly, you must have a very high opinion of me, Mr. Rokesmith, when you believe that in prosperity I neglect and forget my old home" (431). The conversation has one surface topic — clarification of Bella's previous behavior — and basically one implicature, or hidden topic. Here, the implicature involves Bella's exploration of Rokesmith's feelings for her. The reference to Bella's rudeness is clear as usual in Dickens, even though six story lines separate the two episodes: Bella's stormy visit home and "elopement" with Pa; little Johnny's willmaking and death; Mrs. Boffin's and the Milveys' return to Betty Higden's to request that Sloppy succeed Johnny as the endowed orphan; Miss Peecher's cross-examination of Mary Ann and Bradley's attempted grilling of Jenny; Lizzie's, Rogue's, and Pleasant's encounter with the disguised Harmon/Rokesmith; and Harmon's soliloquy.

Like his narrative passages, Dickens's dialogues do not tax our analytic abilities as James's do; instead, they allow us to recall the facts of conversations and events, to make connections rather than to recognize emotional severances. So the hard work we have left to do in reading *Our Mutual Friend* is, rather, to retrace ground we have already covered between a word and its earlier referent — to assess how the scene at hand clarifies our store of information about Bella's and John's feelings toward each other and to review apparently unrelated events in order to discover what they have to do with one another. The effect of these far-flung related conversations, then, is that we focus on them with reference to the social worlds in which we find them. As a consequence, we try to start connecting those worlds.

As James's metaphors tend to shift meaning, so larger units of narration and dialogue are prone to switch topics, syntactic patterns, or both. Topic switches involve shifts in the referent for a reiterated pronoun. In one such conversation, Maggie confides to Adam that Charlotte let her know Adam married for Maggie's benefit and that Charlotte can "so beautifully understand" his reasons for marriage. Adam, after blushing, says "What she does like . . . is the way *it* has succeeded" (367). "It" could be either

Charlotte's telling Maggie why Adam married, Charlotte's understanding of Adam's reasons, or the marriage itself. Unlike the mental search one conducts to find referents for Rogue Riderhood's *it's*, discussed above, our search here is incomplete, for some events are not dramatized within the text. In other words, our epistemological search is thwarted because we do not get all the facts that we need to feel confident that we can know the truth.

Maggie responds to her father's remark with a question, "Your marriage?" and he answers by shifting the topic by replacing Maggie's noun phrase "marriage" with one that is not a reiteration of it: "Yes — my whole idea. The way I've been justified. That's the joy I give her. If for her, either, it had failed —!" (367). Ralf Norrman rightly points out that in *The Golden Bowl*, "yes" is almost invariably the lead-in to an evasion or else a soft, seemingly affirmative beginning to what ends in a negation (89). In other words, "yes" usually means "no," but politely.

To clarify "it" in the above dialogue, we refer cataphorically to "marriage," which is not quite accurate, and so on to "my whole idea," which in turn we can only decipher as a cataphoric reference to the sentences that follow, at which point we start from zero again, analyzing what Adam means by saying he has been "justified." One might assume he means justified in marrying Charlotte as part of his larger plan to allow Maggie to make a life with her husband, but one has to stop and think about "it," to double back over the preceding conversation, and then to look ahead for possible modifications before one can feel certain — if ever.

In addition to ambiguous pronouns, noun ambiguity and shifts in the function of verbs necessitate a recursive reading process. In a scene that is remarkable in James for its sexual explicitness, the prince and Charlotte are alone having tea, Maggie and the principino having gone to spend the day with Adam. The prince bursts out to Charlotte with "How can I not feel more than anything else how they adore together my boy?" (224) and later "They would have done the same for one of yours" (225). Charlotte says that not even her having had numerous children would keep their "*sposi*" apart (the noun *sposi* is an ambiguous word here, meaning either Charlotte's and the prince's spouses, or Maggie and Adam as each other's "spouse"); she follows the remark by saying "we're immensely alone," meaning Amerigo and herself. After the prince moves to stand directly before her, she asks, "What will you say . . . that you've been doing [this afternoon]?" Amerigo's answer is *not* a reply to Charlotte's question; he changes verb forms and, by implication, topics: "Yet I can scarce pretend to have had what I haven't" (226). And Charlotte replies, repeating his verbs, "Ah, what haven't you had? — what aren't you having?" after which Amerigo again changes the subject and replies that they must "act . . . in concert." Here the implicature is more difficult to determine than it is in *Our Mutual Friend*, when Bella spars with Rokesmith. Although elliptical, Bella's reference to "the other day" is clear, while Charlotte's and the prince's elliptical talk has several possible meanings. In addition to causing ambiguity, the prince's change of verb forms, from "doing" to "have had," intensifies the sensual overtones. Charlotte picks up his new verb and uses it twice: "what haven't you had? . . . having?" This switch creates an explicitly sexual context; at the end of this scene the two embrace.

James's references tend toward revision and divergence, whereas Dickens's links tend toward unilinear accumulation of meaning and its consequent epistemological certainty. Tracing Dickens's bird of prey metaphor, we find it connects characters and by implication their text worlds. Comparisons implied by the bird of prey metaphor link characters from different subplots. Each of these subplots evinces a distinct parodic style (e.g., the mock-epic description of Bella and Pa's "elopement" in Book the Fourth, chapter 4; the acerbic Miltonic depiction of the Lemmeles' wedding breakfast in Book the Second, chapter 16). At the same time, these stylistic shifts do not subvert thematic cohesion because the metaphoric links across discourse worlds are so strong that they push us to connect those parodied social spheres. At the end of the novel, Dickens provides us with a sense of interrelatedness, of comedic closure: the mysteries have been solved, and the worlds of the various predators have broken up, but an alternate society is forming. In the penultimate chapter, "Persons and Things in General," disparate worlds come together in a circle around Bella and John Harmon (the man everyone thought had been murdered), minus the villains — the predators — who have acted as serious threats. The second romantic subplot, Eugene's pursuit of Lizzie, has been resolved by Lizzie's transformation of Eugene from bored would-be seducer to grateful, loving husband. Bella and Lizzie come from families whose social status is beneath their husbands', so both couples represent a subversion of social class distinctions that results in social linkage. The cumulative effect of these explicit, interconnected references is a vision of a society that challenges the world of the predators: the class-obsessed Veneerings and Podsnaps, Bradley Headstone, Rogue Riderhood, and Mr. Wegg. The dominant narrative voice in this chapter parodies a newspaper society page announcement and serves notice that a comic resolution has occurred. This chapter begins:

> Mr. and Mrs. John Harmon's first delightful occupation was, to set all matters right that had strayed in any way wrong, or that might, could, would, or should, have strayed in any way wrong, while their name was in abeyance. . . . In all their arrangements of such nature, Mr. and Mrs. John Harmon derived much assistance from their eminent solicitor, Mr. Mortimer Lightwood; who laid about him professionally with such unwonted despatch and intention, that a piece of work was vigorously pursued as soon as cut out; whereby Young Blight was acted on as by that translantic dram which is poetically named An Eye-Opener, and found himself staring at real clients instead of out of window. (874–75)

In revealing the truth about his disappearance, John Harmon has created a network of relationships that causes the truth about the predators to be revealed. At the same time, the text betrays some discomfort about the efficacy of epistemological searches: Harmon and Bella's marital happiness is also in part the result of forces that they could not understand, predict, or control: Bradley's obsession with Lizzie and his attempted murder of Eugene are averted by his own mental collapse, Wegg's bungled "friendly move" against Boffin is thwarted by Boffin's unexpected wit, and, most importantly, Bella's marriage to John is effected by a Boffin who is more wily than either the reader or Bella has any reason to expect. We, like Bella, are taken in by his pretended paranoia and miserliness. This flaw in an otherwise intricate network of subplots is a jarring suggestion that a world that appears to be predictable may not be completely so. This undermining of epistemological certainty is still relatively minor in the context of the entire novel; nevertheless, it does point toward a possible ontological dilemma. Indeed, McHale argues that the weight of foregrounded epistemological and ontological questions may shift: "Intractable epistemological uncertainty becomes at a certain point ontological plurality or instability: push episte-mological questions far enough and they 'tip over' into ontologi-cal questions. By the same token, push ontological questions far enough and they tip over into epistemological questions — the sequence is not linear and unidirectional, but bidirectional and reversible" (11). In *Our Mutual Friend*, the ontological dilemma re-mains only an undercurrent of possibility; it is not what McHale calls "the dominant," or foregrounded, concern (11). *The Golden Bowl* moves closer to foregrounding ontology, making it approach postmodern anxiety.[12] The cumulative effect of James's ambiguous references is a vision not of a society but of four isolated people who act upon the illusion that they understand one another, or them-selves. While the emphasis is upon truth and ways of knowing, truth becomes so problematic that if the sociohistorical context had been larger than the upper-class world that James creates, the nature of reality might also have been made equivocal.

Although Maggie and the prince seem to be glad to be reconciled to each other and parted from her father and Charlotte, who are off to live in America, they are still striking poses for one another. She fears that he seems to be "waiting for a confession," which most readers, I suspect, do not anticipate from the prince. The story concludes with this scene between them: "He tried, too clearly, to please her — to meet her in her own way; but with the result only that, close to her, her face kept before him, *his hands holding her shoulders, his whole act enclosing her,* he presently echoed: '"See"? I see nothing but *you.*' And the truth of it had, with this force, after a moment, so strangely lighted his eyes that, as for pity and dread of them, she buried her head in his breast" (567). She has been given access to a "pagoda," an emotional relationship with her exotic (because Italian and aristocratic) husband, but now, instead of walking around it, she is enclosed by "it," which is, finally, "his whole *act.*" Furthermore, Maggie buries her face to hide from "the truth" in his eyes. One is left wondering, with some skepticism, if the prince's love is feigned, and if what Maggie is hiding from is not the truth of his love, but the truth of his fickleness.

While James and Dickens manipulate syntax and metaphor differently and for different purposes, both of them emphasize narrative self-consciousness about the medium, print, with numbered pages and complex plots that invite us to flip backward and forward, to make marginal notes, to cross-reference the references. At the same time, the characters experience an analogous process. One significant part of the linguistic infrastructure of the novel is anaphoric and cataphoric reference, which disrupts to various degrees a character's relationship with her milieu, causing it to be revised by the process of memory working over time, trying to solve certain mysteries. In the worlds that modernist writers draw upon, conventional assumptions about truth — what it is, how to know when one has found it — are severely disrupted; one's epistemological search is no longer linear but recursive, requiring backtracking and suspending judgment until one reads further to gather more facts. At the end of the modernist novel, the facts yield only more questions. In the worlds of realistic writers, however, the individual character's (and reader's) epistemological assumptions are challenged and examined, usually against conventionality, then reconciled to a revised world view.[13] *Our Mutual Friend* contains some modernist elements, but because epistemological uncertainties are resolved it remains essentially within the bounds of realism. *The Golden Bowl* is modernist in leaving epistemological questions unanswered; in raising ontological questions, it approaches postmodernism. A basic difference between Dickens and James is that — to borrow a metaphor from *The Golden Bowl* — Dickens takes us down the road of realism, into which many paths eventually converge, while James takes us on a modernist circular route, with many side trips and recursions about a fantastic tower.

Notes

1. The term "foregrounding" connotes not only emphasis of some textual feature but emphasis, by means of its extraordinary frequency, for some particular reason (Fowler 1986, 71). The term was created by the Russian formalists (see Mukařovský 1964, 17–30).

2. Levine writes of the Victorians, "Their narratives . . . struggle to reconstruct a world out of a world deconstructing, like modernist texts, all around them." Their response, he argues, is to write "*against* the very indeterminacy they tend to reveal" (4).

3. In "Connexity, Interpretability, Universes of Discourse, and Text Worlds" (forthcoming), Enkvist explains that a writer's text strategies are manifested both on the macrostructural level of text organization (e.g., according to time and place) and on the syntactic level. In "Stylistics, Text Linguistics, and Text Strategies" (1988), he suggests ways in which a text strategy "drives" a set of predications about a story that the writer wants to tell. These essays employ information-processing theory to suggest, among other things, that literary theory and text linguistics can be used together to explicate textual cohesion and interpretability in ways impossible to either discipline alone.

4. I am indebted to Thomas E. Nunnally for this analogy and for his comments on an earlier draft of this paper.

5. For a linguistic treatment of Maggie's internal monologues, see Maini (1988, 151, 155).

6. The nature and function of implicature are discussed in Grice (1975, 43–45) and Fowler (1986). Fowler defines implicature as "roughly, what is said 'between the lines.' This relates to the traditional notion that one can say one thing and mean something else. . . . An implicature is a proposition emerging from something that is said, but not actually stated by the words uttered, nor logically derivable from them. It must therefore be a

product of the relationship between utterance and context; and a vital part of context would be the knowledge and motives of the speaker and addressee" (106).

7. I am indebted to Nils Erik Enkvist for clarifying this relationship between metaphor and its referents and for his comments on an earlier draft of this paper.

8. My term "supralinguistic" is equivalent to Riffaterre's "hypersign," which he discusses in his *Semiotics of Poetry*. I prefer "supralinguistic" to the term "metatextual" because "meta" suggests meaning *beyond* the text, while "supra" means "above," in the sense that symbolic metaphors and networks of referentiality take on meaning above the actual semantics and syntax, yet still building upon, or deriving from, them.

9. Michael Riffaterre (1990) has drawn a stimulating new distinction between *extended metaphor* and a related meaning structure that he calls "subtext"; see his *Fictional Truth* (54 ff.). Riffaterre describes the *mise en abyme* as "a mirroring of text by subtext reminiscent of the Romantic conceit of the oak tree potential within the acorn" (22). According to McHale, the term was adopted from heraldry by André Gide (McHale 1987, 124).

10. For a discussion of the anticipatory subject, see Quirk and Greenbaum (1973, 423).

11. See Ralf Norrman's chapter "Referential Ambiguity in Pronouns" (1982, 6–65).

12. For another, more complex view of the ideological shifts inherent in the English novel, see McKeon (1987, 20–21), in which he gives an overview of the dialectical forces at work in the "narrative epistemologies" of the novel. His category of "naive empiricism" seems to be roughly equivalent to the kind of empirical search underway in *Our Mutual Friend* and *The Golden Bowl*, although in the latter text, this search is perilously close to McKeon's next category, "extreme skepticism," which develops in reaction to naive empiricism.

13. Levine (1981) develops a similar argument about Victorian realism: "Nineteenth-century realism . . . deliberately subverts judgments based on dogma, convention, or limited perception and imagination" (20). He sees the dogmatic Mr. Podsnap as "the enemy not only of Dickens, but of all Victorian novelists" (2). For a thorough discussion of how epistemological uncertainty works within a character, see R. F. Brissenden's analysis of Clarissa in *Virtue in Distress*, especially 176–86.

References

Auerbach, Erich. [1953]. *Mimesis: The Representation of Reality in Western Literature.* Trans. Willard R. Trask. Princeton: Princeton UP.

Booth, Wayne C. 1961. *The Rhetoric of Fiction.* Chicago: U of Chicago P.

Brissenden, R. F. 1974. *Virtue in Distress: Studies in the Novel of Moral Sentiment from Richardson to Sade.* New York: Macmillan.

Dickens, Charles. [1865] 1986. *Our Mutual Friend.* Ed. and intro. Stephen Gill. Middlesex, England: Penguin.

Enkvist, Nils Erik. Forthcoming. "Connexity, Interpretability, Universes of Discourse, and Text Worlds."

———. 1988. "Stylistics, Text Linguistics, and Text Strategies." Keynote address, Symposium on Stylistics and Literary Texts, Bar-Ilan University, Israel.

Forster, E. M. 1927. *Aspects of the Novel.* New York: Harcourt.

Fowler, Roger. 1986. *Linguistic Criticism.* Oxford: Oxford UP.

Grice, H. Paul. 1975. "Logic and Conversation." In *Syntax and Semantics III: Speech Acts,* ed. P. Cole and J. Morgan, 41–58. New York: Academic P.

Halliday, M. A. K., and Ruqaiya Hasan. 1976. *Cohesion in English.* London: Longman.

James, Henry. [1904] 1983. *The Golden Bowl.* Ed. and intro. Virginia Llewellyn Smith. Oxford: Oxford UP.

Levine, George. 1981. *The Realistic Imagination: English Fiction from Frankenstein to Lady Chatterly.* Chicago: U of Chicago P.

Lubbock, Percy. [1921] 1955. *The Craft of Fiction.* New York: Scribner's.

Maini, Darshan Singh. 1988. *Henry James: The Indirect Vision.* 2d ed. Studies in Modern Linguistics 83, ed. A. Walton Letz. Ann Arbor: UMI Research Press.

McHale, Brian. 1987. *Postmodernist Fiction.* New York: Methuen.

McKeon, Michael. 1987. *The Origins of the English Novel 1600–1740.* Baltimore: Johns Hopkins UP.

Mukařovský, Jan. 1964. "Standard Language and Poetic Language." In *A Prague School Reader on Esthetics, Literary Structure, and Style,* ed. and trans. Paul L. Garvin, 17–30. Washington, D.C.: Georgetown UP.

Norrman, Ralf. 1982. *The Insecure World of Henry James's Fiction.* New York: St. Martin's.

Quirk, Randolph, and Sidney Greenbaum. 1973. *A Concise Grammar of Contemporary English.* New York: Harcourt.

Riffaterre, Michael. 1990. *Fictional Truth*. Baltimore: Johns Hopkins UP.
————. 1978. *Semiotics of Poetry*. Bloomington: Indiana UP.
Watt, Ian. 1960. *The Rise of the Novel: Studies in Defoe, Richardson, and Fielding*. Berkeley: U of California P.

Comparison and Synthesis
Marianne Moore's Natural and Unnatural Taxonomies

The selective nomenclature — the chameleon's eye if we may call it so — of the connoisseur, expresses a genius for differences; analogous dissimilarities in Man Ray's **Of What Are The Young Films Dreaming,** *exemplifying variously this art of comparison and synthesis.* (Marianne Moore 1986, 183)

Art and Science in Moore

"Comparison and synthesis" and the discovery of "analogous dissimilarities" are among the most characteristic features of Marianne Moore's own poems. She is famous for her composite images, such as that of the cat "Peter" (1982, 43), who is described in a sequence of comparisons with elements from a great variety of sources: a human thumb, fronds, katydid legs, shadbones, porcupine quills, seaweed, a snake, a prune, alligator eyes, an eel, a mouse, and a frog. This sequence of diverse analogies results in a "synthesized" image; Peter is a mental and verbal construct, the sum of the associations called up in the observer between an actual cat and other creatures and things in the natural world.

The integration and unification of conventionally opposed elements is both a moral and an aesthetic goal for Moore. Her longest poem, "Marriage," is a meditation on the "enterprise" of trying to unite male and female, and "Sea Unicorns and Land Unicorns" takes as its starting point the medieval notion of land and sea as parallel realms and of complementary creatures, such as the lion and the unicorn, which attract one another and together form a powerful whole:[1]

> Thus personalities by nature much opposed
> Can be combined in such a way
> That when they do agree, their unanimity is great.
>
> (77)

Moore cites the perception of unity in diversity as a fundamental principle of poetry. "Didn't Aristotle say," she asked Donald Hall, "that it is the mark of a poet to see resemblances between apparently incongruous things?" (Phillips 1982, 102). In Moore's own work, "apparently incongruous things" are constantly brought together to form harmonious wholes — conceptual and verbal orderings of disparate elements of the natural world.

The creation of mental and verbal structures for the "comparison and synthesis" of natural objects is not, of course, an "enterprise" limited to poets; the taxonomies of the natural sciences serve a very similar purpose. Moore's interest in science and the "scientific" quality of her own work have often been discussed (Donoghue 1968, Ransom 1969, Blackmur 1935). Moore was a biology major at Bryn Mawr College, and her poems often reflect, both in subject matter and in diction, a "relentless accuracy" and "capacity for fact" (Moore 1982, 76) that are more typically associated with scientific writing than with poetry. Her poems are full of specialized vocabulary, quantification, and detailed factual (or ostensibly factual) information: the hedge-sparrow "wakes up seven minutes sooner than the lark" (111); the "pale / tigerstripes — about seven" on a chameleon are the result of "the melanin in the skin / having been shaded from the sun by thin / bars" (196); the musk ox "grows six pounds / of qiviut; the cashmere ram, / ten ounces — that is all — of pashm" (193–94). Copious footnotes to the poems identify sources and provide background information, and *Observations* includes an index — although an odd one, containing such unconventional entries as "orchids, collision of, 67" and "pulled, 20." Moore even uses a scientific simile to describe the process of poetic composition: "I never plan a stanza. Words cluster like chromosomes, determining the procedure" (Hall 1969, 34).

Moore seeks to break down the conventional opposition between literary and scientific writing. In the long version of "Poetry," she explicitly rejects the notion (quoted from Tolstoy) that some types of material should be excluded from the class of "poetry" on the basis of conventional genre or subject matter: "nor is it valid / to discriminate against business documents and // school books; all these phenomena are important" (267). Moore says that both "the poet and the scientist . . . must strive for precision" (in Hall 1969, 44), and she attempts to integrate the scientist's precision, traditionally associated with an objective point of view — an attempt to describe the structure of the world as it "really" exists — with the subjective precision of the poet, who builds a reality that is overtly a mental construct, an image of the world as it is perceived: "What is more precise than precision? Illusion" (151). The goal of both types of precision is integration: to compare and synthesize, to discover or create structure out of the enormous variety of the natural (and created) world.

Compounding and Classification

Both Moore's concern with comparison and synthesis and her interest in the natural sciences are reflected in her most abundant and characteristic linguistic structure: the noun + noun compound. Her use of compounds is so frequent that the concordance to her poems contains a thirty-five-page "second section" that "lists separately the components of the poet's many hyphenated compounds" (Lane 1972, preface, n.p.). The majority of these are noun + noun compounds, and since the list includes only hyphenated forms, many compounds are omitted because they are written either as one word (*moonstone*, 51; *waterfly*, 68) or as two words (*avalanche lilies*, 74; *strangler figs*, 110).

Borroff mentions that "a hallmark of [Moore's] descriptive style" is her "propensity for joining two or more nouns together to form compound nouns and modifiers" (99). She cites the frequency of these and other types of complex noun-phrases in feature writing and advertising as evidence of the influence of Moore's journalistic sources on her diction. As the above examples suggest, however, the noun + noun compound is also characteristic of the diction of the natural sciences. Compounds are often used taxonomically, "for distinguishing different species of a genus (using the term loosely) in the real world" (Zimmer 1971, C11). These taxonomic compounds form nonarbitrary labels for their referents, in that they link them with other referents that are perceived as related: a *bloodhound* is a member of the *hound* class, distinct from but related to other members such as *elkhound, foxhound* and *wolfhound*. The various species are identified in terms of what are seen as their distinctive characteristics — most frequently habitat (*water buffaloes*, 194; *desert thorn*, 201), resemblance (*crape myrtle*, 109; *trumpet flower*, 107) or function (*food grape*, 17; *silkworm*, 110).

There has been much debate as to how noun + noun compounds should be defined (cf. Adams 1973, Bauer 1978, Hatcher 1960, Lees 1960, Marchand 1960, Warren, n.d.). For my purposes, I will consider a noun + noun compound to be any sequence of noun + noun that functions as a unit and contains no overt morphological or syntactic indication of the relation between the two nouns. Four classes of noun + noun compounds are commonly recognized. The first and by far the most numerous group is the *endocentric* compounds, such as *beehive* and *armchair*, in which "the compound is a hyponym of the grammatical head: a beehive is a kind of hive, an armchair is a kind of chair" (Bauer 1983, 30). In an *exocentric* or *bahuvrihi* compound, such as *birdbrain* or *egghead*, the entire compound "is a hyponym of some unexpressed semantic head ('person' in both the examples given here)" (30). An *appositional* compound such as *maidservant* is a hyponym of both its elements; "a maidservant is a type of maid and also a type of servant" (30). In a *dvandva* or *copulative* compound such as *Alsace-Lorraine*, "the compound is not a hyponym of either element but the elements name separately entities which combine to form the entity denoted by the compound" (31).

In discussions of the functional and stylistic characteristics of noun + noun compounds, the first features usually mentioned are unification and conciseness. Marchand says that we form compounds when we "see or want to establish a connection between ideas, choosing the shortest way possible" (22). A compound noun not only names its referent; it also makes an implicit statement about it, a statement of relation between the noun's elements. A *treefrog*'s name contains information about the animal's habitat; the noun could be paraphrased, "a frog that lives in a tree." In the case of an exocentric compound, the situation is even more complex; a third noun, the head, must be posited, and the existing two-noun compound must be related to it. The statement "The spoonbill flew away" thus contains the additional implicit statements: "The (implied) bird is identified by its bill," and "The bill is like a spoon." A great many relations are possible between the elements of an endocentric or an exocentric compound, and often the relation is ambiguous or obscured by the passage of time: a *cat coat* could be a coat either worn by or made from cats; few contemporary speakers of English could define the relation of the elements of *polka dot*.

In addition to directly modifying a noun with another noun, Moore frequently derives adjectives from nouns with the suffix *-ed*: *toothed temples*, 129; *flowered step*, 131. Very often a compound noun is adjectivalized: *sea-serpented regions*, 60; *snipe-legged hieroglyphic*, 48. Like noun + noun compounds, noun + *-ed* adjectives are characteristic of the diction of scientific description (Ljung 1976, 164), commonly specifying the particular feature of a species that most clearly distinguishes it from other related species: a *rose-breasted grosbeak* from other *grosbeaks*, a *three-toed sloth* from other *sloths*. Moore's noun + *-ed* adjectives, like her compound nouns, bring the taxonomic precision of scientific writing to her poetry and call attention to the similarities and differences between the scientist's and the poet's approaches to the natural world. The nonscientist will often be unable to say whether Moore's "taxonomic" designations (*rust-backed mongoose*, 12; *upland meadow mouse*, 17) are scientifically recognized names for actual species or poetic descriptions.

Naming and Identity

Noun + noun compounds are often described as having classificatory or naming functions. Downing calls compounding "a back door to the lexicon" and says that a speaker who creates a compound "is typically faced with a situation in which he wishes to refer to an entity which possesses no name of sufficient specificity. . . . [In such a situation,] compounds are ideally suited to serve as ad hoc names" (quoted in Levi 1978, 62–63).

Naming is a prototypical symbolic act. To pick out one element of the natural world and assign it a label is to impose a conceptual ordering on reality. Although it has long been a tenet of linguistics that "the bond between the signifier and the signified is arbitrary" (Saussure 1966, 67), a compound noun, as I have already suggested, is a less arbitrary label than a monomorpheme, in that it implies a structure of relations between the referent and the referents of other nouns that share an element of the compound. Such forms may be viewed as "diagrammatically iconic," since "like diagrams, they resemble the conceptual structures they are used to convey" (Haiman 1985, vii).

The relation between word and object is, of course, a primary concern for the poet, and Moore frequently plays on the iconic quality of noun + noun compounds to comment on our conceptual acts of comparison and synthesis, as they are reflected in our linguistic structures. Moore is intensely interested in names and the act of naming; she sometimes decomposes a name to play on its real or fancied etymological connections: "Jupiter or jour pater, the day god" (116), "reindeer . . . adapted // to scant *reino*/ or pasture" (96). She sometimes refers to a thing by its technical Latin name, distancing it from everyday experience, presenting it as the object of scientific scrutiny: "*myristica fragrans*" (21), "lion's foot - *leontipodum more* / exactly" (96). In "He Digesteth Harde Yron," the subject of the poem, the ostrich, is never referred to directly by its common monomorphemic name, but is called, at the beginning of the poem, "camel-sparrow" (99) and at the end, "sparrow camel" (101). The ostrich is, of course, neither sparrow nor camel. The compounds appear to be metaphorically copulative; the ostrich is seen as possessing camel-like and sparrow-like characteristics. The word *sparrow* is apparently borrowed from Xenophon, who, confronted with a strange new creature, attempted to fit it into a conceptual taxonomy by comparing it with familiar species.

Within a given language or idiolect, there is generally a one-to-one relationship between referent and linguistic label. This "iconicity of isomorphism" reflects the "commonly accepted axiom that no true synonyms exist, i.e. that different forms must have different meanings" (Haiman 1980, 515). Moore often questions the accuracy or appropriateness of names, or assigns several names to a single referent, each representing a different view of the referent or a different conceptualization of the world in which the referent participates. "The Frigate Pelican" is

> This
> hell-diver, frigate-bird, hurricane-
> bird; unless swift is the proper word
> for him

(25)

The reader is presented with different characterizations of the same creature. This is a bird that *dives* as if into, or like a creature from *hell*; that accompanies or resembles a *frigate*; that has the strength and violence of, or is associated with, the occurrence of a *hurricane*. (We later learn, from "storm omens," that this last reading of "hurricane- / bird" is the "correct" one.) The identifying elements *hell, diver, frigate,* and *hurricane* form a cluster of associations around the *bird,* creating a composite embodiment of a violent marine landscape.

Moore appears dissatisfied with all these attempted characterizations, however, and suggests that perhaps "swift is the proper word /

for him." But *swift* is the name of another very different bird, a small land bird. The adjectival, descriptive sense of the name comes into focus, but the reference slips away from the pelican and onto one of its attributes, speed, which it shares with another bird. Throughout this series of epithets, the reader is shown not the bird itself, but the various natural phenomena and attributes with which it is associated.

In Moore, alternate taxonomic terms for one referent serve as alternate conceptual perspectives from which the referent may be viewed. The identity of a creature or thing is constructed out of a variety of linguistic labels representing different perceptions of its place in the natural world, its relations to other referents. Sometimes, however, these alternate linguistic labels are conflicting, misleading, or obscure. The title, "The Arctic Ox (or Goat)," introduces a creature of one species while suggesting almost in the same breath that it may actually belong to another species. *Ox* and *goat* call up quite distinct images; what sort of creature is this that might belong to either species? A note beneath the title informs us that the poem is derived from an article about "musk oxen." In the body of the poem, Moore refers to the animal in question as *the arctic ox* and then as *the "goat,"* implying that it is, in fact, an ox and not a goat. In the third stanza, however, she states that "The musk ox / has no musk and it is not an ox." The objective precision of the taxonomic labels collapses; neither the species name nor its defining characteristic is accurate. It is, as Moore scornfully puts it, an "illiterate epithet," one reflecting incompetence with *words*. In the fifth stanza, the creature is a *"musk ox,"* the quotation marks serving as a reminder of the inaccuracy of the name. In the sixth stanza, the animals are "these ponderosos," a word I have not yet found in an English dictionary, but one that suggests their massive "ponderous" bulk. Having dismissed the available labels, Moore creates her own "epithet."

In the tenth stanza, a new name appears: "these scarce *qivies*"; we have been prepared for this by a reference to *qiviut*, the creature's fleece. These two words show an apparent morphological relation between the name of the animal and that of the wool for which it is known. This new name also reinforces the notion of the creature's rarity; *qiviut* is one of the very few words in an English dictionary containing a *q* not followed by a *u*. Moore seems now to have abandoned the attempt to fit an Indo-European name to these foreign animals; she adopts a term that appears to be native to their own habitat, a term exotic and opaque to her readers.

Moore's final naming of her subject is a whimsical chain of phonetic association: "our goatlike / qivi-curvi-capricornus." The exotic name is transformed into an Indo-European morpheme which suggests zoological terminology and, by extension, the Latin word for *goat*. By the end of the poem, "The Arctic Ox (or Goat)" has passed through a number of nominal transformations, culminating in a sort of etymology by association.

Moore is always alert to the problem of maintaining the iconic connection between word and referent, where one originally existed. Loss of this connection may lead to unauthentic, hackneyed use of language.

> Even gifted scholars lose their way
> through faulty etymology.
> No wonder we hate poetry.
> and stars and harps and the new moon.

(151)

She says, "I shall purchase an etymological dictionary of modern English / that I may understand what is written" (59), yet she often uses "faulty etymology" for her own purposes. "Logic and the Magic Flute" begins:

> Up winding stair,
> here, where, in what theater lost?
> was I seeing a ghost -
> a reminder at least
> of a sunbeam or moonbeam
> that has not a waist?
> By hasty hop

> or accomplished mishap
> the magic flute and harp
> somehow confused themselves
> with China's precious wentletrap.
>
> (171)

The *winding stair*, as Moore reveals in a note, is a literal translation of the Dutch *"wenteltrap* a winding staircase; cf. G. *wendeltreppe,"* the name given to "the shell of *E. pretiosa*, of the genus *Epitonium"* (288–89). "By hasty hop / or accomplished mishap," the referent of the literal, etymological meaning of the word leads us to the referent of its metaphorical meaning, now semantically opaque. The Dutch *trap*, meaning 'staircase', and the English *trap* "somehow confuse themselves." The false etymology that leads us to understand the English sense of *trap* is encouraged by words such as *lost, catacomb, fetter* and a reference to *Trapper Love*. The word *wentletrap* itself, and indeed the whole poem, is a "trap" for the reader: a chain of associations, visual, etymological, phonetic, and semantic, linking the elements of the poem in a meditation on love, freedom, art, and their interrelations. Here, quirks of association and faulty etymology "illogically wove / what logic can't unweave" (172) — a unified poetic image.

The first stanza of "His Shield" contains a catalogue of spiny creatures and an elaborate lesson in etymology:

> The pin-swin or spine-swine
> (the edgehog miscalled hedgehog) with all his edges out,
> echidna and echinoderm in distressed-
> pin-cushion thorn-fur coats, the spiny pig or porcupine . . .
>
> (144)

The pronoun of the title does not reveal the identity of the poem's subject; we do not know who he is, and the opening lines of the poem do not immediately enlighten us. The compound *pin-swin* is opaque, since *swin* is not a current English word. The next compound, *spine-swine*, seems to elucidate the first; *swin* must be the same as *swine*. But does this mean that *pin* is the same as *spine?* A possible etymological connection between the two is implied.

In the next line, we are shown an explicit example of faulty etymology: "the edgehog miscalled hedgehog." We may have believed that the hedgehog was so called because it lives in hedges. Now we are told that it is because of its many "edges," presumably meaning 'sharp points'. *Hedgehog* is perhaps a hypercorrection; "dropped" *h-* is restored; or maybe *edge* and *hedge* are related, like *ear* and *hear, ax* and *hatchet,* the hedge marking the edge of a field. The historical facts (it appears that *hedgehog* is from *hedge,* OE *hecg,* and not, as Moore would have it, from *edge,* OE *ecg*) are almost irrelevant here. Moore's phonetic-semantic "etymological" associations have a sense of their own. Whether or not they faithfully reconstruct the origins of words (as does "the spiny pig or porcupine"), they set up a series of images and relations among words and their referents — a case-study in the descriptive function of names, of linguistic change, of the elusive quality of words, and of the power of the imagination to reinvent relations between names and things.

Taxonomies of the Imagination — "The Jerboa"

Although it was once customary to think of scientific language as "literal" and poetic language as "figurative," it is by now a commonplace that scientific description is also metaphorical. It is sometimes argued that "There is no difference between the predication of *Water is liquid sunshine* (an apparent metaphor) and *Water is* H_2O (a supposedly literal statement). . . . If we say that one of the expressions is 'poetic' while the other is 'scientific', then we have classified them according to different universes of discourse, rather than drawn a distinction between literal and metaphorical sense" (Di Pietro 1976, 101–2).

In Moore's descriptions of animals, plants and objects, "different universes of discourse" often come together. When the distinction between the scientific and poetic viewpoints is obscured, so, too, are the distinctions between the natural and the man-made, the actual and the imaginary, the arbitrary and the iconic. Moore's use of taxonomic and descriptive compounds helps to create a unifying perspective in which these and other oppositions are reconciled. In "The Jerboa," the unauthentic, exploitative life and art of the ancient courts is contrasted with the genuineness, freedom, and decorous simplicity of the jerboa, which lived in the nearby desert. The poem begins with a description of a man-made object:

> A Roman had an
> artist, a freedman,
> > contrive a cone — pine-cone
> > or fir-cone — with holes for a fountain. Placed on
> > > the Prison of St. Angelo, this cone
> > > of the Pompeys which is known
>
> now as the Popes', passed
> for art.

(10)

This prison ornament, "contrived" on commission by an ex-slave, is of uncertain species: "pine-cone / or fir-cone," not a clear, accurate representation of one or the other. It "passed for art" but was not.

In the decadent Egyptian court, animals were enslaved, hunted, and killed, and their bodies and images were used to create luxury items. The king kept slaves, dwarves, "and tamed"

> Pharaoh's rat, the rust-
> backed mongoose. No bust
> of it was made, but there
> was pleasure for the rat. . . .

(12)

Pharaoh's rat, which is not a rat but a mongoose, leads Moore to "a small desert rat," the "jerboa" of the title, which finally makes its appearance on the fourth page of the poem:

> and the jerboa, like it,

a small desert rat,
and not famous, that
   lives without water, has
   happiness. Abroad seeking food, or at home
      in its burrow, the Sahara field-mouse
      has a shining silver house

of sand. O rest and
joy, the boundless sand
   the stupendous sand-spout,
      no water, no palm-trees, no ivory bed,
      tiny cactus; but one would not be he
      who has nothing but plenty.

(13)

Pharaoh's rat has "pleasure" in its luxurious court life, but the jerboa "has / happiness" living free and unencumbered in the desert. In the description of the jerboa that follows, Moore's taxonomic/descriptive language takes the reader from an objective, zoological perspective on the animal and its environment to a subjective, poetic view of the jerboa as a work of authentic art that brings not only pleasure but also the deeper sense of joy that accompanies moral and aesthetic decorum.

In Moore's first three mentions of the jerboa, she moves from an opaque apparent monomorpheme — the "purest" name: "jerboa," to an apparent descriptive phrase: "a small desert rat," to an apparent taxonomic label: "the Sahara field-mouse." The term *desert rat* prepares one for *Sahara field-mouse* at two structural levels:

Environment	Species
desert	rat
Sahara	field-mouse
field	mouse

But the descriptive phrase and the taxonomic label are in conflict. Is this a rat or a mouse? Is it native to desert or to field? The nonzoologist has no way of being certain whether the phrase *Sahara field-mouse* is an actual taxonomic term, 'a type of field-mouse native to the Sahara', or a metaphor: 'a creature that is to the Sahara as a field-mouse is to a field'. The unifying function of the complex compound is undermined, as the modifying element *Sahara* of the higher-level compound contradicts the modifying element *field* of the lower-level compound. We do not know what this creature "really" is; we have only the sum of the ways it is referred to, various attempts, "scientific" or "poetic," to structure the natural world by means of words.

The second section of the poem begins,

> Africanus meant
> the conqueror sent
> from Rome. It should mean the
> untouched: the sand-brown jumping-rat - free-born; and
> the blacks, that choice race with an elegance
> ignored by one's ignorance.
>
> (13)

The jerboa's new label, *sand-brown jumping-rat*, falls somewhere between the clearly taxonomic and the clearly descriptive. The complex, doubly hyphenated label is taxonomic in form, but specification of color by comparison *(sand-brown)* rather than by simple color-name *(buff, tan,* etc.) is unusual in scientific nomenclature. The jerboa's color reflects its desert environment — the natural adaptation of the "free-born" jerboa to its surroundings, as opposed to the garish ornaments of the ancient Egyptians. Moore's use of the word *sand* in her designation for the jerboa reflects the link between the animal and its surroundings and thus also preserves the connection between the creature's essence and its linguistic label.

The characterization of the jerboa as a *jumping-rat* marks the beginning of a chain of imagery that lifts the jerboa above the earth: it jumps "as if on wings," it has a "bird head," and the fur on its back "is buff-brown like the breast of the fawn-breasted / bower-bird." In *fawn-breasted / bower-bird*, we see another semitaxonomic, semidescriptive label. The bower-bird is a well-known species, although, again, the comparative form of color-designation is more poetic than scientific in tone. The phrase also contributes a new tone to the description of the jerboa. Although *bower* is used taxonomically, identifying the bird in terms of its dwellinglike constructions, for most readers the word is more suggestive of poetic than of scientific diction; a *bower* is a rustic structure where lovers meet. Similarly, *breast*, while it may be used in taxonomic labels (*rose-breasted grosbeak*), is also a word with romantic reverberations. In the context of these other words, *fawn* also participates in the atmosphere of softness, gentleness, and vulnerability. Each element in this long label, then, functions at two levels; it evokes both the language of zoological taxonomy and the language of love poetry. The poetic tone and the scientific tone are inseparable here. Moore weaves two conventionally opposed levels of diction together, creating a form of designation/description that combines the sense of crispness and precision conveyed by the concise referring units of taxonomic compounds with the evocative, personal tone suggested by the constellation of romantic vocabulary and by the metaphorical mode of presentation (rodent-color compared to bird-color compared to fawn-color).

The rest of the noun + noun compounds (and the adjectives derived from them) applied to the jerboa are clearly descriptive rather than taxonomic. Various aspects of the jerboa are characterized in terms of their resemblances to other creatures and things. As Moore focuses in on a particular part of the animal, she simultaneously moves away from it; the jerboa has *chipmunk contours* and a *bird-head*; the tip of its tail is *fish-shaped*, and it moves with *kangaroo speed*. The eye of the naturalist poet sees in the jerboa reflections of many other examples of natural adaptation. Moore's jerboa gradually changes from a "real" taxonomically defined animal to a composite creature of the imagination.

The jerboa's "leap" into the realm of art is reinforced by comparisons with man-made objects; the tip of its tail is "silvered to steel by the force / of the large desert moon," and after this magical transformation, the jerboa becomes, in the poem's final two stanzas, an odd, elegant, composite artifact:

By fifths and sevenths,
in leaps of two lengths,
   like the uneven notes
   of the Bedouin flute, it stops its gleaning
      on little wheel castors, and makes fern-seed
      foot-prints with kangaroo speed.

Its leaps should be set
to the flageolet;
   pillar body erect
   on a three-cornered smooth-working Chippendale
      claw — propped on hind legs, and tail as third toe,
      between leaps to its burrow.

                                                    (14–15)

With the exception of its *kangaroo speed*, the jerboa's attributes are no
longer compared to those of other animals, but to the products of
human art: *the Bedouin flute, little wheel castors, the flageolet, pillar body*, and
finally the elaborate *three-cornered smooth-working Chippendale / claw*.
The jerboa's movement is like music, and the delicate *fern-seed / foot-
prints* it leaves suggest supernatural power (often ascribed to fern-
seed), but even as it moves, it seems immobile, carved. It is upright,
like a pillar, elegant and functional like a Chippendale claw — an
embodiment of decorum. By the end of the poem, the jerboa, this
"simplified creature," has become highly complex. It is both natural
and supernatural, both a zoological specimen and a creation of the
observing mind, given concrete form in the various labels that
specify its perceived relations to other elements of the world.

Integration of Natural Classes — "Virginia Britannia"

In scientific taxonomies, members of different "natural" classes
are distinguished and grouped together in separate categories; an
animal cannot be "related" to a vegetable or mineral. In Moore's
imaginary taxonomies, however, no such limitation holds. Poetic

"relatedness" is based on the precision of illusion, which discovers new ways of integrating diverse objects. Moore's labels and descriptions very frequently link items from a variety of natural classes, breaking down conventional taxonomic barriers and creating new, harmonious structures.

"Virginia Britannia" (107–11) catalogues the inhabitants of Virginia, past and present, and records, indirectly, the process of appropriation and reshaping that has occurred since the arrival of the Europeans. The reader might expect that the human and nonhuman participants in a historical scene would be differentiated from one another, with the landscape forming a passive background against which the humans act. This is not the case in Moore's Virginia, where the chief distinction is not human versus nonhuman or animate versus inanimate, but native versus colonial. The human "actors" do not act; in the five-page poem, the only tensed, active verb (apart from the copula) with a human subject occurs in the sentence "a great sinner lyeth here under the sycamore," — the permanently static "activity" of a dead man's repose. The humans in "Virginia Britannia" are viewed as elements of the densely populated natural landscape; they do not stand out from the surrounding flowers, birds, and other flora and fauna. Moore repeatedly insists on the integration of her humans into the scenery by describing people in terms reminiscent of natural-historical taxonomy and by using words normally associated with humans in her descriptions of animals and plants.

In the first stanza, we are introduced to an assortment of Virginia residents:

> . . . the red-bird, the red-coated musketeer,
> the trumpet-flower, the cavalier,
> the parson, and the wild parishioner.
>
> (107)

The taxonomic-sounding *red-bird* is directly followed by *red-coated musketeer*, a human, but one who is categorized, like the bird, on the basis of the coloration of his "coat." The *trumpet* of *trumpet-flower* picks up the military tone of *musketeer* but removes it to the nonhuman realm; these are not real trumpets, but flowers. The cavalier and the parson are human, but what about "the wild parishioner"? *Wild* animals and flowers are common, but *wild* in the taxonomic sense ('not tamed; not domesticated') suggested by the context here is not generally used of humans; when it is, it carries a connotation of savagery — a less-than-human quality. *The wild parishioner* refers to an original inhabitant of the parish, but whether it is human or an animal (as is suggested by the following image of "a deer / track in a church-floor / brick") is unclear.

In the next stanza, two important humans, one native and one colonial, are introduced. They are not described directly, however; rather, they are represented by their symbols of power, both of which include animal elements: Powhatan's *fur crown* and John Smith's coat of arms "with ostrich, Latin motto, / and small gold horse-shoe" (107). On the following page, we meet another "Virginian":

> Observe the terse Virginian,
> the mettlesome gray one that drives the
> owl from tree to tree and imitates the call
> of whippoorwill or lark or katydid — the lead-
> gray lead-legged mocking-bird. . . .
>
> (108)

It is only in the third line of this description that it begins to be clear that the subject is a bird, and only in the fifth line do we learn what bird. Both the adjective *terse* and the noun *Virginian* lead us to expect a human; the -an suffix meaning 'inhabitant of' is normally used only of people, not of animals, and *terse* is an adjective applied to speech. Moore's extension of these human characterizations to a bird again challenges the notion of human uniqueness and supremacy; birds, humans, plants, and animals are all "Virginians."

We see two sets of pansies, "dressed" in elaborate, human-like finery:

> . . . box-bordered tide-
> water gigantic jet black pansies — splendor; pride —
> not for a decade
>   dressed, but for a day, in over-powering velvet; and
>   gray-blue-Andalusian-cock-feather pale ones
>   ink-lined on the edge, fur-
>   eyed, with ochre
> on the cheek. . . .

(108)

In this flower bed, we see *velvet, cock-feathers, ink, fur-eyes,* and *cheeks,* images which both describe the pansies' appearance and link them with animals, birds, and humans; specifically, the two types of pansies evoke the two humans we have already met. The *splendor* and *pride* of the black flower's *over-powering velvet* suggest the velvet clothing which might have been worn by the Europeans who were about to "over-power" the natives, while the *fur-eyed* pansies recall Powhatan's fur crown: their *cock-feather* coloration suggests the feather head-dresses worn by some native groups, and their "ochre / on the cheek" calls up an image of war paint.

Flowers and humans are again linked in the following passage:

>   Old Dominion
>   flowers are curious. Some wilt
>   in daytime and some close at night. Some
> have perfume; some have not. The scarlet much-quilled
>   fruiting pomegranate, the African violet,
>   fuchsia and camellia, none; yet
>   the house-high glistening green magnolia's velvet-
> textured flower is filled
>   with anesthetic scent as inconsiderate as
>   the gardenia's. Even the gardenia-sprig's
>   dark vein on greener
>   leaf when seen
> against the light, has not near it more small bees than the frilled

silk substanceless faint flower of
the crape-myrtle has. Odd Pamunkey
princess, birdclaw-ear-ringed; with pet raccoon
from the Mattaponi (what a bear!). Feminine
odd Indian young lady! Odd thin-
gauze-and-taffeta-dressed English one! . . .
(109)

In this *inconsistent flower-bed*, flowers are *quilled* like birds or porcupines, *velvet-* / *textured, frilled silk* or *crape* like clothing. The *velvet-* / *textured* magnolia recalls the *over-powering velvet* pansies. The magnolia, too, is powerful and *inconsiderate*, "with anesthetic scent."

The list of flowers is followed without transition by the introduction of two more human beings, but they are not described as "human" in any usual sense of the word. We are given no notion of character, no image of face or body; both women are defined in terms of their ornamentation — their "plumage" — as was the *red-coated musketeer*. The "Pamunkey / princess, birdclaw-ear-ringed; with a pet raccoon" has fierce animal attributes; the *birdclaw* and the *ear* meet with alarming vividness, and it may take a moment for the reader to sort out the syntactic/semantic relations among the elements of the complex *-ed* adjective. The princess's English counterpart, in contrast, is mild and refined: "Odd thin- / gauze-and-taffeta-dressed English one" — dressed in light, man-made fabrics. Each is "odd" to the other, and each is carefully labeled, like a newly discovered specimen, with a description of the most striking features of her appearance. The Englishwoman is covered, ghostlike; the Pamunkey princess may or may not be wearing anything other than her fierce ear-rings. These two images with their contrasting tones are similar to two earlier images of flowers: "The scarlet much-quilled / fruiting pomegranate" and "the frilled // silk substanceless faint flower of / the crape myrtle." *Birdclaws* versus *gauze*, *quilled* versus *frilled silk* — the pairs of women and the pairs of flowers complement each other. There is a stronger resemblance between the pomegranate and the Pamunkey princess and between the Englishwoman and the frilled silk crape myrtle than there is between the two flowers or the two women. The classes here are not *woman* and *flower*, but *wild* and *domesticated*.

Although the native and the imported are in contrast, they are destined to grow closer to one another as the colonists settle in and appropriate the land and its inhabitants. By the end of the poem, the native and imported vegetation have become intertwined:

> The live oak's darkening filigree
> of undulating boughs, the etched
> solidity of a cypress indivisible
> from the now agèd English hackberry,
> become with lost identity,
> part of the ground. . . .

(111)

The separate species have "lost identity"; all are equally "part of the ground," and the word *indivisible* recalls the "Pledge of Allegiance," in which the United States is described as "one nation . . . indivisible." The many diverse elements of the American scene, original and imported, will, it is hoped, unite in an integrated whole: *E pluribus unum*.

Nature, Art and Language — "The Monkey Puzzle"

If words may be used to reflect conceptual structurings of the natural world, they may also be used to reflect the manifold, tangled and contradictory nature of those structurings. Moore's reader is made constantly aware that any relation expressed in language, whether it be the "objective" language of science or the "subjective" language of poetry, is an illusion, a mental construct. The structure of linguistic relations may reveal or conceal the actual properties of natural entities. For Moore, the "pedantic literalist" (37) is rigid, unimaginative, "perfunctory" in his attention; his words merely reflect back the hackneyed conceptual associations of stale convention. The creative observer and speaker uses language to arrive at fresh insights into the unbounded complexities that the natural world presents for our contemplation. I will close with a discussion of "The Monkey Puzzle," a poem that brings together clearly and compactly issues of scientific taxonomy versus poetic description, the integration of natural classes, and the power of language to conceal or reveal reality.

THE MONKEY PUZZLE

A kind of monkey or pine-lemur
not of interest to the monkey,
in a kind of Flaubert's Carthage, it defies one —
this "Paduan cat with lizard," this "tiger in a bamboo thicket."
"An interwoven somewhat," it will not come out.
Ignore the Foo dog and it is forthwith more than a dog,
its tail superimposed upon itself in a complacent half spiral,
this pine tree — this pine-tiger, is a tiger, not a dog.
It knows that if a nomad may have dignity,
Gibraltar has had more —
That "it is better to be lonely than unhappy."
A conifer contrived in imitation of the glyptic work of jade and
    hard-stone cutters,
a true curio in this bypath of curio-collecting,
it is worth its weight in gold, but no one takes it
from these woods in which society's not knowing is colossal,
the lion's ferocious chrysanthemum head seeming kind by
    comparison.
This porcupine-quilled, complicated starkness —
this is beauty — "a certain proportion in the skeleton which
    gives the best results."
One is at a loss, however, to know why it should be here,
in this morose part of the earth —
to account for its origin at all;
but we prove, we do not explain our birth.

(80)

"The Monkey Puzzle" contains no verbs of activity; its "plot" consists of the interaction of subject and object, of observer and observed. The speaker moves through a succession of descriptive phrases, some apparently scientific, others imaginative, building up a characterization of the object — recreating it in words. The reader, in turn, confronts the words of the poem and tries to move back from the poet's description to a mental image of the actual object.

The title compound is both endocentric and exocentric. The exocentric compound, *monkey puzzle (tree)*, is a taxonomic term, the popular name for "the Chile pine *(Araucaria imbricata)*" (275), so called because of the complex pattern of its branches. The endocentric compound refers to a literal puzzle: the poem itself, a riddle-poem in which the reader becomes the "monkey" who must try to solve the linguistic puzzle of the unstated head of the exocentric compound and guess the referent of the title.

The poem tantalizes us with approximations and contradictory restatements. The object at first seems to be an animal — but what sort of animal — monkey, pine-lemur, "Paduan cat with lizard," tiger, or the mysterious "Foo dog" that can become "more than a dog"? "It defies one." The speaker either does not know or will not reveal its "real" identity and offers various incompatible designations, three of them quoted, apparently representing other speakers' views of the "same" object.

Within the first eight lines of the poem, we find six noun + noun compounds, expressing various relations between their elements:

Compound	Head	Relation	Modifier
monkey puzzle	puzzle	to be solved by	monkey
monkey puzzle	(tree)	resembles	monkey puzzle
pine-lemur	lemur	lives in	pine
bamboo thicket	thicket	composed of	bamboo
Foo dog	dog	originates from?	Foo (Chow)
pine-tree	tree	of the species	pine
pine-tiger	tiger?	lives in	pine
		composed of	
		of the species	
		resembles	
		?	

Three of these compounds have *pine* as their modifying element, but their heads contradict one another — is the referent a lemur, a tree, or a tiger? The compound *pine-tiger* has the form of a taxonomic label, but it is ambiguous, and the reader must try to interpret it on the basis of the preceding compounds. Is a *pine-tiger* a type of tiger that lives in a pine, like a pine-lemur? A tiger made out of pine, as a bamboo thicket is composed of bamboo? A cross-class hybrid — a tiger of the species *pine*? The possibilities are unlimited; the more different names this creature or thing is given, the more a "puzzle" it becomes.

In the eighth line, Moore suggests for the first time that the object is actually vegetable rather than animal, a *pine-tree* — but how is the reader to be certain that this taxonomic label is any more scientifically "accurate" than the others, particularly when it is followed by a return to animal names? The object is concealed in a verbal maze, but the object *is* the maze; it is a composite of the many ways it may be seen and referred to. "'An interwoven somewhat,' it will not come out." It *cannot* come out, because it is not separate from that which hides it; it has no autonomous identity. It is not one thing with one name, but a set of perceived relations among various creatures and things. It is not even an unambiguous noun, but a strange, amorphous adjectival-adverbial chimera: "'An interwoven somewhat.'"

The second half of the poem focuses on the artificial quality of its subject. It has already been suggested that the "puzzle" belongs to a fictional world. It lives "in a kind of Flaubert's Carthage," a literary reconstruction of an actual setting — one carefully researched and full of accurate detail, but also highly personal in its imagined incarnation. It is neither animal, vegetable, nor mineral — or rather, it is all of these: a "pine-tree" that is "porcupine-quilled," "a conifer contrived in imitation of the glyptic work of jade and hard stone cutters," — nature imitating art — "a true curio." The object is not autonomous; it is nature *observed*, the creation of the same perceiving mind that sees a "chrysanthemum head" on a lion. It is not a decorative domestic object; it is fierce and wild, "a tiger, not a dog," but its "porcupine-quilled, complicated starkness . . . is beauty." As the end of the poem approaches, the object itself disappears, leaving only its aesthetic virtues; in fact, the statement "this is beauty" serves as the poem's final definition of its title object — of the tree, and of the natural world in general. The "puzzle" of nature, which the human "monkey" tries to unravel, is also the source of beauty, "a certain proportion in the skeleton which gives the best results."

Beauty is functional, the result of natural selection, and Moore's poem seems to nod wryly in the direction of the theory of evolution. Human beings may, from their own point of view, be the most highly evolved species, but this fact seems to do them little good. The natural object has beauty, knowledge, and value: "It knows that . . . 'it is better to be lonely than unhappy.' . . . it is worth its weight in gold, but no one takes it / from these woods in which society's not knowing is colossal." It is indifferent to human attention and to human ignorance. "It defies one. . . . it will not come out," and the human observer is left "at a loss . . . to know why it should be here." Scientific theories based on "proportion of the skeleton" and similar quantifiable data will explain many aspects of the natural world, but they will not "account for its origin." The mystery of "our birth," for Moore, is the province of faith and of the imagination.

The natural object that "imitates" the man-made and the man-made object that imitates the natural are united in Moore's monkey puzzle. The poem, like the tree or the Foo dog's tail, is "superimposed upon itself." It is both real and imagined, since it is constructed out of words, the "objects" in which our thoughts are embodied. This beautiful but almost indecipherable creature is lonely, like the bird in "Smooth Gnarled Crape Myrtle,"

> which says not sings, "without
> loneliness I should be more
> lonely, so I keep it" — half in
> Japanese. . . .

(104)

The work of art is solitary, but it makes a gesture of communication, in its half-foreign language. Its "birth" cannot be "explained," but must be "proven" in its ability to replicate the experience of its creation. The verbal relations of the poem must reproduce the poet's encounter with the object, the network of conceptual relations linking the object to other things and ideas. Readers of "The Monkey Puzzle," making their way gingerly among the strange and apparently disconnected phrases of the poem, experience the amused and admiring bafflement that the "complicated starkness" of the monkey puzzle tree inspired in Moore.

If the "pedantic literalist" believes that the external world may be captured simply in language by means of one-to-one relations between things and words, Moore believes that both the world and the linguistic structures that we use to describe it are "monkey puzzles," complex, "interwoven" networks of relations. These relations, and most particularly the relations between things and words, are, for Moore, by no means one-to-one or "immutable," but are constantly being created, questioned, and redefined through "observations." Metaphor, ambiguity, and paradox are to be cultivated, not avoided, for these nonliteral linguistic strategies realize some of the infinitely varied and complex potential relations among the things of the world and the minds that reach out to grasp them. The only literalists who are of any interest to Moore are her famous

> "literalists of
> the imagination" — [who are] above
> insolence and triviality and [who] can present
>
> for inspection, "imaginary gardens with real toads in them,"
> (267)

who can successfully integrate the real and the imagined, the objective and the subjective in a unified vision.

Note

1. Unless otherwise indicated, page references for poems are to Moore (1982).

References

Adams, Valerie. 1973. *An Introduction to Modern English Word-Formation.* London: Longman.

Bauer, Laurie. 1978. *The Grammar of Nominal Compounding.* Odensee: Odensee UP.

———. 1983. *English Word-Formation.* Cambridge: Cambridge UP.

Blackmur, R. P. 1935. "The Method of Marianne Moore." In *The Double Agent: Essays in Craft and Elucidation.* New York: Arrow Editions. Reprinted in Tomlinson (1969), 66–86.

Borroff, Marie. 1979. "Marianne Moore's Promotional Prose." In *Language and the Poet,* 80–108. Chicago: Chicago UP.

Di Pietro, Robert J. 1976. "The Role of Metaphor in Linguistics." In *Linguistic and Literary Studies in Honor of Archibald A. Hill,* ed. Mohammed Ali Jazayery, Edgar C. Polome, and Werner Winter. 2 vols. Lisse: Peter de Ridder P, vol. 1: 99–107.

Donoghue, Denis. 1968. "The Proper Plenitude of Fact." In *The Ordinary Universe.* London: Faber and Faber. Reprinted in Tomlinson (1969), 165–71.

Downing, Pamela. 1977. "On the Creation and Use of English Compound Nouns." *Language* 53:810–42.

Haiman, John. 1980. "The Iconicity of Grammar." *Language* 56:515–40.

———, ed. 1985. *Iconicity in Syntax.* Amsterdam: John Benjamins.

Hall, Donald. 1969. "The Art of Poetry: Marianne Moore." In Tomlinson (1969), 20–45.

Hatcher, Anna Granville. 1960. "An Introduction to the Analysis of English Noun Compounds." *Word* 16:356–73.

Lane, Gary, ed. 1972. *A Concordance to the Poems of Marianne Moore.* New York: Haskell House Publishers.

Lees, Robert B. 1960. *The Grammar of English Nominalization.* IJAL 26, no. 3, part 2 (Publication 12 of the Indiana University Research Center in Anthropology, Folklore and Linguistics). Bloomington: Indiana UP.

Levi, Judith. 1978. *The Syntax and Semantics of Complex Nominals*. New York: Academic Press.

Ljung, Magnus. 1976. "*-ed* Adjectives Revisited." *Journal of Linguistics* 12:159–68.

Marchand, Hans. 1960. *The Categories and Types of Present-Day English Word-Formation*. Wiesbaden: Otto Harrossowitz.

Monroe, Melissa. 1988. "The Expressive Function of Nominal Structure in Marianne Moore and Wallace Stevens." Ph.D. diss., Stanford U.

Moore, Marianne. 1925. *Observations*. 2nd ed. New York: Dial Press.

———. 1982. *The Complete Poems of Marianne Moore*. Harmondsworth, Middlesex: Penguin Books. First published by Macmillan and Viking, 1967.

———. 1986. *The Complete Prose of Marianne Moore*. Ed. Patricia Willis. New York: Elizabeth Sifton Books, Viking.

Phillips, Elizabeth. 1982. *Marianne Moore*. New York: Frederick Unger.

Ransom, John Crowe. 1969. "On Being Modern with Distinction." In Tomlinson (1969), 101–6.

Saussure, Ferdinand de. 1966. *Course in General Linguistics*. Ed. Charles Bally and Albert Sechehaye. New York: McGraw Hill. Original French edition first published in 1916.

Tomlinson, Charles, ed. 1969. *Marianne Moore: A Collection of Critical Essays*. Englewood Cliffs: Prentice-Hall.

Warren, Beatrice. n.d. *Semantic Patterns of Noun-Noun Compounds*. Göteborg: Gothenburg Studies in English 41.

Zimmer, Karl E. 1971. "Some General Observations about Nominal Compounds." *Working Papers in Language Universals* 7, Stanford U, C1-C21.

PART 3

Voice

First-person narration is especially problematic in fictional narrative. The *I* of a story can be interpreted in varying degrees to represent the author, who, of course, as a living or dead human being, must remain outside the text. Because the real author can be known only partially and primarily from evidence outside a fictional text, the term *implied author* is sometimes used to refer to the authorial voice within the text. Yet the fictional *I* may not represent the author at all but a fictional character whose voice is very different from the author's own. The two chapters included in this section consider texts in which the voice of a first-person narrator represents multiple perspectives. For further treatment of the subject, see Karen A. Hohne's "Dialects of Power: The Two-Faced Narrative" in part 7.

In an essay on Gordon Weaver's *Eight Corners of the World,* Cynthia Goldin Bernstein and Ewing Campbell suggest that the narrator's speech is set apart from the author's speech and from all other speech. The narrator, in an attempt to discover his own identity in an alien world, combines American slang, movie jargon, Japanese, Latin, and pig Latin, only to find himself an outcast from both Japanese and American cultures. The whole communication process is brought into question by the failure of all the narrator's personal written records to endure the bombs and fires of World War II.

Joyce Tolliver traces the linguistic markings of the dual perspective in the story "Mi suicidio," by Spanish author Emilia Pardo Bazán. The use of deixis, adjective placement, and reference suggest two mutually contradictory "scripts" of erotic love. The first script, activated by the ingenuous protagonist and corresponding to an initial, ingenuous reading of the text, rests on post-romantic literary and cultural clichés that idealize erotic love and posit woman as diaphanous, passive angel. The second script, called up by the disillusioned narrator and corresponding to a second, parodic reading of the text, revolves around the cynicism of the betrayed sentimentalist and defines woman as deceitful seductress. The clash between the two scripts serves to undermine this angel/whore dichotomy and to reposition woman as subject of her own erotic discourse.

CYNTHIA GOLDIN BERNSTEIN AND
EWING CAMPBELL

Appropriated Voices
in Gordon Weaver's
Eight Corners of the World

In defining the West *by what it is not* through the contrasting image of the Orient, we have made the Orient an exotic place, what Edward Said (1979) identifies as one of our "deepest and most recurring images of the Other." So it is thematically and imagistically significant that Gordon Weaver chooses an Oriental as narrator of *The Eight Corners of the World*. Set in the periods before, during, and after World War II, the novel takes as its topic alienation as expressed through a lack of linguistic identity. That war, especially the conflict between Japan and the United States, is represented through the narrator's discordant style. Yoshinori Yamaguchi speaks neither standard English nor Japanese, but rather a cacophonous combination of American slang, formal diction, film jargon, fractured clichés, and expressions in Japanese, Latin, pig Latin, Yiddish, and other languages. The linguistic acrobatics of this astonishing work are essential to the novel's representation of conflict, destruction, and alienation.

In the circumstances of its telling, the novel foregrounds the medium of expression in narrating a story. Can one ever explain a set of circumstances *in other words* or through another medium? That is precisely the narrator's concern when he summons tattoo master Terada Seijo to hear and record by means of dermatography the events of his life. Obese and suffering from emphysema, renal

failure, and cancer, Yoshinori Yamaguchi has decided to transform
the spoken word of his life into flesh, thereby making flesh the word.
Upon his death, he is to be flayed and the skin bequeathed to the
Wantanabe Nautical Museum of Tattoo Arts. It would seem that
through the transformation of history into flesh, the narrator seeks
to leave a permanent record of his life.[1] He wonders, however,
whether observers will understand what they view or, as he asks
Seijo, "will they dig what they gander?" (186). In response, the
tattoo artist suggests writing a monograph to accompany and
explain the displayed tattoo. But the narrator rejects the suggestion,
claiming, "Nothing on paper, nor pics neither, as how it don't do not
endure, Jack!" (186).

No medium of representation is lasting. The narrator's family
pictures were destroyed — along with his father, mother, and
sister — during the bombing of Tokyo. His *Redskin* yearbook, with
its class pictures and autographs, was burned as he filmed the
bombing of Pearl Harbor. Everything else was consumed in the
bombing of Hiroshima and Nagasaki, ending the legendary hope of
Japanese domination, to which the adage "the eight corners of the
world" refers.[2] From these episodes, the narrator attempts to extract
a lesson: "What's to conclude? Jack, it ain't nothing don't endure.
No, not peoples nor pics (nor eiga flics!) do last, reet? . . . Got
burned up in series of fires big and small, cinders and also ashes
scatter to eight corners of world. Answer, Jack, is Big Irony of Life,
reet?" (347–48). The narrator is sensitive to the irony of the Japanese words for movie *(eiga)* and English *(Eigo)*, and he has taken
pride in his accomplishments in both media. Yet words and film
alike fall victim to the flames of war. Instead of representing Japanese
domination, the phrase "eight corners of the world" is associated, in
the quotation above, with ashes of pictures and films. Taking a
picture or telling a story is not very different from creating a tattoo.
In fact, the narrator likens the tattoo artist's tool to a camera when
he speaks of "the click and snap of his electric needle" (16) and
storytelling to dermatography when he considers how to *"inject
striking ironics"* (17) into his narration. There is little reason, then,

for the reader to suppose that the narrator's skin picture will be any more permanent than oral narrative, photographs, or films.

Reinforcing this theme are numerous references to inscriptions that aim at but fail to achieve permanence. Yamaguchi refers to the *hanko*, or autograph, in expressing a desire "to go to Hollywood in America to seek the *hanko* autograph signatures of the actors and actresses who appear in the *gaijin eiga*" (21); in gifting baseball player Moe Berg with an expensive ivory "*hanko*, how you say, signature seal, ideograph of his name in *kanji*" (designed by his father, a calligraphy artist) (95); in commenting to Seijo, "Remind me to save you a good spot for your *hanko* signature seal calligraph" (185). Inscriptions are highlighted again in the etching of his name "incised on bronze plaque Honor Roll" (106) and in the cover of his 1940 Oklahoma A&M college yearbook "not unlike unto carved in stone, cast in bronze" (106). The materials used for the inscriptions — ivory, bronze, stone — would seem to suggest permanence, yet these must be read as ironic. In the conflict to come, the narrator is soon to lose his yearbook, his honor, and his identity.

The ambiguity of the narrator's identity is represented by the different names he uses in the four segments of his life. In the first, as a young student of the English language and things American, he is "Yoshinori Yamaguchi," a translator for a troupe of American baseball players barnstorming Japan as that country wages war on China and prepares to do the same with the United States. At the same time, he begins his career as a cinematographer by helping one of the players evade Japanese surveillance in order to photograph military installations. In the episode, as in those to come, he is torn between his native Japanese culture and the American culture and language he admires. In the second episode, the narrator's subversive role is inverted as he comes to the United States to attend Oklahoma A&M University, where he absurdly spies on ROTC drills. Known as "Gooch" in his metaphorical exile, he is no more at home in his beloved America than he was in his native Japan. Harassed by one of the university wrestlers and called into the office of the institution's president because of a report that he is romantically involved with a Caucasian, Gooch is acutely aware of his "otherness." After college, the revenant Gooch, renamed "Lieutenant Benshi" in the third episode, returns to his role as filmmaker. He is commissioned to record, interpret, and glorify on film the war to bring the world's eight corners under Japanese dominion. His documentary, constructed by staging scenes and using clips from old movies, is to be completed at facilities in Hiroshima. However, the flight of the *Enola Gay* brings those plans to a halt. After the war and in need of a cover, Yoshinori in the fourth episode assumes the mask of "Foto Joe," maker of memories for American soldiers and Japanese girls, publisher of army yearbooks, and finally producer of martial arts movies for the vanquished nation. The flier he distributes to advertise his services concludes with words that highlight the theme of the novel: "Motto: is it not ironic, folks, as how nothing don't endure? Hey, Hundred Millions, even life ain't permanent, but Foto Joe Yamaguch via magical illusion of modernist miracle *eiga* flics can give YOU satisfactory illusions to contrariwise, reet?" (350). The novel in postmodern fashion foregrounds ontological questions of world and self.[3] Permanence and identity can only be illusions.

Having many different names can be as unsettling as having no name at all. In fact, the narrator sometimes calls himself "orphan child of no name." At other times, he renames himself with a string of appositives: "*wataschi*, . . . Student Yamaguchi Yoshinori (me!)" (37). The different names represent the ambiguity of his identity, both literally during the four phases of his life and figuratively or essentially during the whole course of his life. And the shifting perspectives of the novel emphasize the relativity of identity. As the narrator describes it: "What's in a name, reet, Jack? Fact is, like, how we say in celluloid world, cinema-land, film biz, it depends, man. On how you shoot it, reet? Like, what's in the frame and what's ain't. Camera angle. Depth of focus. Soundtrack (music, etcetera blah). Additional dialogue. Special effects. Like, man, what your average person, any Joe Schmoe, John Q. Public, man-in-the-street might say: depends on your point of view, reet, Jack?" (8). A different name, then, is a way of signaling the unrooted nature of his condition.

Yamaguchi does not speak like the "man-in-the-street," and he is deeply concerned as to whether the common person will understand his story. Yamaguchi has good reason to question whether he can succeed in getting his message across. He endeavors to keep the big picture in mind while focusing on particular episodes (17); yet Seijo confesses to having "no expertise in this regard" (186), to which Yamaguchi responds, "Reet! Like not your job to figure significance of bits and pieces, piths and also gists, reet?" (186). Seijo, in fact, often seems to miss the message. Rather than responding to the ironies of the narrator's story, he responds to Foto Joe's financial success in post-war Japan. "'Ah, Mr. Yamaguch, how wondrous rich is the life you have enjoyed!' says Terada Seijo. . . . Obvious deduction to be made therefrom: he do not dig, reet? No sensibilities rendered sensitive to chronicles of ironics (large and small!) I is done enumerated so far, reet?" (298). Seijo, the internal audience of the narrative, has been given the responsibility of interpreting Yamaguchi's story and retelling it through a visual medium. If he cannot understand the story, how can he re-present it in a coherent way?

Those questions of telling and interpreting are raised by Weaver's creation of the narrator's unique language, an idiolect appropriated from the speech of others but distorted by him and implying an alien way of knowing and conveying what is seen. That aspect of Otherness is never far from Bakhtin's assertion, "Someone else's words introduced into our own speech inevitably assume a new . . . interpretation and become subject to our evaluation of them" (195). The narrator's speech, set apart from both the author's and all other speech, is destined to be an instrument of failed negotiation as he attempts to find his identity in an alien world.

It is through the narrator's unusual speech patterns that Weaver establishes the *double-voicedness* (Bakhtin 1984) of *The Eight Corners of the World*. Narration that is perceived to be spoken by a storyteller apart from the author is a type of narration Russian critics refer to as *skaz* (Bakhtin 1984, 185–92; Fleischman 1990, 120–23). It is characterized by the oral language of the common people, as opposed to the literary language an author would ordinarily use. Even more than the oral quality of skaz, Bakhtin emphasizes its "orientation toward another person's discourse" (192). The narrator's use of language reflects that Otherness.

Seijo's aim in interpretation is to create a unified picture out of the multiple identities and multiple voices in one man's life. One thing that makes that task so difficult is that language itself is fragmented. Instead of being a medium of communication used to bring people closer together, the narrator's language in this novel reflects his alienation from both Japanese and American cultures. As one of his redneck antagonists at Oklahoma A&M says to him, "I don't understand a word you're saying half the time, you little yellow dwarf!" (136). The strange diction and manner of expression that constitute the narrator's idiolect reinforce and define his difference from all other established identities.

Yamaguchi's way of speaking might be called, to use Halliday's (1978) expression, an *anti-language*, a private code that sets the speaker against the dominant speech and practices of a culture. The term is problematic in suggesting that it is somehow outside language. Such, of course, is not the case; no matter how nonstandard anti-language may be, it is still a kind of language. Rather, anti-language is "against language" in implying a code whose function opposes the reinforcement of the established values of a society, making it the language of society's outcasts. In this sense, the term is similar to *anti-hero*, implying a character who performs the role of a hero but whose attributes are the very opposite of a hero's. An anti-hero is not just another kind of hero; the concept depends for its meaning on what people believe a hero ought to be. Similarly, anti-language is not simply another language, for the sense of alienation it creates depends upon the norm from which it deviates.

The use of anti-language complements the creation of a narrator whose values differ from those of the implied author. This is the link, as Roger Fowler (1981) has pointed out, between anti-language and Bakhtin's concept of the polyphonic novel. According to Bakhtin, the characters of Dostoevsky's novels are not "illuminated by a single authorial consciousness" but represent instead "a *plurality of consciousnesses, with equal rights and each with its own world*" (Bakhtin 1984, 6). The anti-language of the narrator not only establishes his separateness from the implied author, but it also represents the multiple identities — Yoshinori Yamaguchi, Gooch, Lieutenant Benshi, Foto Joe — contained within the one character.

Multiplicity of identity is a theme reinforced also by the multiple names given to other characters, events, and things. Babe Ruth is introduced to the Japanese by the inept American interpreter, Mr. Walter Wetherell, who says, "Mr. Ruth's immortality is signified in the many names he assumes," and "The utterance of his many appellations — Babe, The Bambino, The Sultan of Swat — strikes horror in the bellies of his bitter enemies" (48). The "blundering Wetherell" (48) misses the mark in his explanation of multiple names. Rather than signifying immortality, they would seem to refute the simplistic notion that any one word will do in representing multiple perspectives.

The narrator uses multiple names for the baseball players who visit Japan:

> George Herman (a.k.a. Babe, a.k.a. Bambino, a.k.a. Sultan of Swat) Ruth; Louis (a.k.a. Lou, a.k.a. Iron Man) Gehrig. (36)

And for his friends at Oklahoma A&M:

> Stevie Keller (a.k.a. Mighty Mouse, a.k.a. Yukon Strongboy), co-ed Miss Clara Sterk (a.k.a. Petty Girl). (105)

And for the leaders of nations:

> Schicklgruber in Germany — *Hitler-san* to you, Terada! — Mussolini, also knowed as *Duce*, in Italy. (104)

> Russki maximum *honcho* Uncle Joe Stalin (a.k.a. Dzhugashvili). (335)

And, to ironic purpose, for events:

> how you say, Korean Conflict (a.k.a. Police Action). (336)

And for words:

> keimpe, shamus, tail. (72)

> "Money," he says, "*genkin.*" . . . I feel thick pad of bills, green-
> backs, lucre, kale, cabbage, moolah, betwixt my fingers, hear
> crispy crackle of banknotes, bucks. (125)

The strategy of renaming names, events, and words is used throughout the novel to bring into question the nature of language and identity.

A similar strategy is evident in the treatment of clichés, where variant versions of familiar expressions produce unfamiliar constructions. When Weaver has the narrator substitute apparent synonyms for words the reader expects, he, in effect, deconstructs the cliché and destroys the dead metaphor of habit. To call something "a portion of confection" (29) is, after all, not the same as calling it "a piece of cake"; and "ten cents per twelve" (191) does not produce the same effect that "a dime a dozen" does. In similar fashion, the novel is filled with such expressions as these:

> yank your limb (5)
> [f]ickle digital appendage of Fate (28)
> exert collegial style effort (95)
> lead conduit cinch (98)
> loose as gander (153)
> steer excrement (154)
> If you don't see cottonwood felled on river's bank, do it really
>   fall? (195)
> Does ursine defecate in forest? Is Papacy prelate not member in
>   good standing of mackerel-snapper faith? (215)
> commence to harvest straws whilst sun is up (304)
> when vessel I envision ties up a berth (336)
> if designs of rodents and peoples go not awry (336)

By having the narrator substitute unexpected words for familiar expressions, Weaver forces the reader to reconsider the metaphors of clichés and, at the same time, establishes the alienation of the narrator as he tries to negotiate his identity within the language.

The question of the relation of language to meaning, raised by the deconstructed clichés, is foregrounded again in the translation from one speech style to another. Following his formal introduction to a crowd of Japanese baseball fans, Babe Ruth uses the vernacular in expressing his gratitude: "Hey, thanks a lot, folks! I hope to hit a bunch of homers when we ever get out there on the field, and I promise to do my damn best, okay?" (39). That speech is then rendered as follows in the speech style of the Japanese High Court: "The Honorable Babe Ruth pledges to struggle versus all opposition with both the strength of the arm which wields the sword and the moral imperative bestowed upon him by his venerable ancestors" (39). Babe Ruth's own words are as incongruous in the formal Japanese assembly as the words of the interpreter would be at an American baseball game.

The narrator's mixture of speech styles goes beyond the informal and formal varieties used by Babe Ruth and his interpreter. In addition to the Japanese expressions dotting every page of the novel, his diction includes unusual words from many languages: schlepp, shnozz, schtick, shamus (Yiddish); avoirdupois, brouhaha, ducat, mis-en-scene (French); et alia, nexus, terminus (Latin); hoi polloi (Greek); kowtow (Chinese). The narrator is also fond of pig Latin (ix-nay, anks-thay) and slang expressions (dig, gizmo, natch). He borrows the jargon of the film industry (camera angle, depth of focus, soundtrack) and baseball (Texas League bloop). His fascination with words is summed up in his comment, "Lingo, . . . words, funny strange, reet?" (139, also 41).

In spite of his familiarity with English, the narrator uses many nonstandard constructions. At the level of diction, he comes up with such morphological oddities as "disremember" and "solitude-ness." Syntactically, he produces double and even triple negatives ("it ain't nothing don't endure" [347]), struggles with subject-verb concord ("I is," used throughout), and invents a bizarre relative pronoun "than which." His nonstandard constructions emphasize the narrator's foreignness and his alienation from the culture whose language he has appropriated.

The narrator's unique discourse exercises a powerful influence on the quality of the narrative. The manipulation of language in this astonishing work is not mere virtuosity. Rather, it is essential to the opposition between the language of a hegemonic culture and the irreconcilable ideologies represented by the narrator's potpourri of jargons. This is a person who has witnessed both the attack on Pearl Harbor and the bombing of Hiroshima. His anti-language plays out the devastation and alienation of a war in which all is consumed by "fires big and small" (348).

Notes

1. Weaver (1991) was asked where he got the idea for the tattoo as the vehicle of expression. He responded that he had read in *Argosy Magazine* how sailors in Japan would have tattoos, done and paid for in installments, prepared for permanent display.

2. In an alternative ending for the novel, Weaver had the museum burn down as well, but he decided that that would be too much (Weaver 1991).

3. See Curry's discussion of postmodernism in this volume.

References

Bakhtin, M. M. 1984. "Discourse in Dostoevsky." In *Problems of Dostoevsky's Poetics*, ed. and trans. Caryl Emerson, 181–269. Minneapolis: U of Minnesota P.

Fleischman, Suzanne. 1990. *Tense and Narrativity: From Medieval Performance to Modern Fiction*. Austin: U of Texas P.

Fowler, Roger. 1981. *Literature as Social Discourse: The Practice of Linguistic Criticism*. Bloomington: Indiana UP.

Halliday, M. A. K. 1978. *Language as Social Semiotic*. London: Edward Arnold.

Said, Edward W. 1979. *Orientalism*. New York: Vintage Books.

Weaver, Gordon. 1991. Personal interview with Cynthia Bernstein. September.

———. 1988. *The Eight Corners of the World*. Chelsea, Vt.: Chelsea Green.

Script Theory, Perspective, and Message in Narrative
The Case of "Mi suicidio"

In narration told in the first person, a dual perspective[1] is present due to the temporal separation between the narrator and the protagonist, although both are signaled by the pronoun "I." The distinction between these two perspectives, and a consideration of their relationship, may be crucial for the expression of what Prince (1983) has called the narrative "message" of the story. The examination of the function of discourse-level linguistic elements is very helpful in making this distinction. In the case of the 1894 story "Mi suicidio" ("My suicide") by the Spanish writer Emilia Pardo Bazán,[2] the tracing of the development of the two perspectives, that of the narrator and that of the protagonist, through the emergent organization of the narrative discourse, depends critically on a consideration of deixis and other linguistic features such as adjective placement and reference.[3]

"Mi suicidio" has an unnamed, autodiegetic narrator[4] who relates his experience shortly after the death of his lover. The narrator/protagonist decides to kill himself in order to be with this woman in the other world, to kill himself while he contemplates the portrait of her, so as to aid the transition. But before he shoots himself, he decides to reread the letters she'd written to him, which he'd returned to her. He begins to look over what he thinks are her love letters to him and finds out that they are, in fact, love letters written by her, but to another man.

The interplay between the two divergent perspectives of narrator and protagonist, especially noticeable in the uses of free indirect discourse, gives rise, in this story, to two very different messages about erotic love. These messages are related to the activation of two different sorts of "scripts" on the part of both the protagonist and the reader.

Schank and Abelson (1977) define a script as "a structure that describes appropriate sequences of events in a particular context" and "a predetermined, stereotyped sequence of actions that defines a well-known situation" (41). They use what they call "the restaurant script" to exemplify this notion: one can easily process the simple story, "John went to a restaurant. He asked the waitress for coq au vin. He paid the check and left." This ease of processing is remarkable, given the use of definite articles here: normally, definite articles are used to refer to "given," as opposed to "new," entities.[5] That the listener has no trouble identifying what waitress is referred to, and what check, even though they have not been identified previously in the discourse, is due to the fact that the listener, upon hearing that the story involves a restaurant, immediately applies the "restaurant script," based on previous experience with restaurants, which includes such elements as ordering, the waitress, and the check. The waitress and the check are part of the restaurant script. This relationship becomes clear when we replace those words with others that are not part of the script: "John went into a restaurant. He ordered a hamburger and a Coke. He gave the elephant a peanut and left."

Further, the mention of "coq au vin" evokes in the listener a particular track of the restaurant script, one that Schank and Abelson (1977) call the "fancy restaurant track" and that "includes within it the possibility of a maitre d', a wine steward, tablecloths, paying with credit cards, fancy desserts, and so on" (40). Schank and Abelson point out that there is "imagery (mainly visual) associated with each action in the sequence [of the script]. Often, descriptive visual information is given in a story, but even if it is not, the listener hearing about a restaurant will typically call to mind impressions of the shapes, colors, relative positions and other properties of objects implicitly or explicitly present in the scene" (44).[6] I suggest that, just as these elements of style form an important part of a script, so may a script be activated, not only by mention of elements familiar to the listener/reader, but also by certain stylistic features of the discourse itself that reports the events forming part of the script.

In "Mi suicidio," one "script" conforms to the conventions of romantic and postromantic sentimental idealizations of erotic love and of woman, while the other corresponds to a vision of erotic love as a manipulative game and woman as duplicitous schemer. The activation of the second script causes the first script to be "reframed" as parody, and both combine to create a new "subtext," which questions this dichotomous view of woman as erotic object and redefines her, rather, as subject of her own eroticism.

The story's title itself signals the necessity of reading this text in a way that questions the literal level, for it presents a puzzling conflict between possible pronominal referents and semantic meaning. The use of the first person singular possessive pronoun indicates (because of the convention that the title and narrative form continuous, although separate, parts of the same discourse) that the story will be told in the first person. However, the convention that narratives recount events that took place in the past[7] makes this title seem semantically deviant. The deictic "mi" indicates the presence of the speaker, but the meaning of "suicidio" is such that an agent of this action would no longer exist after having carried out the action. The meaning of the phrase, then, must be other than that which could be derived simply from its compositional semantic meaning. The reader must then formulate a hypothesis to explain the possible meaning of the title. At least three possible hypotheses present themselves:

1. If the title is to be taken literally and the suicide as a fait accompli, then this story might be interpreted as the recounting of a supernatural event; the narrator is then speaking from beyond the grave.
2. The meaning of the word *suicidio* might include the implicit modifiers *planned, attempted,* and, crucially, *failed.*
3. The word *suicidio* is to be taken figuratively, representing,

perhaps, a complete psychological transformation in the speaker.

In any case, the reader must infer a temporal gap between the moment of the narration and the moment of the narrated: no matter which hypothesis we accept, this is, in some way, a story of a suicide told after the fact, by the agent of the act of suicide, since the simultaneous narration of an act of suicide could not, by its very nature, be completed. This gap is essential to the interpretation of the title and of the entire narrative.

Problems of the specification of focalization and of referential identity are immediately raised in the first clause of the story: "Muerta 'ella'" ("[With] her dead").[8] First, a sudden switch in topic is effected from the title to the opening of the story. In a story titled "Mi suicidio," one would expect to be told about the death, real, planned, imagined, or otherwise, of the protagonist/narrator; the "script" evoked, impossible as it is, is that of the self-inflicted death of the speaker. However, in the story's opening, the death referred to is not that of the speaker but that of a third person. A momentary confusion may result from the appearance that the one who says "mi" in the title is no longer speaking in the first instance of narration, that the speaker of "mi" in the title is now referred to in the third person.

Second, the deletion of the verb indicates a lack of consideration of the narratee: even though the deleted verb would be a form of the copulative *estar*, and thus would be of reduced semantic content, the morphology would necessarily indicate tense and aspect and thus provide the listener/narratee with information regarding the relative temporal situation of narration and of the narrative.

Finally, the use of the pronoun *"ella"* is highly anomalous. As Brown and Yule (1983) point out, "pronouns are . . . the paradigm example of expressions used by speakers to refer to 'given' entities" (214). But the referent of this pronoun is not at all identifiable. Because of the nature of the written narrative, extralinguistic cues cannot be relied upon; and, more important, there is no previous context from which the reader might hope to retrieve the identity of the referent. The initial utterance, then, seems to break normal discourse rules, just as the title breaks, or at least bends, rules of narrative semantics. In the same way that the logical processing of the title necessitates the formulation of some hypothesis that would explain the semantic deviance, so this utterance, in order to be processed mentally, demands the formulation of some sort of hypothesis that might explain this irregular use of a pronoun to refer to a "new" referent. In addition, the deletion of the copulative verb, as well as the apparent change in topic from title to initial utterance, must be explained.

This last (short-lived) narrative mystery is cleared up in the rest of the first sentence. The topic has changed but momentarily, as we find that the discourse is still "about" the speaker of the "mi" of the title, to the extent that the speaker is affected by the death of *"ella"*:

> Muerta 'ella': tendida, inerte, en el horrible ataúd de barnizada caoba que aún me parecía ver con sus doradas molduras de antipático brillo, ¿qué me restaba en el mundo ya?" (26)

> (With "her" dead; stretched out, inert, in the horrible coffin of varnished mahogany that I seemed to still see with its unpleasantly shining gold moldings, what was left for me in the world now?)

The utterance "¿qué me restaba en el mundo ya?" ("what was left for me in the world now?") reveals the use of indirect free style: if this utterance were attributable directly to the narrator, as opposed to the protagonist, the function would be to ask the question of the narratee, or of himself as narrator. A more appropriate reading of this sentence would posit the temporally deictic *ya* as meaning *en ese momento* ("at that moment"), i.e., at the moment represented in the narrative. The sentence would then be the narrator's representation of the protagonist's utterance, "¿Qué me resta en el mundo ya?" ("What is left for me in the world now?"), thus marking tangibly the simultaneous, but distinct, vocal presences of the protagonist and of the narrator.

The use of this technique might explain, in part, the strange initial utterance: if this utterance is attributable to the character rather than to the narrator, the sentence needs no copulative verb, since the character would have no reason, at the moment of the utterance, to take into consideration the processing needs of an interlocutor. And since the utterance, originating with the character, implicitly is situated in some previous (mental) discourse, the use of the pronoun would be perfectly in keeping with normal discourse rules, marking, as it might, a given referent.

But we are given more information about the referential nature of *"ella"* in the next sentence: "En ella cifraba yo mi luz, mi regocijo, mi ilusión, mi delicia toda . . ." ("In her I found my light, my joy, my hope, all of my delight . . .") (26). This *ella* is not set within quotation marks; there are, in addition, several other instances later in the narrative in which *"ella"* is contrasted with *ella*. This second *ella* is truly anaphoric; that is, it is used to refer to a previous referent, namely, *"ella." "Ella"* must be functioning as if it were a more explicit noun phrase, such as a proper name, rather than as an anaphoric pronoun. Why does the narrator not use a full noun phrase, rather than this highly marked quasi pronoun? The contrast between *"ella"* and *ella* indicates that the entire explanation does not rest with the use of indirect free style, for the character would have no need to differentiate between discursively new and given referents in a mental discourse. The marked deletion of the proper name or any other explicit full noun phrase would indicate an awareness of the interlocutor/narratee and a concomitant need, for some reason, to suppress any identifying references.

One possible reason for the refusal explicitly to name *"ella,"* for the reduction of identifying references to the sole reference to sex, might relate to the nature of the personal relationship between *"ella"* and the narrator/protagonist.[9] The narrator might be protecting the identity of *"ella"* because they were engaged in an illicit affair. Further evidence for such interpretation is given later in the narrative: the reference to "aquel mismo aposento donde se deslizaron insensiblemente tantas horas de ventura" ("that same room where so many hours of happiness slipped by unnoticed") (27), suggesting that perhaps the site of the couple's bliss was limited to one room, that it was not public; and, more important, a later explanation on the protagonist's part of his practice of returning all love letters which *"ella"* had written to him, "por precaución, por respeto, por caballerosidad" ("as a precaution, out of respect, out of chivalry") (29).

The replacement of the proper name (or other full noun phrase) by *"ella,"* then, might connote an acknowledgment of that societal convention that proscribes erotic relationships outside marriage, to the extent that the participants in such a relationship cannot be referred to by their proper names or even by terms that might allude to the nature of the relationship. Attention is drawn to this societal convention through the flouting of linguistic/discursive convention. At the same time, since there is only one possible referent for this pronoun, because of the given versus new discursive convention, the use of *"ella"* might also carry the implicature that, for the speaker, there is only one female to whom he might conceivably refer; there is only one woman in his life. This anomalous use, then, might carry a double connotation: one that relegates the referent to the role of the speaker's partner in an illicit affair, and one that exalts the referent to a position of unique and absolute dominion.

The first three paragraphs of the story function to activate a literary "script" that is an extension of this second connotation of the quasi pronoun *"ella,"* in which the protagonist, grief stricken over the sudden death of his beloved, decides, in the best (or worst) tradition of sentimentality, to commit suicide and join his loved one in the afterworld.

In keeping with this sentimental script, which the narrator establishes through the use of indirect free style, the protagonist decides to commit his passionate act in the room which served as a site for his liaisons with *"ella,"* contemplating her portrait as he does so. Upon entering the room, the objects in the room trigger an overwhelming series of memories of *"ella."* These associations are represented at length, again in a section of indirect free style, in which the central structuring device is the literary anaphora of the word "allí" ("there"). The deixis of this word, in combination with the use of the past tense, indicates that the deictic center[10] rests with the character. The protagonist is in the room being described; the narrator is not, as indicated by the use of the past rather than the present tense. The technique, then, is again that of indirect free style: the character's thoughts are represented directly with the modification that the verbs are changed to the past tense, and inquits are not used:

> Allí estaba el amplio sofá donde nos sentábamos tan juntos como si fuera estrechísimo; allí la chimenea hacia cuya llama tendía los piececitos . . . allí la gorgona de irisado vidrio de Salviati. . . . Y allí, por último, como maravillosa resurrección del pasado, inmortalizando su adorable forma, ella, ella misma . . . ; es decir, su retrato. (27)

> (There was the wide sofa where we used to sit so close together, as if it were very narrow; there the fireplace toward whose flame she used to stretch her little feet; there the vase of iridescent glass from Salviati. . . . And there, finally, like a marvelous resurrection of the past, immortalizing her adorable form, she, she herself . . . that is, her portrait.)

The description of the portrait of *"ella"* is emblematic of the overly sentimental sensibility that permeates the protagonist's "script":

> su gran retrato de cuerpo entero, obra maestra de célebre artista, que la representaba sentada, vistiendo uno de mis trajes preferidos: La sencilla y airosa funda de blanca seda que la envolvía en una nube de espuma. (27)

> (her great full-length portrait, masterpiece of a celebrated artist, which represented her seated, wearing one of my favorite dresses: The simple, frothy white satin sheath which enveloped her in a cloud of foam.)

"She" wears a dress that makes her appear diaphanous: "The simple, frothy white satin sheath which enveloped her in a cloud of foam" strongly suggests the appearance of an angel in her white "cloud," the outlines of her body simultaneously covered and delineated by the shape of the sheath. The painting captures not only the ethereal quality of *"ella"* but also the physical details; it is a "fidelísimo trasunto de los rasgos y colores, al través de los cuales me había cautivado un alma: imagen encantadora que significaba para mí lo mejor de mi existencia" ("very faithful likeness of the features and coloring through which a soul had captivated me: enchanting image which signified for me the best of my existence") (27).

The protagonist decides to contemplate the portrait as he shoots himself. In the sentence relating the motive for this decision, once again we find evidence of that double perspective made possible by indirect free style: "Así no se borraría de mis ojos ni un segundo su efigie: los cerraría mirándola, y volvería a abrirlos, viéndola no ya en pintura, sino en espíritu. . . ." ("In this way her image would not fade from sight for even a minute; I would close [my eyes] looking at her, and I would open them again, seeing her now, not as a painting, but in spirit") (28). The conditional can be used either modally, to express the resulting condition of a hypothetical action or as an expression of probability, or temporally, as a report, set within the past tense, of an utterance originally set in the future tense. Since there are no accompanying expressions of hypothetical actions (which would, according to prescriptive grammar, be set in the imperfect subjunctive), either explicitly or implicitly, and there is no indication that the conditional is being used to express probability in the past, this use of the conditional clearly must be taken to be the temporal use. The original utterance, then, must be attributed to the protagonist; this is the narrator's reporting of the protagonist's "así no se borrará de mis ojos. . . . los cerraré. . . . y volveré a abrirlos" ("in this way her image will not fade from my eyes. . . . I will close them. . . . I will open them again"). Once more, indirect free style reveals the presence of two separate perspectives, that of the protagonist and that of the narrator.

After contemplating the image of his beloved, the protagonist becomes further distracted from his suicidal task when he decides to light a candelabrum so that the falling dusk will not obscure his view of the portrait as he pulls the trigger. The candelabrum happens to be located on top of a *secrétaire*, and the sight of the latter suggests to the protagonist that perhaps the letters comprising their amorous correspondence might be found inside. Continuing his retrospective, he forces open the *secrétaire* and discovers a packet of letters written in "her" hand. He assumes that these are the letters he had chivalrously returned to her, "y mi corazón agradecía a la muerta el delicado refinamiento de haberlas guardado allí, como testimonio de su pasión, como codicilo en que me legaba su ternura" ("and my heart was grateful to the dead woman for the delicate refinement of having kept them there, as a testimony of her passion, as a codicil in which she bequeathed to me her tenderness") (29).

Although the protagonist attempts to assume the role of the letters' implied reader, he soon sees that he is not the intended reader: the *"tú"* to which *"ella's"* letters are addressed is, in fact, another, a "third person" for the protagonist. Likewise, he is excluded from the erotic discourse established between the *"yo"* uttered by *"ella"* and the unidentified *"tú"* of the letters. In the new discursive context, he himself is only a third person, whose participation is limited to that of reader of a text belonging to and concerning others. In order to read (and understand) the text of the woman's erotic discourse, the protagonist must reread the entire text of his representation of the relationship between himself and *"ella."* He must reject the sentimental, idealized script and replace it with one that might accommodate his status as third person. Further, he must completely reorder his representation of that entity to which *"ella"* refers; the identity of the referent of *"ella"* is in question, not only for the reader of the story, but also, now, for the protagonist himself.

The discovery that the erotic discourse of his lover has been directed, all along, to another, forces the protagonist to redefine qualitatively the nature of *"ella."* She is obviously not waiting for him in the other world, as he had imagined. In fact, he himself has not been the object of her desire in the material world. The script of sentimental passion has been effectively destroyed.

But the culmination of that script, the suicide of the protagonist, need not change. In fact, the narrator tells us, "una voz irónica gritábame al oído: '¡ahora sí . . . ahora sí que debes suicidarte, desdichado!'" ("An ironic voice shouted in my ear, 'Now, now you really should kill yourself, you wretch!'") (31). Now the script is that of a suicide motivated by desperation rather than by a tender desire to join the beloved in the spirit world. The suspense that, at this point, forms an essential element of the story is underlined and augmented by the use of ellipses and semicolons rather than commas, as well as by the markedly lengthy adverbial section intercalated between the penultimate and the last perfective verb:

> Lágrimas de rabia escaldaron mis pupilas; me coloqué, según había resuelto, frente al retrato; empuñé la pistola, alcé el cañón . . . y, apuntando fríamente, sin prisa, sin que me temblase el pulso . . . , con los dos tiros . . . (31)

> (Tears of rage scalded my eyes; I placed myself, as I had resolved, facing the portrait; I took hold of the pistol, I lifted the barrel . . . and, pointing coldly, unhurriedly, my pulse steady, with two shots . . .)

This sentence is filled with what Iser (1971) has called "gaps of indeterminacy" (13) that the reader must fill by actively hypothesizing about what will happen next. If the protagonist were indeed to shoot himself, the fact of the story's narration in first person would represent a break with the laws of the natural world, and so the story would represent an example, unusual in Pardo Bazán's works, of the marvelous. A voice, whose origin is not clear, has suggested to him that now he has even more reason to kill himself, but it is a voice that speaks ironically, shouts rather than murmurs.

The irony present in the shouting voice is also perceivable in the very ending of the story, as we discover, finally, whether the title,

"Mi suicidio," can be taken literally: "reventé los dos verdes y lumínicos ojos que me fascinaban" ("I shot through the two luminous green eyes that fascinated me") (31).

The phrasing of this final sentence is almost an exact echo of part of the narrator's earlier description of the portrait of *"ella,"* before which he intends to shoot himself: "y eran sus ojos verdes y lumínicos que me fascinaban" ("and they were her luminous green eyes that fascinated me") (31). The two phrases are identical superficially but for the placement of the adjectives. But there is another, contextual difference: the verb, "fascinaban," is temporally ambiguous in the second utterance, between a reading in which the eyes still fascinate the protagonist at the time of the action (i.e., the sentence is the narrative representation in the past tense of the protagonist's "Reviento los dos ojos . . . que me fascinan" ["I shoot through the two eyes . . . that fascinate me"]) and a reading in which the eyes are no longer fascinating (i.e., "fascinaban" is equivalent to "habían fascinado" ["had fascinated"]). In the first reading, the narration is still focalized through the protagonist; the utterance is mediated only to the extent that it is presented in the past tense rather than a present tense that would make the utterance simultaneous with the act it represents. In the second reading, the focalization is through the narrator; the time of the utterance is posterior to the moment of the action of shooting. Using this second reading, the last sentence works as an ironic allusion to and comment upon the protagonist's earlier adoring description of the fascinating eyes of the beloved and signals the possibility of "rereading" the entire narrative in an ironic way.

The discovery that his lover's erotic discourse was in discordance with his own leads the protagonist to discard his previous sentimental script and to construct a second one, this time a script of Avenged Infidelity. Likewise, the two conflicting discourses of desire formed by that of the sentimental protagonist and that of the unfaithful *"ella"* reveal another sort of discursive duality in the narrative itself. This duality is formed by the ingenuously sentimental discourse of the deluded protagonist (which might correspond to a first, ingenuous reading of the narrative) and a second voice, attributable to the informed narrator, which represents the parodic presentation of that same narrative. Just as the protagonist must reread his own discourse of desire for "*ella*," so must the reader now "reread" this narrative as parody.

Bakhtin (1978) speaks of parody as a type of "double-voiced discourse" in which "the author employs the speech of another, but, in contradistinction to stylization, he introduces into that other speech an intention which is directly opposed to the original one. The second voice, having lodged in the other speech, clashes antagonistically with the original, host voice and forces it to serve directly opposite aims. Speech becomes the battleground for opposing intentions" (185).

Gilbert and Gubar discuss the use itself of parody in women's literary texts as precisely the sort of "duplicity" that appears in the narrative discourse of "Mi suicidio": "Parody . . . is . . . one of the key strategies through which . . . female duplicity reveals itself. As we have noted, nineteenth-century women writers frequently both use and misuse (or subvert) a common male tradition or genre. Consequently, . . . a "complex vibration" occurs between stylized generic gestures and unexpected deviations from such obvious gestures, a vibration that undercuts and ridicules the genre being employed" (80).

In this story, it is a second, informed reading of the text that reveals the underlying parodic discourse of the narrator. The title is no longer mysterious; we know that the narrator/protagonist does not kill himself and that "suicide" here means not only "planned, but averted, suicide," but also, possibly, refers ironically to the "death" of the narrator/protagonist's previous ingenuous self. The double connotations attachable to the anomalous use of the pronoun "*ella*," as if it were a full noun phrase, might reflect the dichotomous representation of the woman as idealized, disembodied angel and duplicitous schemer. The use of indirect free style is explained as a device that allows an essential distinction between the perspectives of the narrator and of the protagonist but that also allows the identification between narrator and protagonist essential to a narration told in the first person. Without the temporal narrative gap between the discourses of the protagonist and of the narrator, underlined by the use of the free indirect style, the conflicting voices of character and narrator would not be perceivable, and the parodic duality of the narrative discourse would not be possible. Likewise, were the narrative told in the third person, the clash in the voices of the narrator and the protagonist would be less remarkable, thus weakening the parodic element.

The imagined "voz mágica" ("magical voice") of *"ella"* that suggests to the protagonist that he should follow her into the other world is clearly an anticipation, or an echo, of that other, "ironic voice" that shouts at the protagonist after his discovery of the letters that now he *really* has reason to end it all. The clash between the contexts in which the two voices urge suicide lends this "voz melodiosa" some highly ironic overtones.

The portrait now seems to be described in a parodic "double-voiced discourse" as well: the *"fidelísimo* trasunto de los rasgos y colores al través de los cuales me había cautivado un alma: imagen encantadora que significaba para mí lo mejor de mi existencia" ("very *faithful* likeness of the features and coloring through which a soul had captivated me: enchanting image that signified for me the best of my existence") (27; my emphasis). The "enchanting image" now could refer either to the portrait or to *"ella"* herself; to the "likeness" or to the "features and coloring through which a soul had captivated me." While during the initial reading, within the script of Sentimental Passion, the word "cautivado" ("captivated") might simply represent part of a cliché, the double-voicing made patent by the creation of the script of Avenged Infidelity now lends this word some stronger connotations: the protagonist/narrator had been in a sense "captured" by the woman; the image he had created of her had been "enchanting" also in the sense of putting him under a sort of spell. The verb "significaba" ("signified") now is temporally ambiguous as well, between the narrator's representation of the protagonist's present-tense "significa" ("signifies"), corresponding to the Sentimental Script, and the narrator's own "había significado" ("had signified"). Finally, the word "fidelísimo" ("very faithful") takes on new shades of meaning, for it is now clear that if the representation of her image is faithful, the woman herself is not; she has in fact merely "represented" faithfulness, presented its "image."

The exaggeration of the redundant, cliché-ridden, overblown style, especially tangible up to the point in the narration that represents the protagonist's illumination, cannot now be ignored. It is relevant, in this respect, that the story carries the dedication "a Campoamor." Although this dedication is superficially explained by Pardo Bazán's assertion in the preface to *Cuentos de amor* that it was Campoamor who suggested the story to her (6), it is also true that this story may allude to the style of Campoamor's works and in fact may be seen as emblematic of his poetry in its mixture of ironic disillusion and what D. L. Shaw (1972) calls "cloying sentimentality": "His poetry on the theme of love and the human (especially feminine) foibles related to it, reveals a[n] . . . oscillation between impersonal observation and cloying sentimentality" (66). Del Río (1963) notes that, in spite of Campoamor's supposed anti-romanticism, his works still retain aspects of this literary current in the "sentimentalismo, a veces la sensiblería, que Campoamor no logra disimular bajo sus ingeniosas agudezas" ("sentimentality, sometimes the mawkishness, which Campoamor does not manage to hide beneath his ingenious witticisms") (162). He adds that "sólo en algunas de sus breves 'humoradas' se libra por entero Campoamor del sentimentalismo" ("only in some of his brief 'humoradas' does Campoamor free himself entirely of sentimentality") (163).

But at the same time, it is possible that this very sentimentality may be seen, in Campoamor's works as well as in "Mi suicidio," as encoded in a double-voiced discourse, for, according to Gaos (1971), "podríamos decir que Campoamor casi pretendió este absurdo absoluto: hacer, más que poesía, parodia de la poesía, una poesía que se burla de sí misma, una *antipoesía*" ("we might say that Campoamor almost aspired to this absolute absurdity: to create, more than poetry, a parody of poetry, a poetry that makes fun of itself, an *antipoetry*") (412). The exaggeration of sentimentality is particularly remarkable in the first paragraph of "Mi suicidio":

Muerta "ella;" tendida, inerte, en el *horrible* ataúd de *barnizada* caoba que aún me parecía ver con sus *doradas* molduras de *antipático* brillo, ¿qué me restaba en el mundo ya? En ella cifraba yo mi luz, mi regocijo, mi ilusión, mi delicia toda . . . , y desaparecer así, de súbito, arrebatada en la flor de su juventud y de su *seductora* belleza, era tanto como decirme con *melodiosa* voz, la voz mágica que vibraba en mi interior produciendo acordes divinos: "Pues me amas, sígueme." (26; my emphasis)

(With "her" dead; stretched out, inert, in the *horrible* coffin of *varnished* mahogany that I seemed to still see with its *unpleasantly* shining *gold* moldings, what was left for me in the world now? In her I concentrated my light, my joy, my hope, all of my delight . . . , and to disappear like that, suddenly, carried off in the flower of her youth and of her *seductive* beauty, was tantamount to saying to me in a melodious voice, the *magical* voice that vibrated inside me producing divine harmony: "You love me, follow me then.")

The almost invariable use of prenominal adjectives contributes greatly to this parodically sentimental effect, since this syntactic construction is generally used, in Spanish, for explicative as opposed to specifying adjectives; that is, prenominal adjectives add intensifying description, as in "la blanca nieve" ("the white snow"); postnominal adjectives are used to individuate the entity represented by the noun, as in "la chica rubia" ("the blonde girl").[11] This adjectival construction is appropriate here, since the adjectives used contribute very little semantically: *barnizada caoba, doradas molduras, melodiosa voz (varnished mahogany, golden moldings, melodious voice)*, and so on. Another semantic redundancy is found in the following asyndeton: "mi luz, mi regocijo, mi ilusión, mi delicia toda," ("my light, my joy, my hope, all of my delight"), which is followed by a euphemism for *morir (to die)* ("desaparecer"; "to disappear") and a semantically impoverished cliché "en la flor de su juventud" ("in the flower of her youth").

The parodic exaggeration of sentimental discourse, which is especially strong in the first paragraph of the story, continues to some degree throughout all of the narration, until the last sentence, although it gradually but steadily diminishes as the narration progresses. The central elements of this exaggeration involve redundancy, either through adjective placement or incongruous insertion of minute physical description into narrative moments that should be highly dramatic. The following are examples of the latter:

> allí la gorgona de irisado vidrio de Salviati, con las últimas flores, ya secas, ya pálidas, que su mano había dispuesto artísticamente para festejar mi presencia. . . . (27)

> (there the vase of iridescent glass from Salviati with the last flowers, now dry, now pale, which her hand had artistically arranged to celebrate my presence. . . .)

> allí, al pie del querido retrato, arrodillándome en el sofá, debía yo apretar el gatillo de la pistola inglesa de dos cañones. (28)

> (there, at the foot of the beloved portrait, kneeling on the sofa, I must pull the trigger of the double-barreled English pistol.)

> encendí la lámpara y todas las bujías de los candelabros. Uno de tres brazos había sobre el *secreter* de palo de rosa con incrustraciones. (28)

> (I lit the lamp and all the candles of the candelabra. There was a three-stemmed one on top of the encrusted rosewood *secrétaire.*)

The description of the portrait of *"ella"* is also remarkable in this respect, with its specification that the work was the "obra maestra de célebre artista" ("masterpiece of a celebrated artist") as well as the description of the woman's dress, abounding, again, in prenominal adjectives: *"sencilla y airosa* funda de *blanca* seda" ("*simple and airy* sheath of *white* silk") (27; my emphasis). In addition, of course, the discourse is laden with imagistic clichés, such as the dry, faded flowers mentioned in the first quotation above, the flower of youth alluded to in the first paragraph, and the following: "dulces frases que no habían tenido tiempo para grabarse en mi memoria" ("sweet phrases that had not had time to engrave themselves on my memory") (29).

But the exaggeration becomes less marked as the narration progresses, and at that point in the narrative in which the protagonist first begins to doubt the fidelity of his dead lover, the narrator uses, for the first time, a simile that is not prefabricated: "a la segunda carilla un indefinible malestar, un terror vago, cruzaron por mi imaginación, como cruza la bala por el aire antes de herir" ("on the second page an undefinable uneasiness, a vague terror, crossed through my imagination, as the bullet crosses through the air before wounding") (29). A few lines later, we find the fresh image "hormigueaban rasgos y pormenores imposibles de referir a mi persona" ("features and details that could not possibly have referred to my person swarmed like ants") (30). And, finally, coincidental with the narrative moment in which the protagonist fully realizes the significance of the fact that his lover's erotic discourse is directed toward another, the narrator tells us that the letters "señalaban, tan exactamente como la brújula señala al Norte, la dirección verdadera del corazón que yo juzgaba orientado hacia el mío . . ." ("indicated, as exactly as the compass points toward the North, the true direction of the heart that I judged oriented toward mine . . .") (30).

As the protagonist approaches the moment of illumination, then, the parodically sentimental discourse fades away. However, the narration describing the protagonist's finding of the letters and the moment when he begins to read them marks a change in narrative technique, a shift away from the use of indirect free style and toward mediated, represented thought: *"se me ocurrió"* que allí dentro estarían mis cartas. . . . *Pensé que* acaso ella no había tenido valor para destruirlas. . . . Al pronto *creía* recordar sus candentes frases . . ." ("*it occurred to me* that there inside would be my letters. . . . *I thought that* perhaps she had not had the courage to destroy them. . . . Suddenly I thought I remembered their burning phrases . . .") (29; my emphasis). After the protagonist begins to suspect his lover's deception, once again the narrative is told through the use of indirect free style: "Quizá las demás cartas eran las mías, y sólo aquélla se había deslizado en el grupo. . . . Pero al examinar los papeles . . . hube de convencerme: ninguna de las epístolas . . . había sido dirigida a mí. . . ." ("Maybe the rest of the letters were mine, and only that one had slipped into the group. . . . But on examining the papers . . . I had to convince myself of it: none of the epistles . . . had been addressed to me . . .") (30). The perspectual distance between the narrator and the protagonist is even smaller at that point in the narrative in which the moment of ultimate illumination is narrated. For the first time, the actual verbal thoughts/utterances are recorded through direct speech: "saqué en limpio que *tal vez* . . . , al *mismo tiempo* . . . , o *muy poco antes* . . ." ("it was clear to me that *perhaps* . . . at the *same time* . . . or *very shortly before* . . .") (30; emphasis in original). The italics here signal clearly that the thoughts are those of the protagonist and not those of the narrator; it is easy to distinguish the narrator's from the protagonist's utterances. The double voice is tangibly present, in fact, in the last word of the story; it is this that creates the aspectual ambiguity of "fascinaban."

The dual perspective made possible by the temporal separation of narrator and protagonist facilitates the presence, throughout the story, of what Bakhtin calls heterophony, or "diversity of (individual) voices" (Todorov 1984, 56). The voice that predominates in the superficial text, attributable to the ingenuous protagonist, expresses a cliché script of idealized, spiritual erotic love. The underlying parodic discursive voice, emanating from the narrator (i.e., the disillusioned protagonist) tells a story of a cheap affair, a relationship of desire built on deceit. The existence of the nameless *"ella"* is literally limited to that of her "image." The discovery that the woman herself has not, in life, limited her existence to that of the passive angel represented in her portrait necessitates the literal and figurative destruction of her image by the narrator/protagonist. Postromantic conventionalisms of sentimentality and idealization of erotic love give way, through the manipulation of deictic ambiguity and of conventions of discourse, to a new, more "realistic" (in both senses of the term) view of the text of erotic love, a text in which woman's own discourse, previously hidden, must now be read.

Notes

1. I am employing the word "perspective" in much the same way that Susan Lanser (1981) uses "point of view" in the following quote:

> If we understand point of view to concern the relations between narrating subjects and the literary system which is the text-in-context, then we confront a complex network of interactions between author, narrator(s), characters, and audiences both real and implied. At the very least, the notion of point of view subsumes those aspects of narrative structure that concern the mode of presenting and representing speech, perception, and event; the identities of those who speak and perceive; their relationships with one another and with the recipients of their discourses; their attitudes, statuses, personalities, and beliefs. (13–14)

I believe that "perspective," from Latin *perspicere*, meaning "to look through," expresses a wider range of the phenomena referred to here. In addition to its association with the narratological concept of focalization as posited by Genette (1980) and refined by Bal (1981), this term also connotes the sense of varying degrees of temporal, affective, and ideological distance among the narrative aspects outlined by Lanser (1981) as well as their function within the text as a unit.

2. "Mi suicidio" was first published in *El Imparcial* (12 marzo 1894) and later reprinted in the author's collection *Cuentos de amor*, 26–31.

3. A discussion of the role in literary narrative discourse of these and other linguistic aspects, as well as a shorter version of the analysis of "Mi suicidio" that I present here, is found in my 1990 article.

4. An *autodiegetic narrator* is one in which "the narrator is the hero of his narrative" (Genette 1980, 245).

5. Wallace Chafe (1976) defines "given" information in the following way: "Given (or old) information is that knowledge which the speaker assumes to be in the consciousness of the addressee at the time of the utterance" (30). M. A. K. Halliday (cited in Brown and Yule 1983, 155), in

analyzing the structure of information in discourse, postulates that the unmarked sequence for the presentation of information is first given information and then new information. Brown and Yule add, "Naturally, information units which are initial in a discourse will contain only new information" (155).

6. Schank and Abelson (1977) explicitly prefer to focus their analysis on the action component of scripts, noting that "the nature of the information in images has been the subject of much controversy, . . . and we do not wish to stir up this hornet's nest here" (44). For a general overview of the literature on scripts, see Brown and Yule (1983, 241–45). For an application of the notion of scripts to the analysis of stories, see Schank and Abelson (1977) and Chafe (1976).

7. See Bronzwaer (1970), Hamburger (1957), and Fleischman (1990) for discussion of the role of tense in narrative.

8. This and all other translations are my own.

9. This pronominal use that indicates the nature of the relationship between the speaker and the referent is reminiscent of the Japanese use of personal pronouns in conversation, in which strong connotations of intimacy between speaker and referent are carried by the use of the third person singular pronoun. According to Clancy (1982), "in ordinary Japanese conversation, third person 'pronouns' imply a personal relationship between the speaker and the referent, and convey much more than the number and gender of a referent. In fact, in certain contexts *kare* (*he*) implies 'boyfriend,' and *kanojo* (*she*), 'girlfriend' (64).

10. Levinson (1983) defines deictic center as being constituted by the following "unmarked anchorage points": "(i) the central person is the speaker, (ii) the central time is the time at which the speaker produces the utterance, (iii) the central place is the speaker's location at utterance time or C[oding] T[ime], (iv) the discourse centre is the point which the speaker is currently at in the production of his utterance, and (v) the social centre is the speaker's social status and rank, to which the status or rank of addressees or referents is relative" (64). For the purposes of analysis of narrative discourse, we may modify this formulation, specifying that "speaker" may be either "speaker" (narrator) or "origin of thought or utterance represented." This change would allow for the fact that it is not always only the narrator's utterance/thought that is being represented in the narrative discourse.

11. See Alcina and Blecua (1983, 508–11) and references.

References

Alcina Franch, Juan, and José Manuel Blecua. 1983. *Gramatica española*. Barcelona: Ariel.

Bakhtin, Mikhail. 1978. "Discourse Typology in Prose." In *Readings in Russian Poetics*, ed. Ladislav Matejka and Krystyna Pomorska, 176–96. Ann Arbor: U of Michigan P.

Bal, Mieke. 1981. "The Laughing Mice, or: On Focalization." *Poetics Today* 2(2): 202–10.

————. 1977. "Narration et focalisation: Pour une théorie des instances du récit." *Poétique* 29:107–27.

Bronzwaer, W. J. M. 1970. *Tense in the Novel*. Groningen: Wolters-Noordhoof.

Brown, Gillian, and George Yule. 1983. *Discourse Analysis*. Cambridge: Cambridge UP.

Chafe, Wallace. 1976. "Givenness, Contrastiveness, Definiteness, Subjects, Topics, and Point of View." In *Subject and Topic*, ed. Charles N. Li. New York: Academic.

Clancy, Patricia M. 1982. "Written and Spoken Style in Japanese Narrative." In *Spoken and Written Language: Exploring Orality and Literacy*, ed. Deborah Tannen. Norwood, N.J.: Ablex.

del Río, Angel. 1963. *Historia de la literatura española*. Edición revisada. Tomo 2. New York: Holt.

Fleischman, Suzanne. 1990. *Tense and Narrativity: From Medieval Performance to Modern Fiction*. Austin: U of Texas P.

Gaos, Vicente. 1971. *Claves de la literatura española*. Tomo 1. Madrid: Guadarrama.

Genette, Gérard. 1980. *Narrative Discourse: An Essay in Method*. Trans. Jane E. Lewin. Ithaca: Cornell UP.

Gilbert, Sandra M., and Susan Gubar. 1979. *The Madwoman in the Attic: The Woman Writer and the Nineteenth-Century Literary Imagination*. New Haven: Yale UP.

Hamburger, Kate. 1957. *The Logic of Literature*. Bloomington: Indiana UP. Translation of *Die Logik der Dichtung*.

Iser, Wolfgang. 1971. "Indeterminacy and the Reader's Response in Prose Fiction." In *Aspects of Narrative: Selected Papers from the English Institute*, ed. J. Hillis Miller. New York: Columbia UP.

Lanser, Susan Sniader. 1981. *The Narrative Act: Point of View in Prose Fiction*. Princeton: Princeton UP.

Levinson, Stephen C. 1983. *Pragmatics.* Cambridge: Cambridge UP.

Pardo Bazán, Emilia. 1894. "Mi suicidio." *El Imparcial.* 12 marzo 1894. Reprinted in Pardo Bazán, *Cuentos de amor.* Madrid: V. Prieto, 1898.

Prince, Gerald. 1983. "Narrative Pragmatics, Message, and Point." *Poetics* 12(6): 527–36.

Schank, R. C., and R. P. Abelson. 1977. *Scripts, Plans, Goals and Understanding.* Hillsdale, N.J.: Lawrence Erlbaum.

Shaw, Donald L. 1972. *A Literary History of Spain: The Nineteenth Century.* New York: Barnes.

Todorov, Tzvetan. 1984. *Mikhail Bakhtin: The Dialogical Principle.* Trans. Wlad Godzich. Vol. 13 of *Theory and History of Literature.* Minneapolis: U of Minnesota P.

Tolliver, Joyce. 1990. "Discourse Analysis and the Interpretation of Literary Narrative." *Style* 24(2): 266–81.

PART 4

Conversation

To what extent are the strategies of ordinary conversation exploited in fiction? Although fictional discourse may violate norms of ordinary conversation, conversational norms lying outside the text are crucial to the reader's understanding of conversation within it.

Conversation, generally speaking, is highly structured behavior. Unspoken rules govern such aspects of conversation as what conventional opening is required in a particular situation (such as saying "hello" when one answers the telephone), when it is appropriate to take a turn (overlaps in conversation can be awkward, but prolonged silence is even worse), or how one's contributions should relate to those of others (Grice's Cooperative Principle).

The chapters in this section explore two crucial areas of conversational analysis. First, Rei R. Noguchi considers *conversational style*, especially in dramatic texts: how it can be defined and distinguished from related terms, such as *tone* and *syntax*; what features constitute the variable, and hence potentially stylistic, aspects of conversation; and how the results of stylistic description contribute to the analysis of literary meaning in a nonarbitrary way. Because of widely shared social meaning associated with certain features of conversational style and because of the iconic nature of written conversation itself, descriptions of conversational style can offer convincing linkages between language form and literary interpretation.

The second area of conversation explored here is the effect of conversation conducted outside the text on the production of the text. Exploring the intertextuality of Zelda Fitzgerald's *Save Me the Waltz* and F. Scott Fitzgerald's *Tender Is the Night,* Janet M. Ellerby shows the effects of both conflict and collaboration. Ellerby explains how Zelda came to write her novel despite Scott's bitter opposition and how Scott came to write his with Zelda as his collaborator. Both were writing novels that repeated in idiosyncratic ways the shared experience of Zelda and Scott's married life. In Zelda's insecure mental state, she needed Scott for financial and emotional support, yet at the same time she wished to find autonomy and self-definition through her writing. Scott, however, believed that the "raw material" of their experience was his alone and saw her need for authorship as a threat to his own efforts to write. The effects of their external conversation are evident in the syntax and imagery associated with their main characters. In contrast to Scott's controlled and ordered style in describing Nicole Diver, Zelda's description of Alabama Beggs reflects the character's desire to escape domination and ordinariness. Although Zelda did not succeed in reclaiming herself through the novel, it has contemporary interest for its fluid style and its depiction of a woman's dramatic gesture toward reclamation. Ellerby raises the issue of the relationship between language and gender, discussion of which continues in part 5.

Conversational Style and the Form-Meaning Link in Literary Analysis

For the linguistic stylistician, the investigation of conversational style poses some special problems of analysis. Not the least of these problems is the notion of conversational style itself. What is conversational style? How does it relate to the more general notion of style? To talk about conversational style is, to a large degree, to talk about the ways speech gets structured in exchanges. But not all structural features in exchanges will delineate conversational style. More important for literary analysis, what connection, if any, do features of conversational style have with interpretation? How viable is the connection between the features of conversational style and meaning? What features seem especially promising in relating form to meaning? To help answer these questions, this chapter offers some practical definitions and strategies for investigating conversational style and then examines some features of conversational style where the link between form and meaning seems the least arbitrary and, thus, the most promising for relating stylistic description to literary interpretation.

Probably no term in stylistics has evoked as much attention and disagreement as "style." For example, in his essay "On Defining Style," Nils Enkvist (1964) discusses, among other definitions of style, the following:

1. style as a "shell surrounding a preexisting core of thought or expression";
2. style as a "choice between alternative expressions";
3. style as a "set of individual characteristics";
4. style as "deviations from a norm";
5. style as a "set of collective characteristics";
6. style as "those relations among linguistic entities that are statable in terms of wider spans of text than the sentence." (12)

For various reasons, Enkvist rejects all six of these definitions and then offers his own: style is the "aggregate of the contextual probabilities of its linguistic items" (Enkvist 1964, 28). In a more recent study, Enkvist (1990, 14) advocates defining style in terms of text strategy, or "the principle guiding the textualization of text atoms or predications." He subsequently but provisionally defines text strategy as a "specific pattern of values and weights assigned to decision parameters" (1990, 17). Since the present study requires neither a defense nor a reconciliation of these diverse and sometimes overlapping definitions of style, a general working definition of style will suffice. Style here is defined as a recurrent or characteristic selection from a set of expressive possibilities in language. Although this definition has its deficiencies, it has the benefit of subsuming most of the definitions cited by Enkvist. Thus style as a "shell," or embellishment, around a preexisting thought or expression can be viewed as involving a selection from a set of available rhetorical devices; style as a choice between alternative expressions, as involving a selection from a set of possible expressions; style as a set of individual characteristics, as a selection of features that mark a person's language as unique or idiosyncratic; style as deviations from a norm, as a selection of expressive features, which in certain contexts violate an established standard; style as a set of collective characteristics, as the sum of the distinctive expressive choices an individual makes; style as intersentential relations of linguistic elements, as a selection of expressive features whose occurrences extend beyond the borders of one sentence. Enkvist's earlier definition can be viewed as a selection of expressive features whose probabilities of occurrence can be stated according to certain contexts. Enkvist's more recent definition in terms of text strategy can be recast as a selection of expressive features resulting from a specific pattern of values and weights assigned to decision parameters.

If style is the recurrent or characteristic selection from a set of expressive possibilities in language, then conversational style must involve the recurrent or characteristic selection from a set of expressive possibilities in language found within the structural unit known as conversation. To define conversational style in this manner, however, creates problems since not all recurrent features found in conversation will delineate conversational style. Some features, in particular, recurrent grammatical constructions, delineate sentence style, not conversational style; that is, some features delineate style *in* conversation but not style *of* conversation. This distinction suggests that investigations of conversational style will most profit by focusing not so much on features of the sentence unit but on features that characterize conversation as conversation.

But just what is conversation? Some common dictionary definitions provide a rough idea of what conversation is and also suggest one formal unit on which to focus. The following definitions of conversation are representative:

> interchange of thoughts and words; familiar discourse or talk (*Oxford English Dictionary*, 1989);
> oral exchange of sentiments, observations, opinions, ideas; colloquial discourse (*Webster's New Third International Dictionary*, 1971);
> informal interchange of thoughts, information, etc., by spoken words; oral communication between persons; talk; colloquy (*Random House Dictionary of the English Language*, 1987);
> informal interchange of thoughts and opinions, as by means of spoken language; the speaking of two or more persons alternately with each other; colloquy (*Funk and Wagnalls New Standard Dictionary of the English Language*, 1963).

While some may quarrel with particular details of these definitions,[1] such definitions do capture the fact that the exchange (i.e., interchange) of speech is central to the notion of conversation. Indeed, talk that lacks exchanges usually does not qualify as conversation. Exchanges not only differentiate conversation from other forms of talk (e.g., lectures, eulogies) but also constitute the most distinct iterative formal unit of conversation. All conversations consist minimally of one exchange and, typically, of a series of exchanges.

But what exactly constitutes an exchange of speech? Obviously, it is not merely one utterance followed by another; otherwise, any two utterances juxtaposed to each other, including those in two different but simultaneous conversations, would qualify as a speech exchange. The conversational analyst's notion of "adjacency pair" provides considerable insight here. According to Emanuel Schegloff and Harvey Sacks (1973, 295–96), an adjacency pair consists of speech sequences which exhibit the following features:

1. *Two utterances in length.* Utterances in an adjacency pair may be of variable length, but they must consist of two and only two utterances. Thus, for example, a greeting such as "Hi" or a question such as "Did you take out the garbage?" followed by a terminal silence would not constitute an adjacency pair.

2. *Adjacent positioning of component utterances.* Utterances in an adjacency pair occur back to back; that is, one utterance is immediately followed by another.

3. *Different speakers producing each utterance.* Utterances in an adjacency pair must come from a first speaker who, in taking a turn at talk, produces a first utterance (i.e., a "first pair part") and a second speaker who, in taking the next turn, produces a second utterance (i.e., a "second pair part").

4. *Relative ordering of parts.* Utterances in an adjacency pair exhibit sequential ordering with respect to parts; namely, a first pair part precedes a second pair part. For example, in the utterance pair of question-answer, the question precedes the answer and not vice versa.

5. *Discriminative relations.* The presence of a particular part has implicational, or "conditional," relevance for the selection of the second pair part. Thus a question calls for an answer; a greeting, another greeting.

Sacks and Schegloff's notion of adjacency pair has obvious practical value in investigations of conversational style insofar as it captures the essence of the prototypical speech exchange. Yet the notion has a drawback insofar as it excludes from analysis not only some highly common but, more important, potentially contrastive, two-part conversational interactions. The following sequences help illustrate the case in point:

> X: Get the chalk.
> Y: Okay. (gets the chalk)

> X: Get the chalk.
> Y: (gets the chalk)

> X: (points to chalk)
> Y: Okay. (gets the chalk)

The first interaction clearly qualifies as an adjacency pair. Two utterances, produced by two different speakers, occur back to back, with the first and second parts in proper sequential and selectional relationship with each other. Linguistically and socially competent speakers of English would agree that whatever X's first utterance (i.e., "Get the chalk.") makes conditionally relevant for a response, Y recognizes, attends to, and displays that relevancy by replying "Okay" (and by getting the chalk). The second and third interactions, however, cause problems. Because these interactions lack either a first or a second utterance, they fail to qualify as adjacency pairs, and if this failure is so, they would have to be excluded from stylistic concern.

Yet most linguistically and socially competent speakers of English would agree that, though the two interactions differ in form from the first and from each other, all three exhibit some sort of family resemblance. For example, all three function as discrete interactional units and convey the same sense of completion: X initiates an action with a request for chalk, and Y consummates that action with some subsequent activity, either verbal, nonverbal, or both. Though the second and third interactions lack an utterance, neither of the omissions strikes the observer (and presumably, the participants) as being "officially" (i.e., noticeably) absent. Thus, for example, after Y returns with the chalk in the second interaction, X cannot rightfully say to Y, "You didn't say whether you were going to get the chalk or not." The interaction here can be contrasted with one in which a second utterance is officially absent:

> X: Did you get the chalk?
> Y: (silence)

In this interaction, the lack of a second utterance is a noticeable omission, and X can properly say to Y, "Why don't you answer?" or some similar utterance that calls attention to the absence of the second utterance.

Since investigations centered on recurrent or characteristic interactions in conversations have little justification for excluding such stylistically contrastive interactions, analysts need a more inclusive unit that, unlike the adjacency pair, accommodates both verbal and nonverbal material. This unit is the exchange. An exchange prototypically consists of two parts, a soliciting (or initiating) first part and a responding second part, either or both of which take the form of utterances.[2] Each part of the exchange can be said to consist of a move or moves, either verbal or nonverbal or both. The speech exchange, which by and large coincides with the adjacency pair of the conversational analysts, comprises those cases in which both parts of the exchange manifest themselves as speech.[3]

Insofar as speech exchanges occur as discernible units in conversation, they constitute data for empirical investigation both in everyday life and in literature. At the same time, however, exchanges are more than mere language data. If viewed from a narrow linguistic perspective, exchanges seem nothing more than sequences of sentences (or sentence parts) produced by at least two different speakers; however, if viewed from a broader sociolinguistic perspective, exchanges are sequences of coordinated language use. Since exchanges always involve a sequence of alternately produced speech, they require concerted action between speakers. In the words of Matthew Speier (1973, 31), a conversational analyst: "Talk [of conversation] is not merely sentence production, it is social exchange and social coordination. Talk is interactional." This "interactional" aspect, of course, also holds true for conversations in literature.

To incorporate the broader sociolinguistic view of conversation, I provisionally define conversational style as a recurrent or characteristic selection of expressive resources in verbal interaction. By "verbal," I mean to suggest that conversational style on its most abstract level involves language-producing ability; by "verbal interaction," that conversational style specifically and characteristically involves an interchange between speakers, and with it, an exchange of thoughts, sentiments, and the like. By "expressive resources in verbal interaction," I wish to suggest that, in addition to verbal resources, nonverbal resources (e.g., hand gestures, eye direction, silence) may also play a part in a full account of conversational style.

The preceding definition suggests that conversational style differs significantly from what is often considered conversational style. For one thing, the conversational style is not the same as conversational "tone," although literary critics frequently (and inaccurately) describe conversational style with such adjectives as "formal," "informal," "detached," "humorous," and so on. As we have seen, however, the essence of conversational style deals with distinctive choices among structural elements comprising exchanges, not with the affective responses or the social dispositions that may attach to these choices. Indeed, a stylistic analysis centered on affective responses or social dispositions would be unable to differentiate, for example, a formal conversation from a formal lecture or an informal conversation from an informal sermon.

The proposed definition of conversational style also clarifies another misconception of conversational style. Conversational style proper is not the style of grammatical categories (e.g., pronouns, verbs, phrase types, clause types) or the style of vocabulary found within conversation. Although literary critics are often prone to equate the stylistic patterning of such elements with conversational style, conversational style is generally neither the style of sentences nor, for that matter, the style of any unit below the sentence level. A focus on vocabulary or grammatical categories might capture some aspect of the style of a work (e.g., style of vocabulary, sentence style), but it would not capture the essence of conversational style. Stated in another way, rather than centering on the patterning of elements within sentences, conversational style centers on the patterning of structures larger than the sentence, specifically, the patterning of speech in the context of the exchange unit. The general — and main — point is that what analysts frequently perceive and describe as conversational style is really style in conversation, not style of conversation.

The foregoing suggests that conversational style differs from the more commonly studied sentence-level style in a more fundamental way. In contrast to the study of usually self-contained (and thereby usually isolated) grammatical elements of the sentence, the study of speech in the framework of exchanges is not language in a social vacuum but language in situated use.[4] It concerns not only the language of the text but goes beyond; it is language with, among other things, speakers, hearers, and social context. Because of this contextualization, conversational style, rather than dealing solely with patternings of linguistic variables as sentence-level style does, may also deal with patternings of linguistic and social (or more conveniently, sociolinguistic) variables; that is, conversational style may also involve distinctive patternings in the ways linguistic elements interrelate with social factors in the context of conversational interaction. This contextualization, as we shall see later, has important ramifications in linking conversational style with meaning.

The problem now is to locate and identify some of the potentially stylistic elements of conversation, particularly those that might have relevance in literary analysis. As stated earlier, one of the difficulties in delineating conversational style stems from the fact that, while many variable elements occur in conversation, many of these elements have to do with sentence-level, or grammatical, style, not conversational style. In locating and identifying some of the potentially stylistic elements of conversation, I keep in mind the following criteria:

> (i) To be stylistic, an analysis of a text must focus on variable elements of language.
>
> (ii) To be genuine, a stylistic analysis of conversation in a literary text must delineate the style of conversation and not the style of sentences or sentence units (i.e., grammatical style) or the tone of conversation.

If linguistic stylisticians seek to go beyond mere description and make their analyses more useful to literary critics, a third criterion must be added:

> (iii) To be useful in literary criticism, a stylistic analysis of a literary text must focus on features which are amenable to both linguistic description and literary interpretation.

Furthermore, if linguistic stylisticians wish to propose a link between any identified stylistic feature and a literary interpretation and, more important, make that form-meaning link convincing to literary critics, they need to adhere to still another criterion:

> (iv) To be deemed valid, a stylistic analysis that proposes a form-meaning link must provide nonarbitrary and independent evidence for the form-meaning link.

Criterion (i) follows from the definition of style adopted earlier, namely, style as a recurrent or characteristic selection from a set of expressive resources in language. Without variable elements, there can be no selection, and without selection, there can be no differentiation of style. Criterion (ii) assumes that conversational style and sentence style are distinguishable from each other but does not assume that the delineation of one is a necessary condition for the delineation of the other. Criteria (iii) and (iv) concern the higher aims of linguistic stylistics, particularly that of connecting the results of description with literary interpretation (for elaboration, see Noguchi 1985 and, particularly, Noguchi 1990). Criterion (iii) directs the analysis to those verbal aspects of conversation that have applicability and relevance to literary criticism. Criterion (iv) concerns the validation of any proposed form-meaning link deriving from a stylistic analysis. Because any identified stylistic feature may be open to different (and arbitrary) literary interpretations, analysts should provide additional evidence to support the form-meaning link rather than merely asserting it. (For some general strategies to verify the link, see Noguchi, forthcoming, "Validating Linguistic Analyses of Literary Texts.")

Given criteria (i)–(iv) as guidelines, the exchange unit provides an especially promising place to focus an analysis of conversational style. For one, exchanges seem to exhibit variation. Many exchanges, whether occurring in real life or in works of literature, strike the observer as being intuitively different from others. Equally important, exchanges constitute a central aspect of conversation. To examine exchanges is to examine a unit common to all conversations. To repeat a point made earlier, all conversations consist minimally of one exchange but typically of a series of exchanges. Finally, in contrast to isolated grammatical entities, exchanges constitute a distinct socially meaningful unit of interaction, a series of which may cluster in various ways to form larger socially meaningful structures such as openings and closings, repairs, clarifications, requests, apologies, and the like.[5]

The problem now posed is just what aspects of exchanges undergo variation and, thus, hold promise for stylistic variation and for a plausible link between form and meaning. The discussion has already touched upon one variable aspect, namely, the occurrence and distribution of nonverbal material in place of verbal material in the first and second parts of sequenced pairs. The investigation of nonverbal material in such cases would be an important concern where noticeable silence or pauses are frequent or characteristic in some sense, as in the plays of Beckett (Eliopulos 1975, 100; Ben-Zvi 1980). More central and more common — but no less interesting — are the variable aspects of sequenced pairs in which both parts manifest themselves as utterances.

One obvious variable in such sequenced pairs is the length of utterances. Exchanges in drama (and works of prose fiction) may vary distinctly in the amount of speech found in individual and paired turns of talk. For example, the following two-part interchange between Everyman and Death consists essentially of plea or request followed by a rejection in the next turn:

> EVERYMAN: O Death, thou comest when I had thee least in
> mind!
> Yet of my good will I give thee, if thou will be
> kind:
> Yea, a thousand pound shalt thou have,
> And defer this matter till another day.
> DEATH: Everyman, it may not be, by no way.
> I set not by gold, silver, nor riches,
> Ne by pope, emperor, king, duke, ne princes;
> For, and I would receive gifts great,
> All the world I might get;
> But my custom is clean contrary.
> I give thee no respite. Come hence, and not tarry.
> (*Everyman*, 210)

By way of contrast, filmmaker Ingmar Bergman, in his screenplay to *The Seventh Seal*, renders a similar situation between the Knight and Death with an interchange containing speeches of much shorter length:

> KNIGHT: Wait a moment.
> DEATH: That's what they all say. I grant no reprieves.
> (*The Seventh Seal*, 100)

On a larger scale, earlier forms of drama (e.g., classical Greek, medieval) generally exhibit longer speeches in exchanges than later forms (e.g., contemporary drama); within drama of a specific historical period, some works (e.g., Jean Genet's *The Balcony*) generally exhibit longer speeches in exchanges than other works of the same period (e.g., Samuel Beckett's *Waiting for Godot*). General variance in the length of speeches in exchanges also occurs within the work of a single dramatist (compare Beckett's *Waiting for Godot* and his *All That Fall*). The variable length of utterances in exchanges suggests that some plays may exhibit greater or fewer number of "moves" per turn of talk than others.[6] A long speech could contain several moves (e.g., assertion, promise, evaluation, apology); a shorter one, fewer. On the other hand, the exchanges in a play can conceivably be characterized by relatively long speeches but few moves. The following interaction from Harold Pinter's *The Caretaker* consists of two speeches, both evaluations, but of different length:

> DAVIES: Not a bad pair of shoes. [He trudges round the room.] They're strong, all right. Yes. Not a bad shape of shoe. This leather's hardy, en't? Very hardy. Some bloke tried to flog me some suede the other day. I wouldn't wear them. Can't beat leather, for wear. Suede goes off, it creases, it stains for life in five minutes. You can't beat leather. Yes. Good shoe this.
> ASTON: Good.
>
> (*The Caretaker*, 24)

Conversely, exchanges can consist of short speeches but several moves, as in, for example, the last speech by Teach below (from David Mamet's *American Buffalo*), which conveys, among other things, a request, a promise, and an assertion:

> DON: We're waiting for him.
> TEACH: Fletcher.
> DON: Yes.
> TEACH: Why?
> DON: Many reasons.
> TEACH: Tell me one. You give me one good reason, why we're

sitting here, and I'll sit down and never say a word. One reason. One. Go on. I'm listening.

(*American Buffalo*, 866)

In addition to variation in length (and the possible variation in the number of moves), exchanges may exhibit variation in speech sequencing and speech type. If the core of conversational structure consists of an iterative series of soliciting speech followed by responding speech, then numerous possibilities for variation exist. When analyzing the exchanges in drama, for example, the analyst can and should ask, does the dramatist characteristically construct dialogue through the "chaining" of such two-part interactions as question-answer, request-response, remark-evaluation? Does the dramatist characteristically favor one type of sequence pair over all others? Does the dramatist, in lieu of chaining, characteristically utilize "coupling," whereby a speaker inserts a soliciting speech after a responding speech in the same turn of talk, as Y does in

X: Were you born in Peoria? (soliciting: question)
Y: Yes. Why do you ask? (responding: answer + soliciting: question)

If pairings of question-answer, request-response, and remark-evaluation constitute the most neutral or unmarked form of exchanges, does the dramatist vary the structure by characteristically selecting as a second part of the exchange what Thomas Klammer (1973, 31) calls a "countering speech," by which the second speaker instead of resolving the speech contained in the first part of the exchange "challenges, contradicts, or simply ignores the speech of the first, and instead of giving suitable reply, speaks as if he himself were initiating the dialogue, or at least a part of it, rather than replying to what someone else said." This countering of soliciting speech can be accomplished with different types of speech as the following three interactions suggest:

X: Were you born in Peoria?
Y: Why do you ask? (i.e., question)

> X: Were you born in Peoria?
> Y: Never mind. (i.e., request)

> X: Were you born in Peoria?
> Y: Some people never learn. (i.e., remark)

In the above examples, the question "Were you born in Peoria?" is not followed by an answer that resolves the question; instead, what follows is another soliciting speech (question, request, and remark, respectively) that challenges the soliciting function of the preceding question. But the possibilities for variation need not and do not end here. Countering speeches may vary not only in type (and frequency) but also in distribution, as when two speakers interact in the following way:

> X: Were you born in Peoria?
> Y: Why do you ask?
> X: Never mind.
> Y: Some people never learn.

Here the first soliciting speech (i.e., "Were you born in Peoria?") is countered by another question, which in turn is countered by a request, which in turn is countered by a remark. Obviously, further counterings can occur (e.g., "Don't get smart." "Look who's talking." "What do you mean by that?"). Such serial counters, which appear more in modern forms of drama than in earlier forms, occur frequently in, for example, some of Beckett's plays:

> CLOV: (turning towards Hamm, exasperated) Do you want
>   me to look at this muckheap, yes or no?
> HAMM: Answer me first.
> CLOV: What?
> HAMM: Do you know what's happened?
> CLOV: When? Where?
> HAMM: (violently) When! What's happened? Use your head,
>   can't you! What has happened?
> CLOV: What for Christ's sake does it matter.
>   (*Endgame*, 74–75)

Such serial counters can sometimes appear in one turn of talk and then be responded to in the next turn, as in Shakespeare's *Love's Labour's Lost*:

> ROSALINE: Which of the vizards was it that you wore?
> BIRON: Where? when? what vizard? Why demand you this?
> ROSALINE: There, then, that vizard; that superfluous case That hid the worse and show'd the better face.
>   (5.2.386–89)

Many works of medieval drama typically consist of longer speeches (in comparison to contemporary drama) and often with several moves per speech but with only one of these moves being responded to in the next turn of talk. Indeed, what probably differentiates the conversational style of medieval or Renaissance drama from, say, contemporary drama is not merely the length of utterances in exchanges but just this type of variable feature.

Analyses focused on exchanges may yield even finer kinds of variation. For example, countering speeches themselves may exhibit variation in what they counter or challenge. If X says to Y, "Get me a beer!" Y could conceivably issue a counter by saying, among others, the following:

1. a. Who do you think you are?
   b. Don't be a lush.
   c. My, you're lazy.
2. a. Would you repeat that?
   b. Quiet!
   c. It would help if you spoke so I could hear you.
3. a. Isn't it your turn?
   b. You shouldn't impose on me.
   c. "Please" is a nice word.
4. a. It's Sunday.
   b. I'm paraplegic.
   c. There's no beer.

While all these counters in some way challenge the request "Get me a beer!" they differ widely with respect to their overt target. Counters (1a–c) are, more or less, speaker oriented; that is, they are on the surface directed at some real or imagined attribute of the speaker of the request, "Get me a beer!" Counters (2a–c)–(4a–c), in contrast, orient to certain aspects of the speech act itself. Specifically, counters (2a–c) point to some flaw in the acoustic (or auditory) monitoring of the speech channel[7] while counters (3a–c) point to some flaw in the monitoring of social interaction, particularly in the monitoring of some rule of politeness. Counters (4a–c), on the other hand, orient overtly not so much to acoustic or social interactional technique as they do to certain physical or existential conditions in X and Y's world, in this case, conditions that hinder or prevent the carrying out of the request. In Beckett's *Endgame*, Clov frequently issues counters of this type (see Noguchi 1984), particularly, type (4c):

HAMM: Go and get two bicycle-wheels.
CLOV: There are no more bicycle-wheels.
HAMM: What have you done with your bicycle?
CLOV: I never had a bicycle.

(*Endgame*, 8)

HAMM: Give him his pap.
CLOV: There's no more pap.

(*Endgame*, 9)

HAMM: Life goes on. (Clov returns to his place beside the chair.) Give me a rug, I'm freezing.
CLOV: There are no more rugs.

(*Endgame*, 67)

HAMM: Never! (Pause.) Put me in my coffin.
CLOV: There are no more coffins.

(*Endgame*, 79)

HAMM: Before you go . . . (Clov halts near the door.) . . . say something.
CLOV: There is nothing to say.

(*Endgame*, 79)

A related but slightly different kind of countering results when Hamm and Clov serially dispute presuppositions that underline not commands (as above) but assertions:

HAMM: Nature has forgotten us.
CLOV: There's no more nature.
HAMM: No more nature! You exaggerate.
CLOV: In the vicinity.
HAMM: But we breathe, we change! We lose our hair, our teeth! Our bloom! Our ideals!
CLOV: Then she hasn't forgotten us.
HAMM: But you say there is none.
CLOV: (sadly) No one that ever lived ever thought so crooked as we.
HAMM: We do what we can.
CLOV: We shouldn't.

(*Endgame*, 11)

In sum, by focusing on the exchange unit — the foremost distinguishing structural unit of conversation — analysts can get at the core of conversational structure; by focusing on the variable aspects of the exchange, analysts can get at the core of conversational style. In accordance with criteria (i) and (ii), a focus on several basic kinds of variables (e.g., the length, type, and sequence of utterances that comprise the exchange unit) can help characterize the essence of conversational style (as opposed to characterizing conversational tone or sentence, or grammatical style). In literary analysis, a focus on such basic variables will reveal some of the characteristic choices an author makes in composing the work and delineating characters within it. To the extent that conversation and dialogue coincide, these choices reflect the author's characteristic method of constructing dialogue; to the extent that dialogue and drama coincide, these choices also reflect the author's dramatic style.[8]

Stylistic analyses focused on the variable elements of the exchange, however, may offer an even greater benefit. If analysts aspire to the higher aims of linguistic stylistics, as specified by criteria (iii) and (iv), a focus on the variables of the exchange unit should lead to more fruitful analyses than the more customary focus on variables of the sentence unit. If the chief drawback of the latter focus is that it severs language too much from its human users, uses, and contexts (see Fish 1973), then a focus on the variables of the exchange cannot but help reunite language and the people who use it. Because descriptions of variables of the exchange unit (unlike descriptions of the variables of the sentence unit) must take into account users, uses, and contexts, variables of the exchange unit are more amenable to linguistic description *and* literary interpretation, thus, in keeping with criterion (iii). Descriptions of conversational style, as suggested earlier, depict more than just the distinctive array of linguistic data on the printed page. Whether in imaginary or real worlds, participants of conversations do not merely produce utterances in random fashion. Insofar as participants of conversations in literature, as in real life, produce conversations through a series of concerted actions, the characteristic patterns found in conversations exemplify, or at least reflect, characteristic patterns of social interaction. The analyst who delineates conversational style, in other words, delineates not just the characteristic selection of structural elements but the characteristic selection of meaningful human behavior.

If so, descriptions of conversational style also offer a more convincing link to meaning. Fish (1973, 131) has charged that because abstract grammatical categories (e.g., noun, verb, prepositional phrase) carry no independent cognitive meaning outside the grammatical system itself and because descriptions of grammatical style as a matter of principle or practice deliberately strip language from human experience, such descriptions have no way of constraining interpretation. That is, after having completed a stylistic description of a work, the analyst could easily assert any or all interpretations for the data. Stated in still another way, linguistic stylisticians who focus on sentence-level elements in their analyses run the risk of making arbitrary connections between language form and literary meaning. Such a charge, however, cannot be so easily directed at analysts who focus on the variables of conversational style since, as we have seen, conversational style delineates not the characteristic selection of abstract (and isolated) grammatical categories but rather the characteristic selection of meaningful human interaction, with human speakers, hearers, and contexts of use. In brief, because the human element enters into the analysis from the very beginning and not as an appendage, linguistic form links more easily — and, in the end, more convincingly — to literary meaning.

This link between form and meaning in conversation is undoubtedly reinforced by shared social meaning. For example, socially competent participants of conversation will generally agree that solicitations in the imperative form like "Get me a beer!" are more assertive and less polite than those in the nonimperative like "May I ask you to get me a beer?" not just in English but in all languages (for pragmatics-based accounts, see Leech 1983, 107–10; Brown and Levinson 1987, 132–44) or that "Get me a beer!" followed by no response at all from the addressee is a noticeable and significant silence in conversation (for discussion, see Schegloff 1972, 363–70) or that "Where are you from, sir?" followed by "What it's to you, buddy?" has produced a verbal challenge on the part of the second speaker (see Lakoff 1975, 64–68). Researchers (e.g., Gumperz and Hymes 1972; Gumperz 1982; Moerman 1988; Grice 1975; Sperber and Wilson 1986) have profusely shown how interactants in daily life rely on shared social meanings to interpret and evaluate everyday activities, including conversational activities. Such shared social meanings, formed and buttressed by common experience, of course, make it easier to reach agreement on some links between conversational form and meaning not just in daily life but also in literature.

Besides reinforcement by shared social meaning, however, the form-meaning link with conversational variables is sometimes strengthened by a more fundamental but less obvious factor. Of the three basic conversational variables identified in this study — length, type, and sequence of utterances in exchanges — two (length and sequence) are not only social in meaning but also iconic. By "iconic," I mean the property of replicating or mirroring (i.e., "imaging") either meaning or an associated form in a nonarbitrary manner. Although language is largely noniconic, iconic aspects do exist (Haiman 1983; Givón 1989, 70–125). In vocabulary, for example, iconicity appears most obviously in the phonological mimicry of *bow-wow, meow, cock-a-doodle-doo, bang, thud,* and *sizzle* for the actual noises; in morphology, it appears in the relatively shorter length, or "smallness," of inflections compared to roots to mirror the fact that roots are conceptually more important than inflections; in syntax, iconicity appears in self-referential sentences like "This string of words is a sentence" or "The main clause in this sentence can be said to have a deleted agent" or, rhetorically, in the sequencing of related ideas in ascending (or descending) order (e.g., "I came, I saw, I conquered") to convey their relative importance. Timothy Austin in *Language Crafted* (1984, 112–13) offers the sentence "Behind the door stood a tall man, and behind him, a little girl with bright red hair," where, to mirror the physical situation described, the noun phrase "a tall man" appears spatially (and temporally) "behind" the noun phrase "the door," and "a little girl with bright red hair" appears spatially (and temporally) "behind" the pronoun "him." A more conspicuous and grosser example from literature would be concrete poetry, where the overall arrangement of words and white space on the page visually reproduces a part of the message of the poem (as in George Herbert's "Easter Wings," May Swenson's "Unconscious Came a Beauty," or John Hollander's "Swan and Shadow").

It is easy to overlook the fact that, like concrete poetry, conversation rendered on the printed page also makes use of a gross kind of iconicity. In contrast to the indirect, or reported, speech of fiction, written direct speech, particularly the conversations rendered in drama, mimics the temporal flow of speech with a corresponding spatial arrangement. What occurs in time is reproduced in space. Thus speakers (i.e., characters) and their utterances are spatially arranged to match the temporal order of appearance. Where the speech of each interactant in oral conversation occupies a discrete temporal slot, we find reproduced in written conversation a matching spatial slot.[9]

The iconicity of written conversation becomes particularly apparent in instances where the speech of the next speaker intrudes into the turn of the talk of the preceding speaker, more specifically, in completive speech and purely interruptive speech. Completive speech, produced by a second speaker, interrupts by completing the utterance of the first speaker, as exemplified in Shakespeare's *Richard III*:

> RICHARD: Now, by my George, my garter, and my crown —
> ELIZABETH: Profan'd, dishonour'd,
> and the third usurp'd.
> RICHARD: I swear —
> ELIZABETH: By nothing, for this is no oath.
> Thy George, profan'd, hath lost his holy honour;
> Thy garter, blemish'd, pawn'd his knightly virtue;
> Thy crown, usurp'd, disgrac'd his kingly glory.
> If something thou wouldst swear to be believ'd,
> Swear then by something that thou hast not wrong'd.
> RICHARD: Now by the world —
> ELIZABETH: 'Tis full of thy foul wrongs.
> RICHARD: My father's death —
> ELIZABETH: Thy life hath that dishonour'd.
> RICHARD: Then by myself —
> ELIZABETH: Thyself is self-misus'd.
> RICHARD: Why, then, by God —
> ELIZABETH: God's wrong is most of all.
>
>   (4.4.366–77)

Purely interruptive speech, like completive speech, also interrupts but has no completive function (except, of course, metrically). We see the difference and the differing representation of purely interruptive speech also in the text of *Richard III*:

> BUCKINGHAM: Lord Mayor —
> RICHARD: Look to the drawbridge there!
> BUCKINGHAM: Hark! a drum.
> RICHARD: Catesby, o'erlook the walls.
> BUCKINGHAM: Lord Mayor, the reason we have sent —
> RICHARD: Look back! defend thee! Here are enemies!
>
>   (3.5.14–19)

Despite the lack of overt stage directions, readers interpret completive speech and purely interruptive speech, such as those reproduced above, as being qualitatively different from each other. Because purely interruptive speech cuts off prior speech with no obvious thematic contribution to the interrupted speech, it belongs exclusively to the next turn of talk. Completive speech, however, has a different status and is represented differently. Being produced by a second speaker, it too belongs in the next turn of talk, but, in contrast to purely interruptive speech, it brings linguistic closure to the interrupted speech; thus, syntactically, semantically, and perhaps psychologically, completive speech also belongs in the turn of the interrupted speech. On the printed page, these facts are given physical representation in the placement of completive speech in the next speaker's slot but immediately at the point of interruption. It is worth noting here that in the numbering of lines in Shakespearean texts, editors usually count a line of interrupted speech and a line of completive speech (but not a line of purely interruptive speech) as belonging to the same line, even though interrupted speech and completive speech come from two different characters.

If partially overlapped speech is represented iconically in printed dramatic texts, so also is completely overlapped speech. We find examples of completely overlapped speech in the choral speech of Greek tragedies or in the three witches' incantations in the opening of *Macbeth*, the latter appearing on the page as

> ALL: Fair is foul, and foul is fair.
> Hover through the fog and filthy air.
>
> (1.1.10–11)

Because the incantation of the three witches here is uttered and heard as one united speech, it is iconically represented on the printed page as speech coming from one collective source rather than the speech of three separate speakers, as in

> [*together*]
> FIRST WITCH: Fair is foul, and foul is fair.
>   Hover through the fog and filthy air.

SECOND WITCH: Fair is foul, and foul is fair.
              Hover through the fog and filthy air.
THIRD WITCH: Fair is foul, and foul is fair.
              Hover through the fog and filthy air.

We might contrast the iconic representation of simultaneous united speech with the iconic representation of simultaneous disunited speech, such as in Edward Albee's *Who's Afraid of Virginia Woolf?*:

MARTHA	GEORGE
I have tried, oh God I have tried; the one thing . . . the one thing I've tried to carry pure and unscathed through the sewer of this marriage; through the sick nights, and the pathetic, stupid days, through the derision and the laughter. . . .	Libera me, Domine, de mort aeterna, in die illa tremenda: Quando caeli movendi sunt et terra: Dum veneris judicare saeculum per ignem. Tremens factus sum, ego, et timeo dum discussio venerit, atque ventura ira. . . .

(227)

The main purpose of citing all these examples from dramatic written conversations, from nonoverlappings to partial overlappings to complete overlappings, is to suggest both their iconicity and their natural propensity to convey or, at least, elicit various kinds of social meanings, not only to the interactants who produce them but also to observers (or readers) who witness them. Although variation occurs across different speech communities, people generally and naturally assign specific and fairly consistent sociocultural meaning to partially or completely overlapped speech, to completive or noncompletive speech, to united or disunited speech. The experience — and reality — of such form-meaning linkages in daily life, of course, offers considerable support to such form-meaning links in literature.

Significant for our purposes, two of the three variables of conversational style isolated in this study (length and sequence of utterances) clearly exhibit iconicity, and, because of the iconicity, form-meaning links can be made with considerably less arbitrariness. Consider first the length of utterances in exchanges. Whatever other features characterize utterances in exchanges, the most obvious spatial feature is length (or size). Of importance here, however, is not that utterances have length *per se* (since they all do) but that the degree of utterance length can mirror (as well as generate) certain kinds of social meanings. If, on the one hand, a speaker's utterances are characteristically long relative to his or her interactant's utterances (or to some other relevant norm), the speaker may be judged as talkative, detailed, reluctant to yield the floor, and so on; if, on the other hand, the utterances are characteristically short, the speaker may be judged as laconic, vague, or willing to yield the floor. The important point here is that, although different speech communities (and people within those communities) may vary in what constitutes long or short utterances and may assign different social meanings to the length of utterances, once a social meaning (e.g., talkativeness) is assigned, the spatial (and temporal) parameters of long and short inevitably come into play. If, for example, talking excessively casts a speaker as loquacious, then, other things being equal, talk of greater length by that speaker makes him or her even more loquacious, never less loquacious. That is, the degree of length, as physically represented on the printed page, is largely — and directly — proportional to the degree of such speaker characterizations. The longer (or shorter) the utterance length, the greater (or less) is the degree of, for example, talkativeness. If we keep in mind criterion (iv), which advocates nonarbitrary and independent evidence for any proposed interpretation, this kind of form-meaning link cannot be accidental, for the link occurs not at just one isolated point but is patterned along a continuum. The physical attribute of length — or here, the iconicity of length — helps validate the form-meaning link. Although form-based interpretations require various kinds of verification to make them convincing, it suffices here to say that, because of the iconicity and the shared social meanings involved, the range of interpretations based on utterance length (and the interpretation ultimately selected from that range) is far from being arbitrary or whimsical. To claim that such a form-meaning link fails to hold in literature is, to a large extent, to claim that it fails to hold in everyday life; indeed, it would seem to deny one basic means by which people in daily life gauge talk and assign social meaning in conversation.

If the length of utterances partakes in iconicity, so too does the sequence of utterances, though less transparently. With length of utterances, the relevant spatial dimension was short/long (or small/big) within exchanges; with sequence of utterances, the relevant dimension is near/far across turns of talk. If conversations prototypically consist of paired sequences of soliciting speech and responding speech (e.g., question + answer, request + response, remark + evaluation), we may view soliciting speech as the starting point where a speaker creates expectations for a following responding speech that resolves whatever is sought in the soliciting speech. That is, a proper question sets up expectations for a proper answer, a proper request sets up expectations for a proper response, a proper remark sets up expectations for a proper evaluation, and so forth. Conversations can differ in how near (or how far apart) these two-part sequences actually occur with respect to each other. As we have seen, the paired parts may be split by one or more countering speeches across several turns of talk. Depending on the presence or absence of such intervening speech, the responding speech to an initial solicitation may be far or near. This spatial dimension of near/far has relevance for certain judgments we might make of the participants or their speech. For example, if the proper responding speech is characteristically adjacent to the proper soliciting speech, we often judge the participants as being, for example, attentive, cooperative, or nonchallenging. Because cooperation in conversation is more basic than noncooperation (and politeness, more than impoliteness), the majority of speech exchanges in life and in literature usually proceed with the matched pairings of soliciting speech and proper responding speech. In the opening of Pinter's *The Birthday Party*, for example, the harmonious relationship between Meg and her husband is, to a considerable degree, depicted and conveyed by the typical and mundane pairing of soliciting and responding speech.

MEG: Is that you?
PETEY: Yes, it's me.
MEG: What? (Her face appears at the hatch.)
        Are you back?
PETEY: Yes.
MEG: I've got your cornflakes ready. (She disappears and
        reappears.) Here's your cornflakes. (He rises and takes
        the plate from her, sits at the table, props up the paper
        and begins to eat. Meg enters by the door.) Are they
        nice?
PETEY: Very nice.
MEG: I thought they'd be nice. (She sits at the table.) You got
        your paper?
PETEY: Yes.
MEG: Is it good?
PETEY: Not bad.
MEG: What does it say?
PETEY: Nothing much.
MEG: You read me out some nice bits yesterday.
PETEY: Yes, well, I haven't finished this one yet.
MEG: Will you tell me when you come to something good?
PETEY: Yes.
        (Pause)
MEG: Have you been working hard this morning?
PETEY: No, just stacked a few of the old chairs. Cleaned up a
        bit.
MEG: Is it nice out?
PETEY: Very nice.

(19–20)

If, however, the proper responding speech is nonadjacent and noticeably far from proper soliciting speech, as when a series of countering speeches intervenes, we judge the interactants as being less cooperative, more willing to challenge one another. In *The Birthday Party*, we witness this increasing distance in the less cooperative and more (and here, more playfully) assertive Stanley in his initial exchanges with Meg:

MEG: . . . Was it nice?
STANLEY: What?
MEG: The fried bread.
STANLEY: Succulent.
MEG: You shouldn't say that word.
STANLEY: What, succulent — ?
MEG: Don't say it!
STANLEY: What's the matter with it?
MEG: Do you want some tea? (Stanley reads the paper.)
           Say please.
STANLEY: Please.
MEG: Say sorry first.
STANLEY: Sorry first.
MEG: No just sorry.
STANLEY: Just sorry!
MEG: You deserve the strap.
STANLEY: Don't do that!

(27–28)

If the Meg-Petey interaction cited earlier conveys harmony and mundaneness, we can contrast it with an interaction conveying just the opposite. Near the end of Edward Albee's *Who's Afraid of Virginia Woolf?*, Martha and her husband, George, seek, among other things, to get each other to admit to lying about their (imaginary) son. Given the vitriolic tenacity of the two antagonists, this interactional task requires for its resolution either a direct confirmation (and/or apology) or direct and persuasive denial of the accusation by one of the parties. The following interaction, which typifies the discordant relationship between Martha and George in much of the play, is especially pertinent because it illustrates how the occurrence of countering speeches between a soliciting speech (e.g., accusation) and proper responding speech (e.g., confirmation or denial) and the occurrence of interruptive speech increasingly heighten the sense of uncooperativeness and disharmony.

MARTHA: (Rising to it) Lies! Lies!
GEORGE: Lies? All right. A son who would *not* disown his
           father, who came to him for advice, for information,

for love that wasn't mixed with sickness — and you know what I mean, Martha! — who could not tolerate the slashing, braying residue that called itself his MOTHER. MOTHER? HAH!!

MARTHA: (Cold) All right, you. A son who was so ashamed of his father he asked me once if it — possibly — wasn't true, as he had heard, from some cruel boys, maybe, that he was not our child; who could not tolerate the shabby failure his father had become. . . .

GEORGE: Lies!

MARTHA: Lies? Who would not bring his girl friend to the house . . .

GEORGE: . . . in shame of his mother. . . .

MARTHA: . . . of his father! Who writes letters only *to me!*

GEORGE: Oh, so you think! To me! At my office!

MARTHA: Liar!

(225–26)

One can, of course, plausibly argue that the contentiousness between Martha and George results from the targets of the counters used, with counters directed at more personal targets (e.g., one's inability to make truthful statements) being more contentious and impolite than those directed at less personal things.[10] This interpretation is certainly true, but one can also plausibly argue that the persistence (i.e., length and frequency) of such injurious counters and the resulting lack of (i.e., "farness" from) resolution both reinforce and increase (but never decrease) the contentiousness and impoliteness. In short, the personal targets and the iconicity here complement one another — or more fittingly, provide corroborating evidence for linking form and meaning.

To generalize a bit, the farther away a proper responding speech occurs from its corresponding soliciting speech by intervening countering speech, the more salient (and, possibly, more serious) becomes the interactional "problem," be it local or general, initially small or large. Thus various social meanings arise when a greeting is separated from a reciprocating greeting, or an apology from an acceptance or a rejection, or praise from diminution, or, as in the illustration above, an accusation from a confirmation or denial. Regardless of which particular social meaning is assigned, the degree of certitude of that meaning varies proportionately to a spatial dimension, this time a near/far one. That is, the relative distance of the proper responding speech from its soliciting speech increases (or decreases) our conviction of the assigned social meaning. This kind of iconicity, where form patterns with meaning along a continuum and where form is buttressed by social meaning, gives greater credence to the form-meaning link and, thus, is in accord with criterion (iv).[11]

Linguistic stylisticians can make a more useful contribution to literary analysis. If they wish to do so, however, they will need to set their sights not merely on formal description but on the higher aims of linguistic stylistics as suggested by criteria (iii) and (iv). Among other things, stylisticians will have to be more selective in the features they analyze since not all features of language have equal relevance — or provide equal accessibility — to literary interpretation. This selectivity will necessitate a more careful and constrained search for form-meaning links not only within the text but, more important, beyond the text. Furthermore, to avoid charges of arbitrariness, stylisticians need to offer various kinds of nonarbitrary and independent evidence, linguistic and nonlinguistic, to help verify any proposed form-meaning link. In the context of such guidelines, conversational style, as defined in this study, offers a particularly fruitful area for exploration.

Notes

1. For example, some may argue that conversation, though primarily oral, need not be only oral, as signed conversation between the deaf — or, indeed, conversation in literary texts — readily attests. A more precise word than "oral" is "verbal," which has the advantage of being neutral to spoken and written conversation. Some may also contend that not all conversations are informal or colloquial. Although they are often so, formal conversations, such as in business telephone calls or job interviews,

also exist alongside the more informal varieties. Two other points deserve comment here. Two of the definitions cited (i.e., "interchange of thoughts and words" and "informal interchange of thoughts and opinions, as by means of spoken language") capture rather nicely the fact that conversationalists do not necessarily always use speech to express themselves. Obviously, conversationalists have recourse to many forms of nonverbal communication (e.g., kinesic, parakinesic) to express their "sentiments, observations, opinions, ideas." These other forms presumably partake in systems that often parallel and sometimes interpenetrate the system of speech in conversation. While important in their own right, the other systems will be set aside in this study. The other point follows partly from the first. If other systems coexist with the speech system, it becomes apparent that people in conversational encounters exchange other things besides speech. Just what is exchanged and just what interactional and social contingencies hold provide rich material for analysts of literature. For a compelling study of one comprehensive form of exchange, the ritual interchange — a complex exchange in which speech exchanges form a subsystem, see Goffman (1972).

2. A more comprehensive definition would be one that takes into account two-part interactions in which neither of the parts takes the form of an utterance:

> X: (points to chalk)
> Y: (gets chalk)

Also, just what constitutes an utterance may pose a problem. As a working definition, an utterance here comprises all that a speaker says in his or her turn at talk. (An equivalent term with respect to drama is "speech.") While the definition of utterance involves a certain degree of circularity, it allows for a considerable degree of preciseness insofar as different speaking turns in literary texts are usually unambiguously marked by some form of speaker identification label.

3. Hereafter, for the sake of convenience, I use "exchange" to refer to the speech exchange unless otherwise indicated.

4. Brown and Yule's (1983) work is a classic study of language in use.

5. For more on the structure of conversational openings and closings, refer to Schegloff (1972) and Schegloff and Sacks (1973).

6. See Burton (1980) for further discussion of "moves" in dialogue.

7. Presumably, all aspects of speech that are related by, for example, the audio tuners on a tape recorder would be accessible to monitoring by speakers in conversation. These would, of course, include the turning off and on of speech.

8. Dramatic dialogue is much more than conversation, just as drama is much more than dialogue. Yet, whatever dramatic dialogue may be, one of its most characteristic structural features — i.e., the serially organized exchanges of speech — makes dramatic dialogue similar to and analyzable as conversation.

9. Conversations reproduced on the printed page actually display a more global iconicity if, following Lyons (1977, 637), we view the canonical situation in oral conversation as one that involves "one-one, or one-many, signalling in the phonic medium along the vocal-auditory channel, with all the participants present in the same actual situation able to see one another and to perceive the associated non-vocal paralinguistic features of their utterances, and each assuming the role of sender and receiver in turn." For written dramatic texts, the printed page typically displays this canonical situation by having speaker appellations, which represent the speakers, on the left side of the page followed by a spatial representation of their speech, which flows from left to right and from top to bottom. This representation of speech on the printed page, however, seems not to capture very well, at least spatially, the actual face-to-face exchange of speech. This shortcoming really lies in writing and reading conventions that force us to orient to written texts in a left-to-right, top-to-bottom fashion. If we keep in mind that oral conversation (which written conversation represents) radiates in all directions and if we orient to the written dramatic texts in a slightly different way by turning the text ninety degrees counterclockwise, we get a better picture of the iconicity, where the participants "face" each other and serve alternately as sender and receiver.

10. This analysis coincides with Brown and Levinson's (1987) theory of Face Threatening Acts.

11. The remaining conversation variable (type of utterance), while lacking the kind of iconicity exhibited by length and sequence, does, nevertheless, link form and meaning in accordance with criterion (iii). Inevitably, we characterize people in everyday life and in literature not only by what they say but also by how they say it (i.e., type of utterance). Thus we characterize people who frequently issue commands differently from those who, for example, frequently issue questions and remarks. In

other words, a high frequency of a particular utterance type (or types) has relevance for interpretation and validation. For a seminal work dealing with some social meanings generated by types of speech in dramatic dialogue, see Burton (1980). For other kinds of noniconic variables found in conversational discourse, see Wardhaugh (1985) and, particularly, Tannen (1984, 144–45) and Tannen (1989); for an excellent study of social meanings conveyed by politeness variables in drama, specifically in Shakespearean tragedies, see Brown and Gilman (1989).

References

Albee, Edward. 1975. *Who's Afraid of Virginia Woolf?* New York: Atheneum.
Austin, Timothy R. 1984. *Language Crafted: A Linguistic Theory of Poetic Syntax.* Bloomington: Indiana UP.
Beckett, Samuel. 1958. *Endgame.* Trans. Samuel Beckett. New York: Grove P.
Ben-Zvi, Linda. 1980. "Samuel Beckett, Fritz Mauthner, and the Limits of Language." *PMLA* 95:183–200.
Bergman, Ingmar. 1960. *The Seventh Seal.* Trans. Lars Malmstrom and David Kushner. In *Four Screen Plays of Ingmar Bergman*, New York: Simon.
Brown, Gillian, and George Yule. 1983. *Discourse Analysis.* Cambridge: Cambridge UP.
Brown, Penelope, and Stephen C. Levinson. 1987. *Politeness: Some Universals in Language Usage.* Cambridge: Cambridge UP.
Brown, Roger, and Albert Gilman. 1989. "Politeness Theory and Shakespeare's Four Major Tragedies." *Language in Society* 18:159–212.
Burton, Deirdre. 1980. *Dialogue and Discourse.* London: Routledge.
Eliopulos, James. 1975. *Samuel Beckett's Dramatic Language.* The Hague: Mouton.
Enkvist, Nils Erik. 1964. "On Defining Style: An Essay in Applied Linguistics." In *Linguistics and Style*, ed. John Spencer, 1–56. London: Oxford UP.
———. 1990. "Stylistics, Text Linguistics, and Text Strategies." *Hebrew Linguistics* 28–30:7–22.
Everyman and Medieval Miracle Plays. 1958. Ed. A. C. Cawley. New York: Dutton.
Fish, Stanley E. 1973. "What Is Stylistics and Why Are They Saying Such Terrible Things About It?" In *Approaches to Poetics*, ed. Seymour Chatman, 109–52. New York: Columbia UP.

Givón, T. 1989. *Mind, Code and Contexts: Essays in Pragmatics.* Hillsdale, N.J.: Erlbaum.

Goffman, Erving. 1972. *Relations in Public.* New York: Harper.

Grice, H. Paul. 1975. "Logic and Conversation." In *Syntax and Semantics III: Speech Acts,* ed. Peter Cole and Jerry L. Morgan, 41–58. New York: Academic P.

Gumperz, John J., ed. 1982. *Language and Social Identity.* Cambridge: Cambridge UP.

Gumperz, John J., and Dell Hymes, eds. 1972. *Directions in Sociolinguistics.* New York: Holt.

Haiman, John. 1983. "Iconic and Economic Motivation." *Language* 59:781–819.

Hymes, Dell. 1972. *Foundations in Sociolinguistics.* Philadelphia: U of Pennsylvania P.

Klammer, Thomas P. 1973. "Foundations for a Theory of Dialogic Structure." *Poetics* 9:27–64.

Lakoff, Robin. 1975. *Language and Woman's Place.* New York: Harper.

Leech, Geoffrey N. 1983. *Principles of Pragmatics.* London: Longman.

Lyons, John. 1977. *Semantics.* Vol. 2. Cambridge: Cambridge UP.

Mamet, David. 1981. *American Buffalo. Nine Plays of the Modern Theater.* Ed. Harold Clurman. New York: Grove P.

Moerman, Michael. 1988. *Talking Culture.* Philadelphia: U of Pennsylvania P.

Noguchi, Rei R. 1984. "Style and Strategy in *Endgame.*" *Journal of Beckett Studies* 9:101–11.

———. 1985. "Conversational Interaction, Verbal Strategies, and Literary Response." *Language and Style* 18:192–204.

———. 1990. "Linguistic and Literary Criticism: An Impasse?" *Lingua e Stile* 25:273–87.

———. Forthcoming. "Validating Linguistic Analyses of Literary Texts." *Language and Style.*

Pinter, Harold. 1976. *The Birthday Party. Complete Works: One.* New York: Grove.

———. 1977. *The Caretaker. Complete Works: Two.* New York: Grove.

Schegloff, Emanuel A. 1972. "Sequencing in Conversational Openings." In *Directions in Sociolinguistics,* ed. John J. Gumperz and Dell Hymes, 346–80. New York: Holt.

Schegloff, Emanuel A., and Harvey Sacks. 1973. "Opening Up Closings." *Semiotica* 8:289–327.

Shakespeare, William. 1971. *The Complete Works of Shakespeare.* Ed. Irving
   Ribner and George Lyman Kittredge. New York: Wiley.
Speier, Matthew. 1973. *How to Observe Face-to-Face Communication.* Pacific
   Palisades, Calif.: Goodyear.
Sperber, Dan, and Deirdre Wilson. 1986. *Relevance.* Cambridge: Har-
   vard UP.
Tannen, Deborah. 1984. *Conversational Style: Analyzing Talk Among Friends.*
   Norwood, N.J.: Ablex.
———. 1989. *Talking Voices.* Cambridge: Cambridge UP.
Wardhaugh, Ronald. 1985. *How Conversation Works.* Oxford: Blackwell.

Conversation and the Fitzgeralds
Conflict or Collaboration?

The novels that Zelda and Scott Fitzgerald wrote about France and the expatriates of the 1920s were significantly different, though both were semiautobiographical. In *Save Me the Waltz*, Zelda wrote about Alabama Beggs and her quest for a career of her own. In *Tender Is the Night*, Scott wrote about Nicole Diver and her quest for sanity and self-sufficiency. However, the personal quests of Zelda and Scott as they wrote these novels are as compelling as their protagonists'. Were they collaborators or competitors? How did their conversation concerning their shared material influence their writing and its production? Furthermore, what drove Zelda to write her novel? Was she justified in writing the book and using Scott's and her experience?

    Save Me the Waltz is most often taught as a flawed but interesting companion piece to *Tender Is the Night*, but the biographical context of Zelda's madness and desperation that enshrouds the novel too often negates its artistic sophistication and innovation. While writing *Tender Is the Night*, Scott was struggling with alcoholism, Zelda's illness, and financial burdens. Nevertheless, having published *The Great Gatsby* as well as two other novels and many short stories, he was taken as a serious writer from whom a great novel could and would evolve, given the right circumstances. Zelda was recognized as Scott's unstable, beautiful wife, who interfered with his writing.

Yet both had stories to tell that emanated from experiences they shared as a married couple. Scott and Zelda waged a battle over who had claim to these experiences as material for fictionalization.

Scott's advantage came from his gender, his formal education at Princeton, and the expectations and encouragement of friends, family, and teachers, who believed he could and would be a fine writer. Writing from the male tradition, Scott was prepared to struggle with the Bloomian precursor (Bloom 1973). His precursor was not one writer whom he misread, but a history of writers who provided him with a background of literary styles that he emulated and then betrayed by taking his determinative stylistic swerve. He had a strong tradition with which to converse, but he knew his genius lay in his invention of a new style. He was able to announce while writing *Tender Is the Night* that he had found "something really NEW in form, idea, structure — the model for the age that Joyce and Stein are searching for, that Conrad didn't find" (Bruccoli 1981, 231).

Nevertheless, if all writers have precursors from whom they must swerve if they are to step beyond mediocrity, who was Zelda's precursor? From whom did she have to swerve in order to create her own innovative discourse? Scott acknowledged that Zelda was "a great original in her way, with perhaps a more intense flame at its highest than I ever had" (Bruccoli 1981, 274), but it was Scott's writing that she knew best and most admired. He was the writer she wished to emulate, yet in order to establish her own creative style, she had to break from his influence as well. Could she, without the advantages of a formal education and a host of precursors from which to draw, establish herself as a writer? As a diagnosed schizophrenic, could she draw from the same private sphere of married life as did her husband for inspiration and ultimately separate herself enough from his influence in order to write a fictionalized version of her own?

It is helpful to apply Harold Bloom's (1973) antithetical theory to Scott and Zelda as each wrestled with precursors and sought authorship. During the years that produced *Tender Is the Night*, Scott had become the Bloomian "strong poet," having successfully published *The Great Gatsby* and effectively swerved from the "Poetic Father," but he was still struggling to define his most advantageous relation to that precursor. When Zelda wrote *Save Me the Waltz,* Scott had already gone through seven frustrating drafts of *Tender Is the Night.* The novel was finally completed after twelve drafts.

In contrast, Zelda can be seen as a female Bloomian ephebe, the beginning writer actively pursuing her own identity. Although Zelda admired Scott's writing, she fits Yeats's description as one "who seeks [her] own opposite" (Bloom 1973, 65). She did not collaborate with Scott on *Save Me the Waltz* but wrote the first draft while a patient in a sanatorium. The novel was a response to Scott's writing that had used their courtship and marriage as material. It was her attempt to tell the antithetical story, to redeem Scott's words, and to render them as newly fulfilled and enlarged words of her own.

Scott had power over her, however, as husband and provider. Moreover, he was the only person from whom she did not feel emotionally isolated. In her insecure mental state, Zelda lacked the strong ego that would allow her independence. By invading the subject matter that Scott considered his territory, Zelda was putting her emotional and financial security at risk. As a result, Zelda was denied the movement toward discontinuity with her precursor. The book was (and still is by some) considered "only a copy or a replica" (Bloom 1973, 80) of the writings of Scott. Zelda had encroached on material that Scott, in fact, was using for *Tender Is the Night.* Though both husband and wife sought autonomy in their writing, only Scott, as the already proved "strong poet," could isolate himself from his own precursor's stance. Scott accomplished what Zelda could not — the attainment of an authoritative stance. Zelda, on the other hand, attained no such position from which to write and received only profound disapproval from Scott.

Sandra Gilbert and Susan Gubar in *The Madwoman in the Attic* (1979) have rewritten Bloom's theory so that it might account for women writers by using the term "anxiety of authorship" rather than "of influence." Their theory provides an explanation for Zelda's urge to write and the anxiety this caused Scott. He believed it necessary that he maintain himself as the author/authority of the family, for he was the provider not only for his wife's and daughter's livelihood, but also for the expensive medical care Zelda required. That Zelda infringed upon his authority by writing her novel in less than three months in the secluded, disciplined, and expensive setting of the sanatorium infuriated Scott. He had been forced continually to postpone completion of *Tender Is the Night* to write and sell short stories in order to maintain Zelda. As author and father, Scott believed himself to be the owner of the text of their life.

Yet Zelda reclaimed herself from that text in which she had become the female character over which Scott assumed rights of ownership. In his three previous novels and many of his short stories, Zelda, serving as model for his female protagonists, had become a "framed" aesthetic object. Scott had even felt free to use portions of her diary and letters. He saw her as the model for a new heroine. In an interview, he contrasted the traditional heroine to Zelda. He said: "We find the young woman of 1920 flirting, kissing, viewing life lightly, saying damn without a blush, playing along the danger line in an immature way — a sort of mental baby-vamp. . . . Personally, I prefer this sort of girl. Indeed, I married the heroine of my stories" (Tavernier-Courbin 1979, 34). One of the criticisms of *The Beautiful and the Damned* by John Peale Bishop was that the "fictional heroine did not come up to Zelda as she was in life" (Hardwick 1970, 96). In *Tender Is the Night*, Scott used her again — this time her mental illness specifically — to create Nicole Diver.

While writing *Save Me the Waltz*, the "anxiety of authorship" must have been for Zelda painful, yet at the same time exhilarating. In writing her novel, Zelda could free herself from Scott's aesthetic ideal by defining and asserting herself and replacing "the 'copy' with the 'individuality'" (Gilbert and Gubar 1979, 19). But she dreaded Scott's antagonism and sent the manuscript off to their publisher without letting Scott see it first. Later she explained: "I was afraid we might have touched the same material. Also feeling it to be a dubious production due to my own instability I did not want a scathing criticism such as you have mercilessly — if for my own good given my last stories, poor things" (Milford 1970, 220). Zelda was the "inferiorized" female. *Save Me the Waltz* was Zelda's attempt to "make herself whole by healing her own . . . diseases" (Gilbert and Gubar 1979, 76). She turned to writing as a form of curative self-assertion, a form of self-expression rather than a mode of literary production providing her income and self-sufficiency.

Gilbert and Gubar's (1979) theory revolves around the woman as artist and creator, made either whole or mad in her attempt to realize herself as a writer. She creates; but what does she create? Herself. It is easy to see why this humanistic ideology would be attractive to women struggling to establish as writers viable self-identities that had been denied them by a society that historically invalidated women writers. Nevertheless, such an ideology, says Pierre Macherey (1978), is "profoundly reactionary both in theory and in practice" (67), for the primary activity allowed to such a writer is the preservation of identity. Macherey sees such an aesthetic as no more than an impoverished religion because it omits any account of production, defined as the process of making. He maintains that writers and artists produce works. They do not work on themselves (67–68).

For Scott, the conditions under which he produced his work were complicated by his dependency on alcohol, a continual need for money, and his relations with Zelda, who was not only his wife and dependent but also his collaborator and critic. However, because of the success of his first novel, he always had a publisher and magazines waiting to publish his short stories. He was expected to produce work, and he did so. For Zelda, the specific determinate conditions under which she worked were not only complicated by alcohol, depression, and Scott, but also by a belief that through her writing, she somehow could work on herself and perhaps even heal herself.

Zelda, thus, had a highly emotional investment in her writing, for she believed that through writing, she could somehow re-create by better defining herself as a unified woman separate from Scott. When this re-creation did not happen, she was bitterly disappointed and more vulnerable than ever to mental illness. But a humanistic quest for self through writing also contributed to Scott's problems, for he too believed that as a writer he worked on himself, though not as the means to heal. Instead, he saw the artistic endeavor intimately tied to his character and his experience. His success depended on his ability to render this experience via language. An excerpt from the diaries of Alexander McKaig demonstrates Scott's self-absorption. Wrote McKaig, "Fitz remark[ed] . . . [that he] cannot depict how any one thinks except himself & possibly Zelda" (quoted in Milford 1970, 79).

Scott decided, furthermore, that because he was more stable than Zelda, he was the writer worth saving. He wrote, "I compromised on the purely utilitarian standpoint that I was the wage-earner, that I took care of wife and child, financially and practically, and beyond that that I was integrated" (Milford 1970, 270). The notion of the unified or integrated self, implicit to humanism, was here used against Zelda in determining her worth, for even though she could and did produce literary texts, she lacked "wholeness" and "integration." Scott continued to perceive Zelda's novel as a threat even after he had revised it extensively and taken out all the sections that might have portrayed him negatively. Collaboration had turned into competition over who would create from what they knew.

Macherey (1978) recognizes a potency in thought that Scott was unable to realize. "Thought," says Macherey, is a "capacity to generate novelty, to actively transform initial data" (6). As a task, thought involves "material, means and product" (7), but for Scott the vital ingredient was material. Moreover, he believed that the material could be depleted. Thus he was driven to keep Zelda from also using "his" material. Ironically, he depended on her to retain access to the raw material of experience, for she had a better memory than he. As he wrote *Tender Is the Night*, he often went up to her room and asked her "advice about things they had done together, conversations they had" (Milford 1970, 267). As *the* author, he believed his task was to organize and control their given reality as it offered itself empirically. His work existed only as long as he had material to receive and describe. He had no faith in a "clear imaginative space" (Lentricchia 1980, 319), no confidence in his ability to accomplish the Bloomian act of willful misreading, and little hope of making the creative swerve from the "enabling model" (Macherey 1978, 50).

It is unfortunate that Scott could not have more faith in the individual interpretive efforts both he and Zelda made as they created the illusion of the real in their novels, for neither was simply imitating empirical data. Between their intersecting, raw material was a hermeneutical distance that assured difference. In fact, their differences were all the more pronounced because their relationship was dialectical rather than static; theirs was a "continuously sustained, elaborated and recapitulated" (Macherey 1978, 53) conversation constructed from a string of differences: male/female, masculine/feminine, husband/wife, provider/helpmate, professional/amateur, father/mother, and sane/insane. These name only a portion of the opposing roles they sustained within their dialectic; however, Zelda's side of the opposition was always the supplement.

To pursue the Derridean understanding of Zelda as supplement is to keep in mind that the supplement compensates for a lack in that which is supposed to be complete in itself (Culler 1982, 103). This notion of the supplement as crucial ingredient to the opposing side of the hierarchical arrangement and that which gives the opposing side its power helps to explain why Scott was threatened by Zelda's possible achievement of an autonomy separate from their relationship. His self-definition as male, husband, provider, and writer was inextricably bound to her participation in the relationships they shared. Yet even as supplement, Zelda wrote an extraordinary novel that angered Scott so much that he admitted he would never be able to forgive her for competing with him. He used all his power along with that of his publishers and Zelda's psychiatrists to try to ensure that the novel would be buried and that Zelda would not publish fiction again.

Such power was only temporary, and *Save Me the Waltz* has resurfaced. When it was brought back into print in 1967, some 550 emendations had to be made in the copy-text for correctness, a fact that hints that Scott may have purposively undermined the quality of its first publication by not insisting on careful editing. Nonetheless, as a modern expressionistic text, it has, as Sara Mayfield observes, a "surrealistic, 'real unreal' quality derived from the persistence of tradition in the South and the advent of the 'avant-garde' abroad" (1971, 184).

Save Me the Waltz is the story of Alabama Beggs, the Southern Belle, the beautiful object, the stunning accompaniment to a successful husband, yet driven to become an independent person, separate from her husband, psychologically and financially, and to create herself based on her own action and her own accomplishment. Alabama's story fits the "kunstlerromane" paradigm described by Rachel Blau DuPlessis (1985) of the female artist struggling between her designated feminine role of passivity and invisible private acts and her meaningful vocation in which she strives for improvement and visible public works (84). This is a narrative of binary choice, and the opposition is constructed within Alabama when she is young.

As a child Alabama wants to know herself as some kernel of unchanging identity. By understanding what she was like as an infant, she believes that she might begin to discover who she will be. When she asks her mother, her mother (whose efforts to be anything more than a maternal figure have all been thwarted) can only reply, "You were a good baby" (*Save Me the Waltz*, 5), but Alabama wants more: "The girl had been filled with no interpretation of herself. . . . She wants to be told what she is like, being too young to know that she is like nothing at all and will fill out her skeleton with what she gives off. . . . She does not know that what *effort she makes* will become herself" (81; emphasis added). In her attempt to create herself, she makes herself into the most audacious of the Southern Belles. She is considered the "thoroughbred" of the town: "Relentlessly she convinced herself that the only thing of any significance was to take what she wanted when she could. She did her best" (29). David Knight, the handsome and gifted young painter, is her ticket out of what has become an oppressive South and away from her authoritative father. But as Jacqueline Tavernier-Courbin points out, the emancipation David offers her is a deceptive emancipation (34). Marriage and New York seem to promise

Alabama a law unto herself, but she receives an early hint in David's letters that this might not be so:

> "City of glitter hypotheses," wrote David ecstatically, "chaff from a fairy mill, suspended in penetrating blue! . . . The tops of buildings shine like crowns of gold-leaf kings in conference — and oh, my dear, you are my princess and I'd like to keep you shut for ever in an ivory tower for my private delectation."
>
> The third time he wrote that about the princess, Alabama asked him not to mention the tower again. (40)

Despite Alabama's hopes for the promises of a modern marriage and a large city, she finds she has made herself *nothing* more than David Knight's wife and Bonnie's mother. Unlike many novels written by women before the turn of the century where marriage provides a culmination of the search for the "raison d'être" and, therefore, a fitting conclusion for these novels, Alabama's quest for meaning is fulfilled by neither marriage nor motherhood. The family moves on to France, but life continues for Alabama as a series of indolent parties interrupted only by a trifling love affair with a French aviator. She seems lethargically resigned to taking "what you wanted from life, if you could get it, and you did without the rest" (98). She realizes she is only a minor character in a world where David considers modern women as "flowers — flowers and desserts, love and excitement, and passion and fame" (111). Her former insistence "on the magic and glamour of life . . . was already feeling its pulse like the throbbing of an amputated leg" (118).

Alabama finds she must do something else in this quest for selfhood and seizes upon the suggestion that she become a ballet dancer, although the suggestion is made only because it would make David and her appear an even more exotic couple if she were a dancer and he a painter. Her dabbling in a career is seen to others as only an improved accompaniment to her husband's image. But it is in the dance that Alabama finds the place where she can pour all her energy; it is not for her a hobby. "It seemed to Alabama that, reaching her goal, she would drive the devils that had driven her — that, in proving herself, she would achieve that peace which she imagined went only in surety of one's self — that she would be able, through the medium of the dance, to command her emotions, to summon love or pity or happiness at will, having provided a channel through which they might flow" (124). It is in her telling of Alabama's training that Zelda enters a world diametrically opposed to anything Scott could have ever hoped to write about. Here she writes about the sensual body, the thin tight wire Alabama's body becomes as she dances, "Miles and miles of pas de bourree, her toes picking the floor like the beaks of many feeding hens, and after ten thousand miles you got to advance without shaking your breasts" (127). The empty skeleton, which has been her self since childhood, is filled in "with the effort she makes" as she becomes a dancer. Again Zelda's narrative is disruptive here from the more traditional nineteenth-century narrative where the woman is "filled in" by the husband who impregnates her. In 1931 Zelda is able to write as Hélène Cixous challenges women of the future to write. Zelda tells of a woman who has won her body as she describes Alabama's arduous physical training. In "The Laugh of the Medusa," Cixous (1981) unknowingly describes Zelda appropriately as the woman writer filled with an urge to inscribe in language her woman's style — making "all metaphors possible and desirable" (quoted in Marks and de Courtivron 1980, 252) by writing through her own dancer's body.

Zelda also ruptures the conventional plot by creating a female hero who is selfishly and defiantly committed to a career at the expense of her family. Alabama identifies with and becomes a part of an unromanticized, unidealized community of women. She writes of the dancers' rivalries for the approval of their teacher, of their petty jealousies, of the sweat as it rolls into their eyes until they cannot see, of their mended and remended tights, of the starch of their organdy skirts that sticks to their hands. Although none of the school's poor ballerinas can understand Alabama's compelling need to succeed as a ballerina when she has such a rich husband to care for her, it is here that Alabama finally finds a community in which she does feel a part. She earns her own place through her own hard work, fierce determination, and perseverance.

Alabama does what Zelda did not do as a dancer, though Zelda was offered the chance to dance professionally. Alabama accepts a debut in Naples and insists on living there alone. When her daughter comes to visit, the result is disastrous; the child is unhappy, but Alabama cannot care — instead, she mends her tights and works harder. Still, Zelda does not create for Alabama an ending of glorious success as a prima ballerina that Zelda must have dreamed of for herself. Alabama's ankle tendons are severed in order to save an infected foot, and her career as a dancer ends abruptly.

Yet even here Zelda subverts the conventional ending of the guilty and self-absorbed woman, reprimanded for her selfish ways by some form of mutilation, who finally learns the lesson that her real value is as wife and mother. The reunion with David is neither happy nor sentimental for Alabama. Upon their return to the United States to see Alabama's dying father, the novel ends in poignant resignation as Alabama accepts her return to being "David's wife" and "Bonnie's mother." She remembers her father saying to her, "'If you want to choose, you must be a goddess.' That was when she had wanted her own way about things. It wasn't easy to be a goddess away from Olympus" (204). The empowerment she received from creating herself as a dancer is gone; she has lost her chance to determine her own future. The opposition between empowerment and passivity is still firmly intact, and Alabama, who has lost the talent that allowed her to move out of passivity toward empowered self-direction, now seems forever denied another chance at such a possibility. Alabama ruminates as the novel ends: "We trained ourselves to deduce logic from experience. . . . By the time a person has achieved years adequate for choosing a direction, the die is cast and the moment has long since passed which determined the future . . ." (210).

There are many silences in this text that must be noted. There is no romanticization of marriage; the reunion of David and Alabama as the novel ends is due only to Alabama's defeat in what she thought might save her. Nor is there sentimentality attached to the relationship between mother and daughter. David is clearly the provider of affection and security for Bonnie. There are no other women of Alabama's social class attempting what Alabama attempts; all are thoroughly a part of the society she rejects, and they find her compulsion appalling, her dancing abominable. There is also no self-pitying whine from Alabama; she poignantly accepts her lot as Zelda ends the novel with stark realism rather than romantic idealism — Alabama is emptying ash trays after enduring yet another party and its trivial conversation. She had once refused the tower that her prince (or knight) offered, and Zelda accordingly declines to produce the more conventional ending of the chastened or humbled woman welcomed back into the family where she truly belonged all along. Instead, she has accomplished what Cixous calls "the woman's gesture" (1981) by "flying in language . . . jumbling the order . . . changing around the furniture, dislocating things and values, breaking them all up, emptying structures, and turning propriety upside down" (258).

How does *Tender Is the Night* differ from Zelda's novel? Scott finished *Tender Is the Night* after reading and editing *Save Me the Waltz*, and his novel clearly becomes a defense of their marriage. In this sense, we can look upon Zelda as Scott's precursor, the one from whom he had to take an imaginary swerve not only to create a new plot from their shared experience but for reasons of self-justification as well.

In *Tender Is the Night* we are no longer interacting with primarily a female character but are instead dealing with Dr. Dick Diver; however, I shall focus on Dick's wife, Nicole, and what she achieves in spite of Dick and because of him. Again the novel can be seen in terms of opposition, but this time it is one of control and loss of control.

Nicole, seduced by her father at sixteen, falls "madly" in love with Dick, the promising young psychiatrist, as she recovers from schizophrenia, a consequence of the seduction. I use the term "madly" quite literally, for Nicole's attraction to Dick is diagnosed as sublimation of the abused love for her father now transferred to the safe haven of both doctor and acceptable lover. Dr. Diver knows this is the case, but Dick Diver, the man who must be loved, revels in her adoration of him and marries her despite the knowledge that he will be caring for her for a good part of their life together. As the novel begins, the marriage has survived ten years, Nicole is still vulnerable to occasional "loss of control," and Dick is the center of a group of idolaters that includes a young actress, Rosemary. For much of the novel Scott unobtrusively allows Nicole to get well and to regain control as Dick falls deeper and deeper into the morass of his own neurotic need for love and loses control of himself and others because of this overwhelming need. Rosemary wants him, finally has him, and then discards him. Other women use him for entertainment, for self-aggrandizement, for getting out of embarrassing situations, and still, "the old fatal pleasingness, the old forceful charm, swept back with its cry of 'Use me!' . . . On an almost parallel occasion, back in Dohmler's clinic on the Zurichsee [when he decided to marry Nicole], realizing this power, he had made his choice, chosen Ophelia, chosen the sweet poison and drunk it. Wanting above all to be brave and kind, he had wanted, even more than that, to be loved" (*Tender Is the Night,* 302). Dick Diver is the tragic hero with the tragic flaw, the need to be loved by weak women that he might control them. His is a flaw for which he finds no cure. As the novel ends, he is exiled from the glimmer of the life of the rich in Europe to "a very small town" in New York and entanglements with girls who work in grocery stores.

It is Nicole who not only survives but flourishes. As Dick crumbles in alcoholic excess, bitterness, and self-pity, Nicole frees herself from the man who made her well in return for her devotion: "Suddenly, in the space of two minutes she achieved her victory and justified herself without lie or subterfuge, cut the cord forever. Then she walked, weak in the legs, and sobbing coolly, toward the household that was hers at last. . . . The case was finished. Doctor Diver was at liberty" (302). The beautiful Nicole is still the object of male desire, and now with Tommy, who has loved her much more faithfully than Dick was ever able to do, has a sexual encounter that is in utter contrast to all Dick's unsatisfying liaisons outside their marriage. By freeing herself from her illness and, consequently, from

Dick, she is able to revert to the sexual woman she had always been. By thinking for herself, she no longer has to let "others think for you and take power from you, pervert and discipline your natural tastes, civilize and sterilize you" (290). "Her ego began blooming like a great rich rose as she scrambled back along the labyrinths in which she had wandered for years. She hated the beach, resented the places where she had played planet to Dick's sun" (289).

If Scott wrote *Tender Is the Night* as self-justification for the obligatory role he had played in his marriage to Zelda, he failed in a very odd way. The story of Dick Diver is attended to faithfully on his downward plunge through loss of self-control, the respect of others as well as his self-respect, yet Dick garners little sympathy as the novel ends. In contrast, Nicole's quiet quest for sanity and selfhood is achieved at the close of the novel. If Scott's intent was to make Nicole look selfish and self-serving, his novel works instead against such an impression.

Scott's ending is more conventional than Zelda's. Nicole is healed and is successful in her new courtship, which results in a better marriage to a more faithful man. The flawed hero is left to wander in the wilderness of Upstate New York. Zelda seems to have written a more subversive narrative in that she has explored the issue of a woman's access to vocation and not provided a Cinderella "happily ever after" resolution. She has followed the narrative pattern of the romance plot up to a point by repressing the female character's quest, but she has not valorized the heterosexual ties of marriage. Her reincorporation of Alabama and David as a couple is not seen as a sign of their personal and narrative success but as Alabama's personal and narrative failure. Zelda produces what DuPlessis (1985) describes as "a narrative that denies . . . seductive patterns of feeling that are culturally mandated" (5). Zelda is able to make this narrative rupture by creating a hero who breaks with the social and ideological organization of gender in her time. In so doing, she accomplishes what the most recognized woman modernist, Virginia Woolf, recommended: "not repeating your words and following your methods but . . . finding new words and creating new methods" (quoted in DuPlessis 1985, 5).

Save Me the Waltz thus stands as a modernist novel in which Zelda ruptures the romance plot and employs a unique style. She writes to Scott about her style: "It is distinctly Ecole Fitzgerald, though more ecstatic than yours — Perhaps too much so" (quoted in Milford 1970, 102). This ecstatic style has too easily been attributed to madness rather than skill. Such criticism is an example of what Shoshana Felman (1975) sees as the critic's attempt "to 'normalize' the text, to banish and eradicate all trace" of disconcerting eccentricity in order to "cure" the text from what is incurably radical (Felman 1975, 10). Because Zelda does not adjust her "ecstatic style" to the accepted norms of "Ecole Fitzgerald," her writing has been judged even by her usually sympathetic biographer, Milford, as "eccentric," "uneven," and "flawed," though charged nonetheless "with her own fiction energy and voice" (224).

It is useful to compare passages from the two novels — both descriptions of a woman walking through a garden. The first, from *Tender Is the Night*, is exemplary of Scott's controlled, efficient prose:

> Following a walk marked by an intangible mist of bloom that followed the white border stones she came to a space overlooking the sea where there were lanterns asleep in the fig trees and a big table and wicker chairs and a great market umbrella from Sienna, all gathered about an enormous pine, the biggest tree in the garden. She paused there a moment, looking absently at a growth of nasturtiums and iris tangled at its foot, as though sprung from a careless handful of seeds, listening to the plaints and accusations of some nursery squabble in the house. When this died away on the summer air, she walked on, between kaleidoscopic peonies massed in pink clouds, black and brown tulips and fragile mauve-stemmed roses, transparent like sugar flowers in a confectioner's window — until, as if the scherzo of color could reach no further intensity, it broke off suddenly in mid-air, and moist steps went down to a level five feet below. (26)

The second, from *Save Me the Waltz*, illustrates a hallucinatory quality that could be said to reveal Zelda's madness or her genius:

White things gleam in the dark — white flowers and paving-stones. The moon on the window panes careens to the garden and ripples the succulent exhalations of the earth like a silver paddle. The world is younger than it is, and she to herself appears so old and wise, grasping her problems and wrestling with them as affairs peculiar to herself and not as racial heritages. There is a brightness and bloom over things; she inspects life proudly, as if she walked in a garden forced by herself to grow in the least hospitable of soils. She is already contemptuous of ordered planting, believing in the possibility of a wizard cultivator to bring forth sweet-smelling blossoms from the hardest of rocks, and night-blooming vines from barren wastes, to plant the breath of twilight and to shop with marigolds. She wants life to be easy and full of pleasant reminiscences. (7)

Although apparently complex, at heart the syntactic structure of Scott's passage is fairly simple. He uses standard syntactic structures in standard places, stretching three simple sentences by using participial phrases and compound noun phrases. The three sentences share the same subject, "she" (Nicole), and the verbs chart her progress through the garden: "she came"; "she paused"; and "she walked." When listed independently, they resemble the well-known pattern of "I came; I saw; I conquered" (and, in fact, nature has been conquered in this passage, though not by Nicole). Scott begins the first sentence with a fronted participial, "Following a walk marked by an intangible mist of bloom that followed the white border stones," then the subject and verb, "she came," followed by a prepositional phrase, "to a space," and another participial phrase, "overlooking the sea." He concludes with an adverbial clause, "where there were . . . ," which lists the items she will pass by: "lanterns," "table," "chairs," "umbrella," and "pine." These objects are described with plain adjectives that emphasize their size: "big," "great," and "enormous."

Even though there is one section in the garden that looks "as though sprung from a careless handful of seeds," this effect is as calculated as the rest. It is clear that the beds of flowers and the furniture have been carefully chosen and arranged, just as the words, phrases, and clauses that describe them have been precisely chosen and ordered. Even the disturbance in the nursery is a "squabble" rather than a "tantrum." The adjectives provide us with an image of full daylight saturated with color: "kaleidoscopic peonies," "pink clouds," "fragile mauve-stemmed roses." The simile "like sugar flowers in a confectioner's window" underscores how contrived these surroundings are. The use of the lively musical metaphor "scherzo" to describe the intense color is unusual, but since a scherzo is a crafted movement in three-quarter time, it is not a metaphor that suggests recklessness or mysteriousness. Instead, the syntactic choices Scott makes produce a garden meticulously cultivated by hard-working gardeners. Nicole moves down the path as an observer; she lacks all agency and can only look "absently" at her surroundings. Not only has the garden clearly been created by others, but it is also not a place where Nicole's thoughts or daydreams elicited by the garden can be observed. Instead, she is no more than a moving object in a lovely but static picture postcard.

Zelda's description moves against standard syntactic convention. She uses several different subjects and verbs — "things gleam," "moon careens and ripples," "world is," "she appears," "There is," "she inspects," "She is," and "She wants" — which, when taken independently, do not fit into any recognizable pattern. In her opening sentence, she immediately makes use of a divergent way of treating syntactic structure by placing the appositive, "white flowers and paving-stones," at the end of the sentence after a dash, which immediately gives a heightened dramatic sense to the paragraph. The independent clause "The world is younger than it is" is anomalous in that it claims that the thing, "the world," is different from itself. Zelda continues this sentence in a bizarre fashion by moving the prepositional phrase "to herself" before the verb so that it reads, "she to herself appears so old and wise." In addition, she chooses to combine striking semantic features; for example, the moon "careens to the garden." Here she is using a verb that suggests a wild kind of motion, but the moon's movement is predictable, not wild. By juxtaposing a noun phrase with a contradictory verb, Zelda creates a mysterious garden full of the unexpected movement of a moon that "careens" and "ripples." In a simile, she compares the moon to "a silver paddle" that disturbs an eerie gaseous moisture (described as "succulent," an unpredictable modifier) that the earth is exhaling.

Unlike Scott, who denies Nicole agency, Zelda gives Alabama creative agency in a supernatural garden. Rather than meticulously describing the actual garden, Zelda shows instead how Alabama imagines an extraordinary garden of possibility. From Alabama's perspective, the world should be like Eden was, capable of spontaneous growth; she does not want to be expelled from that garden. Given the images of white in darkness, Alabama conjures up a magical space for a "wizard cultivator," who will not only be able to make flowers and vines grow from rocks and waste but will be able to bring on the magical hour — "The breath of twilight." As she walks, she proudly inspects not only the garden but "life" itself, as if she were the "wizard cultivator" who could create lushness out of "the least hospitable soils." The entire garden, then, becomes a metaphor for the way Alabama would like to live, not dependent on the ordinary and expected, but on the unusual and exotic. The only color in the passage comes with "the marigolds," which are connected to the unexpected verb "to shop." Everything in the description up to this point has been natural or magical, and it is surprising suddenly to come upon a verb that means commerce and social order. "To shop" seems to infringe on the unrealistic possibilities that Alabama would like to believe in, and it prepares us for the closing sentence that returns us to "life" and the likelihood that it will not be "easy and full of pleasant reminiscences."

Zelda's poetically fluid yet decisive passage is not meant to be reasonable. Instead, it is perhaps "the woman's gesture" (Cixous 1981, 253) as Zelda dips into a different consciousness and, like her protagonist, seems "contemptuous of ordered planting," such as predictable modifiers and sensible metaphors. Hers was a "new way of writing . . . which, for centuries," as Felman observes, "has signaled antithesis to dominant values" (1975, 109).

Zelda did not heal herself by writing her novel; a unified, integrated self could not be claimed from the novel's production. Scott's controlled, polished work was the standard against which Zelda's was judged, and the novel is still considered as an imperfect companion to *Tender Is the Night*. But the swerve Zelda took to reclaim herself from Scott's reification of her did create a new character — Alabama Beggs. Zelda did not find herself in Alabama, and her disappointment in the novel's failure led her to another more severe collapse, but the novel has contemporary interest. In fact, Charles Scribner's Sons released in 1991 *Zelda Fitzgerald: The Collected Writings*, edited by Matthew Bruccoli, which includes *Save Me the Waltz*. By recognizing the poetic nature of Zelda's unique and inventive style in telling Alabama's story, we can welcome *Save Me the Waltz* into our literary sphere, not as a biographical curio or as the failed companion piece to *Tender Is the Night*, but as a provocative modern novel in its own right.

References

Bloom, Harold. 1973. *The Anxiety of Influence: A Theory of Poetry*. New York: Oxford UP.

Bruccoli, Matthew J. 1981. *Some Sort of Epic Grandeur: The Life of F. Scott Fitzgerald*. New York: Harcourt.

————, ed. 1991. *Zelda Fitzgerald: The Collected Writings*. New York: Scribner's.

Cixous, Hélène. 1981. "The Laugh of the Medusa." Trans. Keith Cohen and Paula Cohen. In *New French Feminisms*, ed. Elaine Marks and Isabelle de Courtivron. New York: Schocken.

Culler, Jonathan. 1982. *On Deconstruction: Theory and Criticism after Structuralism*. Ithaca: Cornell UP.

DuPlessis, Rachel Blau. 1985. *Writing Beyond the Ending: Narrative Strategies of Twentieth-Century Women Writers*. Bloomington: Indiana UP.

Felman, Shoshana. 1975. "Women and Madness: The Critical Phallacy." *Diacritics* (Winter), 2–10.

Fitzgerald, F. Scott. 1934. *Tender Is the Night*. New York: Scribner's.

Fitzgerald, Zelda. 1967. *Save Me the Waltz*. Carbondale and Edwardsville: Southern Illinois UP.

Gilbert, Sandra M., and Susan Gubar. 1979. *The Madwoman in the Attic: The*

Woman Writer and the Nineteenth-Century Literary Imagination. New Haven: Yale UP.

Hardwick, Elizabeth. 1970. *Seduction and Betrayal: Women and Literature*. New York: Random.

Lentricchia, Frank. 1980. *After the New Criticism*. Chicago: U of Chicago P.

Macherey, Pierre. 1978. *A Theory of Literary Production*. Trans. Geoffrey Wall. New York: Routledge.

Marks, Elaine, and Isabelle de Courtivron. 1980. *New French Feminisms: An Anthology*. Amherst: U of Massachusetts P.

Mayfield, Sara. 1971. *Exiles from Paradise*. New York: Delacorte.

Milford, Nancy. 1970. *Zelda: A Biography*. New York: Harper Colophon.

Tavernier-Courbin, Jacqueline. 1979. "Art as Woman's Response and Search: Zelda Fitzgerald's *Save Me the Waltz*." *Southern Literary Journal* 11:22–42.

PART 5

Language and Gender

This section expands our discussion of discourse style by exploring how sex roles affect representation of language. The authors have chosen two contexts that have received relatively little critical attention: the first looks at how gender considerations affect the essays of a Mexican woman writer; the second investigates how sex roles are displayed in the discourse of a once popular television program.

Mary Gomez Parham examines the work of Rosario Castellanos, whose essays are characterized by thematic and stylistic innovation. Much of this innovation derives from her willingness — indeed, her daring — to "write like a woman." Thematically, her focus is on women's problems and on women writers; her images are those of a woman. Stylistically, her writing exhibits many of those traits that sociolinguists associate with women. Castellanos prefers a discursive, conjunctive style, for instance, involving the use of fragments, interrogatives, and a conversational, informal tone. Her essays are filled with emotion, often manifested by the use of various intensifiers, though she, like many women writers, favors humor over direct expressions of anger. Women's tendency to favor the reduction of authorial distance is also apparent in Castellanos's essays. Her courage in writing in her own way on unpopular topics in a strongly male-dominated culture should be recognized, as should her success in manipulating a woman's style to achieve her own ends. Her writing is an important part of what is new in the New Essay in Latin America.

June M. Frazer and Timothy C. Frazer explore the effects of gender in the discourse of "Policewoman," a popular television series from the seventies. Despite the apparent authority given to the female title character, Sgt. Pepper Anderson's discourse is diffident compared to that of her male partner. In analyzing empowered and powerless language, the authors emphasize the need to take into account the illocutionary force of the speakers' utterances. Because traditional speech-act or discourse models fail to account for what actually happens in cross-sex conversation, the authors formulate a model based on the function of statements and questions. Applying their model to an episode of "Policewoman," they find that "male dominance of discourse in this example of 'feminist' programming is as great as in real life."

Gender issues are often entangled with the consideration of how language represents and reinforces relations of dominance and submissiveness. In part 6, the emphasis shifts away from gender to the discourse of power.

Rosario Castellanos
and the New Essay
Writing It Like a Woman

In Latin American literature, as in other literatures, the essay has often been a stepchild among genres, rarely able to capture for long the attention of any substantial number of literary scholars. This neglect has been the case in spite of the fact that in Latin America production in the genre has been prodigious and high in quality. What has happened is that a body of talented scholars have dedicated themselves to the task of almost single-handedly nurturing the essay. Well-known names such as those of José Martínez, Peter Earle, Robert Mead, Donald Bleznick, and Juan Loveluck come to mind.

These scholars have been laudably successful in their endeavors on behalf of the essay except in one area, that of the essay written by women. Anthologies and histories largely omit women essayists, and when they are included, as women such as Victoria Ocampo, Concha Meléndez, and Rosario Castellanos are in Peter Earle and Robert Mead's history, for example, entries devoted to them are generally exceedingly brief.[1] Furthermore, critical work on women essayists is rare, perhaps because they have simply been commonly excluded from the canon. The essay, with its traditional emphasis on logical discourse, has never been considered to be a "feminine" genre. Women have been — sometimes grudgingly — accorded the right to excel in the sentimental, the gothic or the detective novel, for instance, or in lyric poetry, but not in the essay. Earle and Mead's comments on Ocampo and Castellanos, respectively, typify critical attitudes toward these writers: "A esta ensayista la apreciamos por su sensibilidad y visión más que por sus ideas" ("We appreciate this essayist for her sensitivity and vision more than for her ideas"), and "Su método es más bien descriptivo que teórico; su intuición es profunda" ("Her method is descriptive rather than theoretical; her intuition is deep") (117, 151).[2]

In such a climate, it is not surprising that the important essayistic work of the Mexican writer Rosario Castellanos, the focus of the present study, has been neglected. This lapse is unfortunate, for Castellanos's work in the essay is both extensive and high caliber.[3] In addition to novels, poetry, and theater, Castellanos wrote four volumes of collected essays (*Juicios sumarios: Ensayos* [1966], *Mujer que sabe latín . . .* [1973], *El uso de la palabra* [1974] and *El mar y sus pescaditos* [1975]), nearly a hundred uncollected essays, and a long study, her master's thesis (*Sobre cultura femenina* [1950]), which Elena Poniatowska regards as the "point of departure for the contemporary women's movement in Mexico" (quoted in Ahern and Vásquez, 133).

Rosario Castellanos's essays are worthy of much more serious investigation, however, not only because they constitute a sizable corpus and are well written, but also because they participate in a rebirth of the genre itself in Latin America. A number of male essayists have been studied as practitioners of this "New Essay." For example, Angela Dellepiane in a study titled "Sábato y el ensayo hispanoamericano" finds Ernesto Sábato's contribution to the genre to be his thematic innovation, his treatment of topics more universal than those that traditionally have preoccupied the Latin American essayist, namely the social ones, principally the questions of Latin American identity and destiny. Jaime Alazraki studies Jorge Luis Borges's groundbreaking treatment of traditional philosophical notions in the essays of the latter ("Tres formas del ensayo contemporáneo: Borges, Paz, Cortázar"), and Martin Stabb points out the wide-ranging textual innovation that Julio Cortázar brings to the genre ("Not Text But Texture: Cortázar and the New Essay"). These men are seen, then, as players in a modern essayistic game characterized by a concentration on new, more universal themes and by a great deal of formal freedom.[4]

No women, however, have been seriously discussed as participants in the current awakening among Latin American essayists, and one of the most surprising omissions in this context is Rosario Castellanos.[5] Whether this situation has arisen because her preoccupation with women's issues and women writers has not interested traditional critics or because, as I have noted, her work may seem too descriptive and intuitive to some or because Castellanos's admirers have been occupied with her fiction and poetry, the lack of attention to her essays is inappropriate, for the essays are innovative in many ways.[6] Certainly, a man writing like Castellanos would without a doubt be counted among Latin America's most important New Essayists.

However, Castellanos's "New Essay" differs in an important way from that of men like the above or Carlos Monsiváis and Gabriel Zaid, her countrymen. In a word, she writes like a woman. And it is precisely in allowing herself to write like a woman — the possible cause, ironically, of the lack of interest in her work — that she rejuvenates the Latin American essay. She brings a woman's voice to the genre, vigorously and unmistakably, more clearly than it has ever been heard before in the Latin American essay. It is the purpose of this paper to illustrate the ways in which Castellanos writes (essays) like a woman. The study will hopefully contribute to both a deeper understanding of her work in all genres and, in more general terms, the growing appreciation of the woman writer not merely as a "lacking" man, to use Lacan's terminology, but as an artist in her own right with a canon, preoccupations, and style that often deviate significantly from the established norm.

The notion that men and women speak and write differently is neither a new nor a geographically limited one. In some languages, there are objectively identifiable lexical differences between men's and women's discourse; in other cultures, the notion of some kind of difference exists as a subjective experience, a popular intuition that the sexes simply do not handle language in the same way. In any case, the judgment by male evaluators that women's discourse is flawed and inferior to men's is pandemic, with such judgments expressed in terms ranging from the jocular to the solemn. To cite a few literary examples, Dr. Johnson, Boswell states, jests that "a woman's preaching [read: expressing herself verbally in any manner] is like a dog's walking on his hind legs. It is not done well; but you are surprised to find it done at all" (287). Later, Jean-Jacques Rousseau in a more serious tone declares that, as writers, "women, in general, show neither appreciation nor proficiency nor genius in any part" and that "that burning eloquence, those sublime raptures which transmit delight to the very foundation of the soul will always be lacking from women's writings" (quoted in Kamuf, 290). And later Flaubert acknowledges the differences between men's and women's style while disdaining the latter when he rhapsodizes, "I love above all else nervous, substantial, clear sentences with flexed muscle and a rugged complexion. I like male, not female, sentences" (quoted in Schor, 185). And similar, though usually more subdued or covert, perceptions have been expressed in this century by prominent literary figures.

Since Flaubert's day a new breed of scholar and writer has begun to study differences in men's and women's discourse. Unlike writers like those quoted above, however, they are studying these differences nonjudgmentally and in depth. The effort has been almost as universal as traditional notions of gender-based language and style differences have been and has found expression in terms ranging from the general to the specific, touching areas from thematism to linguistics. Among those working in this area are French feminists led by Hélène Cixous, Julia Kristeva, and Luce Irigaray, who speak of women's need to "write the body," to write from their own reality, and of their duty to write in a way that subverts the ideals of traditional phallocentric discourse.[7] With greater specificity, the theories of Virginia Woolf, who lamented the difficulties encountered by women writers straining to imitate the established male idiom (76), have been amply expanded upon by a number of American literary scholars, such as Elaine Showalter,

Julia Penelope (Stanley), and Susan Gubar. And finally, male-female discourse differences have been studied in the greatest depth and detail in the recent work of a number of American sociolinguists, among them Robin Lakoff, Nancy Henley, Barrie Thorne, Cheris Kramarae, and Deborah Tannen, all of whom have documented significant gender-based speech and/or writing (in general, "style") differences in many languages.[8] The work of pioneers such as these will form the framework for this examination of Rosario Castellanos's essays.

Castellanos's version of the new Latin American essay is, like that of other New Essayists, characterized by thematic innovation. She is not obsessed with the old question of Latin American identity and looks abroad for her models. Although her writings exhibit a deep concern for issues related to Mexican life, her most favored topics — world literature, especially that written by women, and women's rights — are what I believe contribute most to the writer's far-reaching relevance. In choosing themes, then, as in her style, Castellanos's place among the New Essayists is related to, if not contingent upon, her femaleness. It could be said of her as it has been of Virginia Woolf that "her attitude as a feminist was intimately bound up with her attitude as an artist" (Marder, 21).[9] Indeed, including her master's thesis, at least half of Castellanos's essays concern women in some way. Many of these are in two collections: *El uso de la palabra*, which contains an especially large number of essays on women's issues, and *Mujer que sabe latín . . .*, which is devoted entirely to women writers and the sociopolitical dimensions of women's place in Mexico and the rest of the world.

The second of the two volumes mentioned, *Mujer que sabe latín . . .*, is both one of Castellanos's most representative works and thematically one of the most interesting. In the case of the essays therein on women writers, the author's intent is clearly to focus the public's — and scholars' — attention on these writers, to validate their work as well as to contribute to an understanding of it. In general, her tone is equanimous, though at times she voices her defense of the writers in strong terms, as in "Bellas damas sin piedad." Here Castellanos attempts to emphasize the talent and importance of several women writers of detective novels. She laments their neglect and in convincing terms condemns the perpetrators of this neglect: "Los misóginos afirmarán que, siendo el policiaco un género menor, naturalmente que las mujeres no temen aproximarse a él porque una aspiración más alta desembocaría en el fracaso" ("Misogynists will assert that, since the detective novel is a minor genre, it is natural that women not fear it, for any greater aspiration would end in failure") (73).[10] In other essays in *Mujer que sabe latín . . .*, in which the author turns her attention to social questions, the tone is generally one of relentless assault on the bastions of injustice toward women. Castellanos is alternately calm, angry, and mocking in these essays, but she is never irrational. She jeers at exaggerated stereotypes in quite emotionally charged, mocking language: "¡Loor a las cabecitas blancas! ¡Gloria eterna a la que nos amó antes de conocernos! Estatuas en las plazas, días consagrados a su celebracíon, etc., etc." ("All praise to the little white-haired ladies! Eternal glory to the woman who loved us before she even knew us! Statues in the plazas, days dedicated to honoring her, etc., etc.") (16). Yet a few lines later she makes it very clear that she is in complete and sober control of her topic, citing sources or statistics as appropriate:

> Dejemos a un lado las diatribas, tan vulgarizadas, de Schopenhauer; los desahogos, tan esotéricos, de Weininger; la sospechosa ecuanimidad de Simmel y citemos exclusivamente a Moebius quien, con tenacidad germánica, organizó una impresionante suma de datos para probar científica, irrefutablemente, que la mujer es una "débil mental fisiológica." (17)

> (Let us leave aside Schopenhauer's vulgar diatribes; Weininger's esoteric emotional outbursts; Simmel's suspect equanimity and let us cite only Moebius who, with Germanic tenacity, organized an impressive body of data in order to prove scientifically, irrefutably, that woman is a "physiologically retarded creature.")

This thematic overview of Rosario Castellanos's essays and especially of those in *Mujer que sabe latín* . . . confirms the importance for her of women's issues as well as her control of the subject matter.

Related to thematic choice in Castellanos's writing-like-a-woman, to borrow Peggy Kamuf's term,[11] are certain motifs and images that appear repeatedly in her essays. Again, they spring from her experience of and preoccupation with womanhood: they are those of a writer daring to write from a frame of reference completely distinct in many ways from the canonical one — that is, from a woman's frame of reference. In *Mujer que sabe latín* . . . , for instance, the feminine perspective is everywhere in evidence. Castellanos writes in at least two essays therein, "La mujer ante el espejo: cinco autobiografías" and "María Luisa Bombal y los arquetipos femeninos," of women and mirrors. In the latter, making use of this "imagen feminista del espejo" ("feminist image of the mirror"), as Sharon Keefe Ugalde calls it (123), she analogizes that "[c]uando una mujer latinoamericana toma entre sus manos la literatura lo hace con el mismo gesto y con la misma intención con la que toma un espejo: para contemplar su imagen" ("[w]hen a Latin American woman takes literature into her hands, she does so with the same gesture and with the same intention with which she picks up a mirror: to contemplate her image") (144).[12] Other traditional feminine focuses for Castellanos include the home, and she writes in one instance that one of Clarice Lispector's bored heroines "decide poseer su casa de la manera que las mujeres la poseen: arreglándola" ("decides to take possession of her house in the manner in which women take possession of it: by straightening it up") (130). Again the author is viewing the world, for the reader, as a woman.

Another primary and typically feminine focus for Castellanos is pregnancy and motherhood. Her intense interest in this area brings to mind that of Hélène Cixous, except that Castellanos's treatment of it is not as consistently positive or, some would say, romanticized as the Frenchwoman's.[13] The Mexican deals more with the sometimes harsh realities of motherhood. In *Mujer que sabe latín* . . . , for example, she discusses motherhood in her social pieces, decrying above all society's distortion of it:

Si la maternidad no fuera más que una eclosión física, como entre los animales, sería anatema. Pero no es ni una eclosión física porque eso implicaría una euforia sin atenuantes que está muy lejos del espíritu que la sociedad ha imbuido en la perpetuación de la vida. (15)

(If motherhood were no more than a physical eclosion, as it is with animals, it would be anathema. But it is not even a physical eclosion, for that would imply an unmitigated euphoria which is very far from the spirit with which society has imbued the perpetuation of life.)

The author is interested in all aspects of motherhood as a condition that often oppresses women in modern society, but it is also part of her own personal experience (she had three pregnancies and one surviving child) and thus, as a writer, of her aesthetic repertoire. One example of this bringing of a very female experience to art is found in the essay "Natalia Ginzburg: la conciencia del oficio." Here, with a hint of her sometimes-negative attitude toward childbearing, Castellanos uses the fetus as a metaphor for the writer's vocation, which she likens to the "dios" with which the mother of Christ was (probably reluctantly, according to Castellanos) impregnated,

[u]n dios que, a fin de cuentas, no es más que un cuerpo extraño, inasimilable al nuestro, una semilla que se implanta hoy con apariencia insignificante, pero que va a crecer, día a día, a nuestras expensas y alcanzara su plenitud a costa de nuestra extinción. (47)

([a] god who, after all, is nothing more than a foreign body, unassimilable by our own, a weed which implants itself today and appears insignificant, but which will grow, day by day, at our expense and which achieves its fullness at the cost of our extinction.)

Such allusions to motherhood and other aspects of women's lives abound in Castellanos's essays and lend credence to the assertion that much of "the difference between the writing of women and the writing of men derives from a difference in life experience and perspective" (Stanley and Wolfe, 125). This perspective is part of the new life that Rosario Castellanos brings to the Latin American essay.

Besides the fresh perspective that Castellanos brings to the essay, however, there is another way in which she writes essays like a woman, infusing the genre with new dimensions, and this is in her style. Certainly, that her style and her thematic and referential focuses relate to her condition as a woman writer interested in women's issues will not be surprising if we agree with critics such as Todorov and Halliday who believe style should "be perceived not in isolation but as an integral part of the textual whole in which all components cohere and contribute to the realization of its theme" (Alazraki, "The Making of a Style," 77). In the following pages, then, I will demonstrate how Castellanos, in her style, writes like a woman, thereby bringing to the essay textual innovation no less important than that lauded in the works of New Essayists like Cortázar and Sábato. To this end I will draw from essays in *Mujer que sabe latín.* . . .

As I have attempted to make apparent in quoting Flaubert and Rousseau earlier, men — historically the majority of writers — have always had some notion, more or less vague, of how they should and do write. Recently, however, feminist scholars have become quite specific in their characterization of male style, generally concurring with Robin Lakoff that it exhibits "declarative rather than interrogative sentence structure, no hedging or imprecision, and lexical items chosen for their pure cognitive content, not their emotional coloration" ("Stylistic Strategies," 66). On the other hand, women writers, in the opinion of the same scholars, tend to subvert this model, using language that closely articulates thought, emotion, the psychic life, and the creative process. That is, in the words of Julia Penelope (Stanley) and Susan J. Wolfe, men's writing "reflect[s] an epistemology that perceives the world in terms of categories, dichotomies, roles, stasis and causation, while female expressive modes reflect an epistemology that perceives the world in terms of ambiguities, pluralities, processes, continuities, and complex relationships" (126).[14] Women's distinctive perspective and attitude give rise to a style and tone that are described in detailed, concrete terms by scholars like Lakoff, Stanley, and Wolfe and that are readily recognizable in Rosario Castellanos's essays. We will also find that Castellanos often uses this feminine style and tone in the traditional essayistic endeavor of engaging and convincing the reader.[15]

According to Stanley and Wolfe, women writers' desire to express as faithfully as possible thoughts in flux leads to a proclivity for a discursive, conjunctive style of writing; the simultaneity aimed for is best achieved through a cumulative syntax rather than a complex and subordinating one, the former being "the syntax of woman's consciousness, the rush of perception, the speech that tells all as it emerges" (137).[16] In Castellanos, an affinity for such syntax is noticeable, although she is certainly capable of writing traditionally complex, more "male" sentences. But her preference for a conjunctive style is strikingly manifest in her very frequent use of parallel constructions and of fragments, structures that encode thought as it occurs, without hierarchic ordering. In her four-and-a-half-page piece on Clarice Lispector, for example, there are several instances of parallel constructions such as the following:

> Ha permitido que una mirada eche abajo la cuidadosa estructura de su apariencia actual y el vacío permite que emerja a la superficie lo que estaba enterrado por siglos de civilización, de acato a las leyes, de obediencia a las normas, de repetición de las costumbres. Que emerja lo último que se es: la materia, antes de evolucionar en sus especies, antes de encarnar en las criaturas, antes de permanecer en la voluntad, antes de resplandecer en la inteligencia. (131)

> (She has allowed a glance to demolish the careful structure of her present appearance and the emptiness allows to surface what was buried by centuries of civilization, of respect for laws, of obedience to norms, of repetition of customs. To surface what one ultimately is: matter, before evolving into species,

before taking form as creatures, before coming to reside in the
will, before dazzling as intelligence.)

¿Es que G. H. todavía se mueve dentro de la multiplicidad? No
será más que un tránsito mientras su método de visión, que
tiene que ser enteramente imparcial, encuentre el camino de
acceso al Dios "indiferente", que es totalmente bueno porque
no es bueno ni malo; que está en el seno de una materia; que es
la explosión indiferente de sí misma. (132)

(Is G. H. still thinking in terms of multiplicity? Couldn't it be
just a transitional phase while her perceptual method, which
must be entirely impartial, finds the route of access to the
"indifferent" God, who is totally good because he is neither
good nor bad; who is at the heart of matter; who is the
indifferent explosion of himself.)

Fragments are even more numerous and tend to be similar to these:

Por eso, cuando hace algunos años, nos deslumbró la aparición
de *Gran Sertón: Veredas* de João Guimarães Rosa tuvimos que
suponer nombres y obras en torno suyo. Nombres y obras que
ayudaran a explicarla, a situarla, a entenderla, a complemen-
tarla. (129)

(Therefore, when a few years ago we were dazzled by the
publication of João Guimarães Rosa's *Gran Sertón: Veredas*, we
had to imagine for ourselves names and works relevant to it.
Names and works that would help to explain it, to contextual-
ize it, to understand it, to complement it.)

Muchos de los críticos han senalado la afinidad que existe entre
Virginia Woolf y Clarice Lispector. Afinidad. Lo que significa
mucho más que influencia, perspectivas comunes e instrumen-
tos de trabajo semejantes. (128)

(Many of the critics have pointed out the affinity that exists between Virginia Woolf and Clarice Lispector. Affinity.

Which means much more than influence, common perspectives, and similar tools.)

En el claustro materno está sucediendo un hecho misterioso, una especie de milagro que, como todos los milagros, suscita estupefacción; es presenciado por los asistentes y vivido por la protagonista, "con temor y temblor." Cuidado. Un movimiento brusco, una imprudencia, un antojo insatisfecho y el milagro no ocurrirá. Nueve interminables meses de reposo, de dependencia de los demás, de precauciones, de ritos, de tabúes. (15–16)

(In the maternal womb a mysterious event is taking place, a kind of miracle that, like all miracles, evokes stupefaction; it is observed by those present and experienced by the protagonist "with fear and trembling." Careful. One false step, one imprudent act, one unsatisfied craving and the miracle will not occur. Nine interminable months of rest, of dependence on others, of precautions, of rituals, of taboos.)

All these examples are textual evidence of the importance for Castellanos of the spontaneous communication of the writer's thoughts.

Another facet of the conjunctive in Castellanos is her use of interrogatives. This trait has been much studied in women's writing and speech, and additional possible implications of its popularity both with Castellanos and women writers in general will be discussed later. At this point, in the context of the discussion of Castellanos's efforts at expressing simultaneity, it should be mentioned that the interrogative for her seems to be a mode of thinking aloud, allowing the reader to be privy to her thoughts before she has filtered and ordered them, much as the use of the fragment does. The following passages, from three consecutive pages of "La participación de la mujer mexicana en la educación formal," are illustrative of this very common phenomenon in Castellanos's essays. Discussing women's history, she questions herself — and her reader — as she writes: "¿Que diferencia hay entre esta mujer y la matrona romana?" ("What difference is there between this woman and the Roman matron?") (22); "Y ¿por qué había de darse preferencia a un simple vehículo para la perpetuación de la especie y no a lo que tiene más valor: una persona?" ("And why should preference have been given to a simple vehicle for the perpetuation of the species and not to that which has more value: a person?") (23); and again, "¿Pero es que no hubo excepciones?" ("But were there no exceptions?") (24). The reader thus becomes an active ally in Castellanos's search for solutions and at the same time will be more strongly convinced of the correctness of Castellanos's conclusions as a result of having been led by the author through the reasoning process that she deems appropriate to the question under consideration. In this case, then, a favored feminine stylistic device seems to serve dual purposes as the writer struggles to win over readers whom she undoubtedly perceived as resistant to her message concerning the wisdom of promoting equality between the sexes.

Related to women's wish closely to reproduce the thought process on paper is the apparent importance to them of the expression of emotion in both speech and writing. Sociolinguist Mary Ritchie Key writes of women's "emotional, expressive language" (71), and her colleague Lakoff has documented women's tendency to "speak in italics," that is, to express greater emotion than men, often by making ample use of various intensifiers (*Language and Woman's Place*, 56).[17] In Castellanos, this tendency is notable in her use of exclamatories, a form of intensifier. The frequency of their occurrence in her essays of social content attests to the writer's own deep emotional involvement in the women's issues treated therein and possibly serves to help her, again, persuade a skeptical reader, as Lakoff says intensifiers may (*Language and Woman's Place*, 56). In "La participacion de la mujer mexicana en la educacion formal," describing the plight of any woman seeking employment outside the home in Mexico, Castellanos exclaims, "¡No vaya a ir alguno con el chisme a su familia y se le venga abajo el teatrito! Y en cuanto a espíritu competitivo, ¡vade retro, Satanás!" ("Heaven forbid that someone should snitch to her family and bring the whole thing to a halt! And as for competitive spirit, get thee behind me, Satan!") (30–

31). Here the writer, herself excited about her subject, seeks to inflame the reader with her own indignation through the use of the exclamatory mode. This is one more demonstration of the use of a typically feminine stylistic trait skillfully manipulated to assist in the task of winning the reader over to the writer's point of view.

Another aspect of style that has been found to be especially characteristic of women's writing involves tone and authorial distance. Josephine Donovan, discussing Virginia Woolf's well-known example of a "man's sentence," writes of "a certain lofty arrogance, a certain sureness, indeed smugness" that she finds in Woolf's invented sentence and in men's writing in general (342). Experts generally agree that women's writing, on the other hand, tends toward a less authoritative, more informal, more conversational tone that shrinks distance among writer, reader, and subject matter (Farrell, 909). It is characterized by a great deal more self-disclosure than is men's writing (Kramarae, 150). Women, who show more interest than men in the "social function of talking" (Kramarae, 105) and whose penchant for politeness in discourse has been well documented by linguists such as Lakoff and Deborah Tannen, will of course adopt a tone different from that favored by men whom "societal norms encourage . . . to learn to be inexpressive as a part of being tough, courageous and competitive" (Kramarae, 150).[18] Not taught as commonly as men to value competitiveness and often conditioned to doubt the competence of their intellect, women will adopt a tone of greater humility than men in their speech and writing.

In Castellanos's essays, these tone-related characteristics — informality, minimal authorial distance, and a tendency to self-disclosure and humility — are all abundantly in evidence. The author's mentioned use of exclamatories and fragments, to begin, imparts a mood of conversational informality to the text. The conversational tone is further enhanced by the use of asides or digressions, as in the following examples from "La mujer y su imagen": "Rudinger (¿quien será ese lustre señor?) encontró en una mujer bavara un tipo de cerebro semejante en todo al de las bestias" ("Rudinger [who could this illustrious gentleman be?] found in a

Bavarian woman a type of brain similar in all respects to that of an animal") (18). Elsewhere in the same essay, Castellanos describes the misogynist theories of Moebius: "En la vida común se usan dos términos contrapuestos: inteligente y estúpido. Es inteligente el que discierne bien. (¿En relación con qué? Pero es una descortesía interrumpir su discurso.) Al estúpido, por el contrario, le falta la capacidad de la crítica" ("In everyday life, we use two opposing terms: intelligent and stupid. He who has good judgment is intelligent. [In relation to what? But it's impolite to interrupt his discourse.] The stupid person, on the other hand, lacks critical capacities") (17). The informality and reduction in authorial distance noticeable here are also artfully achieved elsewhere through the use of the first person plural: "Basta de anécdotas y de historia. Estamos en 1970 . . ." ("Enough anecdotes and history. We're in 1970 . . .") (21). This connecting with the reader also occurs when the author directly addresses the reader, as she often does: "Por algo es hombre y tiene a su cargo una familia que sostener, ¿no?" ("There's a reason why he's a man and is responsible for maintaining a family, right?") (31). Later in this collection of essays, Castellanos discusses the work of Silvina Ocampo and concludes by remarking to the reader, "Y . . . aun lo que está usted haciendo en este momento — leer — no es, pese a la promesa de Valéry-Larbaud, un acto impune" ("And . . . even what you're doing right now — reading — is not, regardless of Valéry-Larbaud's promise, an irreproachable act") (154). Castellanos's already documented predilection for the use of interrogatives is yet another device for the minimizing of authorial distance, for it is, like the declarative address cited, a way of talking to, and not at, the reader. And finally, the conversational informality of many of Castellanos's essays is to some degree a result of her tendency to self-disclosure, a distance-diminishing characteristic of much of women's writing, particularly in the genre of the journal or diary. This trait finds expression in the several important essays in which Castellanos discusses her life (including intimate, painful aspects of it) and her work and the interaction of the two. Among these essays are, in *Mujer que sabe latín* . . . alone, "Lecturas tempranas," "Si 'poesía no eres tú,' entonces ¿que?" and "La angustia de elegir." In other essays not specifically devoted to her own life and work, Castellanos nonetheless reveals much about herself, injecting personal opinion on the subject matter and even on occasion on her own critical competence, as in the following passage. It is part of a section in which she discusses the use of a questionnaire in an attempt to begin dealing with the problems of working women in Mexico.

> El cuestionario podría ser formulado con mucho más rigor, y por lo tanto con mucho más fruto, por un especialista en estas cuestiones. Yo sólo me guío por la intuición estética, por la observación de lo que ocurre en torno mío y por algunas experiencias en cabezas ajenas y en la propia. Nada más. (37)

> (The questionnaire could be formulated with much more structure and precision, and therefore with much better results, by a specialist in these matters. I am guided only by aesthetic intuition, by the observation of what is happening around me and by some experiences in other people's heads and in my own. Nothing else.)

The self-effacement exhibited here is often found in Castellanos's works, as it is in those of many women writers whose discourse may be affected by insecurity or excessive deference (Lakoff, "Women's Language," 144–45). At any rate, whatever the etiology of this and the other tonal characteristics discussed here, it should be noted in conclusion that Castellanos's informal, intimate posture in her essays serves a persuasive purpose, much as her frequent interrogatives do: such a tone tends to disarm a skeptical, resisting reader and encourages reader involvement in the discussion and, consequently, a more receptive attitude on his or her part.

There is one final aspect of Castellanos's style in her essays that seems to be influenced by her condition as woman, and this involves her handling of anger and her use of humor. Researchers who agree that women as writers and speakers express a great deal more emotion than men often point out that anger is the one emotion they do not express as readily as men do (Lakoff, "Women's Language," 142), although some assert that it is precisely anger that should be the essence of the feminist writer's consciousness.[19] Women's style, traditionally dominated, as we have seen, by politeness and deference, apparently excludes the expression of this emotion. Castellanos, too, seems to have some difficulty with anger and softens it through the use of humor. Although several scholars have commented, some at length, on the rareness of humor in women's writing (and particularly of sarcasm, satire and irony), Castellanos clearly expresses her favoring of humor in the act of suasion.[20] In an essay in *Mujer que sabe latín . . .* , she contrasts the attitudes and methods of the revolutionary and the reformer, clearly favoring those of the former, "los iconoclastas que aplican 'el ácido corrosivo de la risa' a las instituciones para destruirlas porque son absurdas" ("the iconoclasts who apply 'the corrosive acid of laughter' to institutions in order to destroy them because they are absurd") (183–84). She elaborates that Democritus, for her a revolutionary par excellence, "no se irrita pues sabe que 'el que se enoja pierde,' sino que se divierte desmontando los mecanismos, exhibiendo las incongruencias, reduciendo a cenizas, con un soplo, una construcción que desafiaba a los siglos" ("does not become annoyed since he knows that 'he who gets angry loses,' but rather he amuses himself taking apart the mechanisms, exposing the incongruencies, reducing to ashes, with one puff, an edifice that has defied the ages") (184). In another essay, the author even more explicitly sets forth her belief in the relative superiority of humor over anger in ideological warfare. In this instance the battleground is that of women's rights:

> Ante esto yo sugeriría una campaña: no arremeter contra las costumbres con la espada flamígera de la indignación ni con el trémolo lamentable del llanto sino poner en evidencia lo que tienen de ridículas, de obsoletas, de cursis y de imbéciles. Les aseguro que tenemos un material inagotable para la risa. Y ¡necesitamos tanto reir porque la risa es la forma mas inmediata de la liberación de lo que nos oprime, del distanciamiento de lo que nos aprisiona! (39)

(In the face of this, I would suggest a battle plan: do not fight customs with the flaming sword of indignation or with the pitiful tremolo of tears but rather expose what is ridiculous, obsolete, corny, common, and stupid about them. I assure you that we have inexhaustible material to laugh at. And we need so badly to laugh because laughter is the most immediate means of liberation from what oppresses us and of escape from what imprisons us!)

These passages lead readers to expect a great deal of humor in Castellanos's essays, and they are not disappointed, as the following excerpts delightfully illustrate. Here, in a diatribe against the vagaries of women's fashions, specifically women's shoes, she applies the "ácido corrosivo" of her own particular style of sarcastic, hyperbolic humor to a small, though real and symbolically important, area of the problem of women's place in modern society:

Son feos, se declara, los pies grandes y vigorosos. Pero sirven para caminar, para mantenerse en posición erecta. En un hombre los pies grandes y vigorosos son más que admisibles; son obligatorios. Pero ¿en una mujer? Hasta nuestros más cursis trovadores locales se rinden ante "el pie chiquitito como un alfiletero." Con ese pie (que para que no adquiriera su volumen normal se vendaba en la China de los mandarines y no se sometía a ningún tipo de ejercicio en el resto del mundo civilizado) no se va a ninguna parte. Que es de lo que se trataba, evidentemente.

La mujer bella se extiende en un sofá, exhibiendo uno de los atributos de su belleza, los pequeños pies, a la admiración masculina, exponiéndolos a su deseo. Están calzados por un zapato que algún fulminante dictador de la moda ha decretado como expresión de la elegancia y que posee todas las características con las que se define a un instrumento de tortura. En su parte más ancha aprieta hasta la estrangulación; en su extremo delantero termina en una punta inverosímil a la que los dedos tienen que someterse; el talón se prolonga merced a un agudo estilete que no proporciona la base de sustentación suficiente para el cuerpo, que hace precario el equilibrio, fácil

la caída, imposible la caminata. ¿Pero quién, sino las sufragistas, se atreve a usar unos zapatos cómodos, que respeten
las leyes de la anatomía? Por eso las sufragistas, en justo cas-
tigo, son unánimemente ridiculizadas. (9–10)

(Big, strong feet are ugly, it is decreed. But they're good for
walking, for holding yourself up in an erect position. In a man,
big, strong feet are more than permissible; they're mandatory.
But in a woman? Even our corniest, most pretentious local
troubadours surrender before "the foot tiny as a needlecase."
With that foot [which in the China of the mandarins was
bound so it wouldn't reach its normal size and which never
performed any kind of exercise in the rest of the civilized
world] you can't go anywhere. Which is what it was all about,
evidently.

The beautiful woman stretches out on a sofa, exposing one
of the features of her beauty, her small feet, to the admiration of
the male, exposing them to his desire. She is wearing shoes that
some tyrannical fashion dictator has declared to be an expression of elegance and that possess all of the characteristics with
which an instrument of torture is defined. At its widest part,
they squeeze to the point of strangulation; at the front, they
end in an unlikely point to which the toes must conform; the
heel is heightened by means of a pointed stiletto that does not
provide an adequate base of support for the body, that makes
balance precarious, falling easy, walking impossible. But who,
except the suffragettes, dare to wear comfortable shoes that
respect the laws of anatomy? Because of this, the suffragettes,
in just punishment, are unanimously ridiculed.)

The obvious predilection shown here for a certain biting, caustic
humor on Castellanos's part betrays, I submit, her considerable
anger. The author is personally affected by and concerned and
angry about women's situation in Mexico. But Castellanos, as a
woman, was surely conditioned to avoid or at least soften considerably any expression of anger, if we may extrapolate from the research of the sociolinguists I have referred to here. Having been
taught to prize politeness above all else in their speech, women have

traditionally eschewed direct expression of their anger. And this is what Castellanos does, avoiding overt expressions of anger while nevertheless managing to vent her anger indirectly through the use of humor. Thus the use of humor here is a form of the hedging whose many manifestations in women's speech have been amply documented by Robin Lakoff. However, it is also true that for Castellanos humor serves a purpose similar to that of her use of questions: humor promotes the formation of bonds between reader and writer. As when confronted by Castellanos's humility and openness, the reader is disarmed by her humor and rendered more receptive to her often unpopular ideas.

Castellanos's use of humor is emblematic of her writing in general, writing that is shaped in great part by her condition as a woman of the twentieth century. However, this writing is never limited or constrained by this condition; on the contrary, Castellanos is able to manipulate a woman's style to achieve her own ends in very astute ways. Her writing-like-a-woman is successful and effective and simultaneously refreshes the Latin American essay: Rosario Castellanos's essays are an integral part — too long ignored — of what is new in Latin America's New Essay.

Notes

1. Martin Stabb mentions Elena Poniatowska ("The New Essay of Mexico," 57, 59), but other studies, histories, and anthologies, like Earle and Mead's, generally severely limit the attention accorded women essayists or ignore them altogether. Such works include classics like Bleznick's and Zum Felde's. However, a break with the traditional tendency to neglect women essayists is to be found in Peter Earle's article "The Female Persona in the Latin American Essay: An Overview," in which he both laments the neglect of women essayists and offers an extensive tribute to the essayistic work of Victoria Ocampo.

2. Interestingly, although there has been a great deal of disparagement of women's writing in general, male evaluations have not always agreed on its most damning defect. Kramarae surveys men's historical insistence on

the intuitiveness and irrationality of the female mind (8). However, women have also been accused of being too unemotional, as Rousseau does when he writes that women's writings "are all cold and pretty like their authors. . . . [Women] are a hundred times more reasonable than they are passionate. [They] know neither how to describe nor experience love itself" (quoted in Kamuf, 290).

3. As to critical work on Castellanos's writing, Maureen Ahern and Mary Seale Vásquez wrote the following in their bibliography and collection of essays on Castellanos, published in 1980:

> What surprises when one examines the criticism of Rosario Castellanos's works is its relative paucity, particularly in certain areas. Reviews of her novels and poetry are quite abundant, but are scarce regarding Castellanos's essay collections and short stories and even more so with respect to her theater. Prior to the present volume, more extensive criticism has been almost non-existent on Castellanos's dramatic and essay production. The short story, too, has been little analyzed. On poetry, criticism has been more ample, though most of the critical activity has been thematic and has dealt with earlier lyric poems or those on Indian topics. It is the novel genre which has been the object of the most substantive critical analysis. (36)

While by now much of the neglect of Castellanos's work has been remedied, the neglect of her essays has not, and the "examination[s] of the evolution of her critical stance, her ideas and her style of exposition" in her essays for which Ahern and Vásquez called in their book have not been forthcoming (37). Two studies that have been done, however, are Mary Gomez Parham's "Intellectual Influences on the Works of Rosario Castellanos" and Naomi Lindstrom's "Rosario Castellanos: Pioneer of Feminist Criticism."

4. The question of when the New Essay may overstep the bounds of the essay genre and no longer be an essay in any sense is currently being widely discussed. The old problem of defining the essay has become exacerbated by the daring of Latin America's New Essayists. See Skirius, Stabb ("The New Essay of Mexico"), and Earle ("On the Contemporary Displacement of the Hispanic American Essay") for cogent treatment of this question.

5. Even Earle and Mead, who include in their history a substantial section specifically treating these "Nuevos," do not discuss Castellanos as

one of the New Essay's possible standard-bearers, but rather relegate their brief discussion of her work to another section of their book.

6. See note 3.

7. For an amplified discussion of these women's work, see Ann Rosalind Jones, "Writing the Body: Toward an Understanding of l'écriture féminine." A useful bibliography is *French Feminist Criticism: Women, Language, and Literature. An Annotated Bibliography,* by Elissa D. Gelfand and Virginia Thorndike Hules.

8. In the area of Spanish language and literature, study of male-female differences has been limited. Some doctoral dissertations have treated the topic, usually tangentially. Two are D. G. Lybrand, "Gender-Specific Speech Features: A Sociolinguistic Inquiry into the Language of Males and Females in an Andalusian Agrotown," and W. L. Mitchell, "Male and Female Counterpoint: Gender Relations in an Andean Community." Three noteworthy articles on women's discourse in Latin American litera-ture are Naomi Lindstrom, "Women's Discourse Difficulties in a Novel by Marta Lynch"; Sandra M. Cypess, "I, Too, Speak: 'Female' Discourse in Carballido's Plays"; and Sharon Keefe Ugalde, "El discurso femenino en *Misiá Señora:* ¿un lenguaje nuevo o acceso al lenguaje?" Why there has been so little work of this type in Hispanic language and culture is an interesting question. Ann Bodine discusses a traditional tendency among European scholars "to serve forth as obvious fact, in need of no further investigation, what 'everyone knows' about the 'different' way women speak" and pre-sumably write (131). Certainly, in the near future we can expect new writers with new attitudes to begin addressing the issue in depth. In the meantime, discourse theorists working in Hispanic literature may gener-ally assume, as I do here, that they may "predict universals in linguistic usage based on universals in the position of women cross-culturally; to the extent that women occupy similar social-structural loci with similar social-structural constraints on behavior, women will behave similarly at the strategic level" (Brown, 134). The position of women in Mexico, the United States, France, or Virginia Woolf's England varies primarily in degree; hence the validity for purposes of the present study of the obser-vations of Woolf and others referred to herein. (See Sandra Cypess's comments on Mexican patriarchalism in this regard [45].)

9. See Butturff and Epstein, 105.

10. Notwithstanding the dedication to women writers obvious here, Castellanos is able when necessary to point out flaws in their writings. In "La mujer mexicana del siglo XIX," discussing the lack of accurate portraits

of women in Mexican literature and history, she asserts that even books by women on these subjects are useless because they are "tan teñidos de narcisismo, de autocomplacencia que es imposible tomarlos sin el grano de sal de la ironía, de la desconfianza" (160) ("so tainted with narcissism, with self-complacency that it is impossible to take them without the grain of salt of irony, of distrust").

11. See her article titled "Writing Like a Woman."

12. Ugalde in the article from which the quote is taken (see note 8) discusses the image of the mirror in Albalucía Angel's *Misiá Señora*, comparing Angel's use of the image with that of Mary Elizabeth Coleridge in her poem "The Other Side of the Mirror" (123). The motif is of sufficient importance in women's writing to have prompted one scholar, Jenijoy La Belle, to dedicate to it a book-length study, titled *Herself Beheld: The Literature of the Looking Glass.*

13. Besides Cixous's works, such as "The Laugh of the Medusa," see the intriguing discussions of women writers and maternity in Nancy K. Miller's "Women's Autobiography in France: For a Dialectics of Identification" and in Tillie Olsen's *Silences.* A helpful bibliography on the topic is to be found in Showalter (393–94).

14. Western European languages in general, whose writers share Greco-Roman, in particular Aristotelian, philosophical and aesthetic ideals, will have in common this tendency, although writers in Romance languages may tend overall to a slightly less linear style of development. In the essay the differences among these languages would be quite minimal, however, because of the nonfictional, analytical nature of the genre. (For an examination of variations in cultural thought patterns, and therefore expository styles, the reader is directed to Robert B. Kaplan's "Cultural Thought Patterns in Inter-Cultural Education.")

15. Some contemporary male writers, such as Joyce and Genet, are greatly admired by today's women writers because they dare to diverge stylistically from norms of "good" writing, as women so often have. See Ann Rosalind Jones (365) for a discussion of this topic.

16. A discussion of Stanley and Wolfe's theory is to be found in Carolyn Allen's study of Djuna Barnes (106–7), which also contains a broader consideration of the question of women's style.

17. Readers who may doubt the validity of applying sociolinguistic research findings to the aesthetics of writing should consult Mary Louise Pratt's *Toward a Speech Act Theory of Literary Discourse,* in which she argues for the existence of a close affinity among the various forms of discourse. At

any rate, for the purposes of this paper, one should keep in mind Peter Earle's observation that "the essay comes closest among literary genres to formal conversation" ("On the Contemporary Displacement of the Hispanic American Essay," 331).

18. Of interest in this regard is Penelope Brown's article on politeness in women's speech in a Mayan community.

19. See Jane Marcus, *Art and Anger: Reading Like a Woman*, as well as Gilbert and Gubar's now-classic *The Madwoman in the Attic*.

20. Lakoff asserts in *Language and Woman's Place* that women make little use of humor (52). Kramarae discusses the scholarship on women's humor in greater depth and concludes that more careful research is needed in the area, as it is one that has been far too neglected (52–63).

References

Ahern, Maureen, and Mary Seale Vásquez, eds. 1980. *Homenaje a Rosario Castellanos.* Valencia: Albatros Hispanófila.

Alazraki, Jaime. 1984. "Tres formas del ensayo contemporáneo: Borges, Paz, Cortázar." In *El ensayo hispánico: Actas del simposio,* ed. Isaac Jack Levy and Juan Loveluck, 113–26. Columbia: U of South Carolina P.

—————. 1986. "The Making of a Style: Borges's *Universal History of Infamy.*" In *Textual Analysis: Some Readers Reading,* ed. Mary Ann Caws, 74–90. New York: MLA.

Allen, Carolyn. 1978. "'Dressing the Unknowable in the Garments of the Known': The Style of Djuna Barnes' *Nightwood.*" In *Women's Language and Style,* ed. Douglas Butturff and Edmund L. Epstein, 106–18. Akron, Ohio: Studies in Contemporary Language, vol. 1. Published with the assistance of the English Department, University of Akron.

Bleznick, Donald W. 1964. *El ensayo español del siglo XVI al XX.* Mexico: Ediciones de Andrea.

Bodine, Ann. 1975. "Sex Differentiation in Language." In *Language and Sex: Difference and Dominance,* ed. Barrie Thorne and Nancy Henley, 130–51. Rowley: Newbury House.

Boswell, James. 1791. *Life of Dr. Johnson.* Vol. 1. N.p.: Everyman.

Brown, Penelope. 1980. "How and Why Are Women More Polite: Some Evidence From a Mayan Community." In *Women and Language in Literature and Society*, ed. Sally McConnell-Ginet, Ruth Borker, and Nelly Furman, 111–36. New York: Praeger.

Butturff, Douglas, and Edmund L. Epstein, eds. 1978. *Women's Language and Style*. Akron, Ohio: Studies in Contemporary Language, vol. 1. Published with the assistance of the English Department, University of Akron.

Castellanos, Rosario. 1975. *El mar y sus pescaditos*. Mexico: SepSetentas.

———. 1974. *El uso de la palabra*. Mexico: Excelsior.

———. 1973. *Mujer que sabe latín. . . .* Mexico: SepSetentas.

———. 1966. *Juicios sumarios: Ensayos*. Mexico: Universidad Veracruzana.

———. 1950. *Sobre cultura femenina*. Mexico: Ediciones de "América."

Cixous, Hélène. 1976. "The Laugh of the Medusa." Trans. Keith Cohen and Paula Cohen. *Signs* 1:875–93. In *New French Feminisms: An Anthology*, ed. Elaine Marks and Isabella de Courtivron, 245–64. Amherst: U of Massachusetts P, 1980.

Cypess, Sandra Messinger. 1984. "I, Too, Speak: 'Female' Discourse in Carballido's Plays." *Latin American Theatre Review* 18(1): 45–52.

Dellepiane, Angela B. 1966. "Sábato y el ensayo hispanoamericano." *Asomante* 22(1): 47–59.

Donovan, Josephine. 1972. "Feminist Style Criticism." In *Images of Women in Fiction: Feminist Perspectives*, ed. Susan Koppelman Cornillon, 341–54. Bowling Green: Bowling Green UP.

Earle, Peter G. 1978. "On the Contemporary Displacement of the Hispanic American Essay." *Hispanic Review* 46:329–41.

———. 1985. "The Female Persona in the Latin American Essay: An Overview." In *Woman as Myth and Metaphor in Latin American Literature*, ed. Carmelo Virgillo and Naomi Lindstrom. Columbia: U of Missouri P.

Earle, Peter, and Robert Mead. 1973. *Historia del ensayo hispanoamericano*. Mexico: Ediciones de Andrea.

Farrell, Thomas J. 1979. "The Female and Male Modes of Rhetoric." *College English* 40:909–21.

Gelfand, Elissa D., and Virginia Thorndike Hules. 1985. *French Feminist Criticism: Women, Language, and Literature. An Annotated Bibliography*. New York: Garland.

Gilbert, Sandra M., and Susan Gubar. 1979. *The Madwoman in the Attic: The Woman Writer and the Nineteenth-Century Literary Imagination*. New Haven, Conn.: Yale UP.

Jones, Ann Rosalind. 1981. "Writing the Body: Toward an Understanding of l'écriture féminine." *Feminist Studies* 7:247–63.

Kamuf, Peggy. 1980. "Writing Like a Woman." In *Women and Language in Literature and Society*, ed. Sally McConnell-Ginet, Ruth Borker, and Nelly Furman, 284–99. New York: Praeger.

Kaplan, Robert B. 1966. "Cultural Thought Patterns in Inter-Cultural Education." *Language Learning* 12(1-2): 1–20.

Key, Mary Ritchie. 1975. *Male/Female Language*. Metuchen, N.J.: Scarecrow P.

Kramarae, Cheris. 1981. *Women and Men Speaking: Frameworks for Analysis*. Rowley: Newbury House.

La Belle, Jenijoy. 1989. *Herself Beheld: The Literature of the Looking Glass*. Ithaca, N.Y.: Cornell UP.

Lakoff, Robin. 1975. *Language and Woman's Place*. New York: Harper.

———. 1978. "Women's Language." In *Women's Language and Style*, ed. Douglas Butturff and Edmund L. Epstein, 139–58. Akron, Ohio: Studies in Contemporary Language, vol. 1. Published with the assistance of the English Department, University of Akron.

———. 1979. "Stylistic Strategies Within a Grammar of Style." In *Language, Sex, and Gender: Does "La Différence" Make a Difference?* ed. Judith Orsanu, Mariam K. Slater, and Leonore Loeb Adler. *Annals of the New York Academy of Sciences* 327:53–78.

Lindstrom, Naomi. 1980. "Rosario Castellanos: Pioneer of Feminist Criticism." In *Homenaje a Rosario Castellanos*, ed. Maureen Ahern and Mary Seale Vasquez, 65–74. Valencia: Albatros Hispanofila.

———. 1983. "Women's Discourse Difficulties in a Novel by Marta Lynch." *Ideologies and Literature* 4(17): 339–48.

Lybrand, D. G. 1982. "Gender-Specific Speech Features: A Sociolinguistic Inquiry into the Language of Males and Females in an Andalusian Agrotown." Ph.D. diss., Southern Methodist University.

Marcus, Jane. 1988. *Art and Anger: Reading Like a Woman*. Columbus: Ohio State UP.

Marder, Herbert. 1968. *Feminism and Art. A Study of Virginia Woolf*. Chicago: U of Chicago P.

Miller, Nancy K. 1980. "Women's Autobiography in France: For a Dialectics of Identification." In *Women and Language in Literature and Society*, ed. Sally McConnell-Ginet, Ruth Borker, and Nelly Furman, 258–73. New York: Praeger.

Mitchell, W. L. 1986. "Male and Female Counterpoint: Gender Relations in an Andean Community." Ph.D. diss., University of Colorado at Boulder.

Olsen, Tillie. 1965. *Silences*. New York: Dell.

Parham, Mary Gomez. 1984. "Intellectual Influences on the Works of Rosario Castellanos." *Foro Literario* 7(12): 34–40.

Pratt, Mary Louise. 1977. *Toward a Speech Act Theory of Literary Discourse*. Bloomington: Indiana UP.

Schor, Naomi. 1980. "For a Restricted Thematics: Writing, Speech, and Difference in *Madame Bovary*." In *The Future of Difference*, ed. Hester Eisenstein and Alice Jardine, 167–92. Boston: G. K. Hall.

Showalter, Elaine, ed. 1985. *The New Feminist Criticism: Essays on Women, Literature, and Theory*. New York: Pantheon.

Skirius, John. 1981. *El ensayo hispanoamericano del siglo XX*. Mexico: Fondo de Cultura Economica.

Stabb, Martin S. 1984. "Not Text But Texture: Cortázar and the New Essay." *Hispanic Review* 52:19–40.

———. 1987. "The New Essay of Mexico: Text and Context." *Hispania* 70(1): 47–60.

(Stanley), Julia Penelope, and Susan J. Wolfe. 1983. "Consciousness as Style: Style as Aesthetic." In *Language, Gender, and Society*, ed. Barrie Thorne, Cheris Kramarae, and Nancy Henley, 125–39. Rowley: Newbury House.

Tannen, Deborah. 1990. *You Just Don't Understand: Women and Men in Conversation*. New York: William Morrow.

Ugalde, Sharon Keefe. 1986. "El discurso femenino en *Misiá Señora*: ¿un lenguaje nuevo o acceso al lenguaje?" *Discurso Literario* 4(1): 117–26.

Woolf, Virginia. 1972. *A Room of One's Own. Collected Essays*, vol. 2. Ed. Leonard Woolf. London: Chatto and Windus.

Zum Felde, Alberto. 1954. *Indice crítico de la literatura hispanoamericana: Los ensayistas*. Mexico: Editorial Guaranía.

JUNE M. FRAZER
AND TIMOTHY C. FRAZER

"Policewoman," Male Dominance, and the Cooperative Principle

As scholars have worked to bring the findings of pragmatics more and more to bear on the study of texts and gender, Pamela Fishman's study of cross-sex conversation (Fishman 1978) has become something of a classic. Fishman's work, and other studies by feminist linguists, show that discourse is controlled by men. Men interrupt more (Zimmerman and West 1982), hold the floor, assert themselves in statement, and control topics. Women, Fishman found in a study of three married couples, ask more questions (two and a half times as many as the men), employ twice as many attention beginnings, use "you know" five times more than men (like "d'ya know" when a hearer's interest is in question), and more frequently use supportive responses. Conversation maintenance is the work women do, what Fishman elsewhere calls "interactional shitwork." Men use fewer supportive responses and make more statements, over twice as many as women.

Fishman's work became an important model in our ongoing study of television discourse. We were interested in finding out the ways in which television discourse was like "real" discourse and whether the conversation interaction we watched on the small screen could tell us anything about interaction in real life. In this paper, we shall examine some problems that arise when we try to apply some assumptions about discourse and interaction to specific cases and at the same time shall show how our interactional analysis reveals the gap between progressive ideologies and audience expectations that bedevil the writers and producers who work in television.

In selecting a text for analysis, we sought an established genre that presented men and women as equals, as were the subjects of Fishman's study. The police procedural we selected was a genre dating from the earliest days of television ("Dragnet") that had evolved during the rise of feminism from a male-dominated drama to one sometimes featuring female detectives, notably "Cagney and Lacey." Nevertheless, among dozens of police procedural dramas that have come and gone on television over the years, only a few have attempted to depict men and women working as partners and equals: "Hunter," "Hill Street Blues," "Magruder and Loud," and "Policewoman." We shall confine this chapter to a discussion of "Policewoman" since it was the first such effort and since it presents a number of interesting analytical problems.

"Policewoman" aired on NBC from 1974 to 1978, starring Angie Dickinson as Sgt. Pepper Anderson and Earl Holliman as Sgt. Bill Crowley. Both the title and the program's logo — a still featuring Dickinson firing a large, obviously phallic revolver in the familiar two-handed, stiff-armed grip — suggest that Dickinson will emerge as the central, proactive character in the series. We conducted our analysis in hopes of discovering whether her apparent empowerment extended to discourse as well.

We assumed that several of Fishman's variables would appear in scripted television discourse as well as in natural conversation, even though those examined in other gender studies might not. We did not, for example, expect to find any overlaps or interruptions like those measured by Zimmerman and West. However, we discovered that an apparent weakness of Fishman's categories lies in the fact that function, or illocutionary force as speech-act theorists would have it, is not considered.

A section of dialogue from the episode we examined, "Father to the Child," illustrates the problem. A twelve-year-old girl, witness to a murder, has been hospitalized, and Sgt. Bill Crowley wants to interrogate her. He invokes the help of policewoman Sgt. Pepper Anderson because, as he has told her earlier, "little girls seem to open up a lot easier to women than they do to men." In the hospital interview with the child, Kerry, Pepper, forced into a traditional caregiver role, initiates and seems to control the interview. However, after the interview concludes, Pepper and Bill discuss it:

> BILL: I'll say this, she's got a mouth on her.
> PEPPER: Well, she probably picked it up in school. What do you think?
> BILL: I think she's scared.
> PEPPER: So do I.

We should note that, despite the superior authority and expertise ceded to Pepper in this situation, Bill is the first to speak in the analysis of it; Pepper's first statement concedes his opinion and is shaped accordingly, beginning with a diffident "well." Pepper does not express an opinion about what they have learned, but rather asks Bill what he thinks, opening the way for him to make a definitive interpretation of the scene, an interpretation to which Pepper simply assents. This is a remarkable example of female/powerless language with a male/empowered figure, even in a scene in which she had apparently been ceded authority of knowledge and interpretation.

Yet if we follow Fishman's model by counting statements in this scene, defining as "statement" any locution not an imperative that we would transcribe as an ending with a period, we would accord Pepper and Bill two statements each, appearing, according to Fishman's categories, to make the exchange seem very democratic and equal. Trying to account for what is happening in this scene tells us, therefore, that in terms of analyzing empowered and powerless language, we need more finely tuned criteria for what counts as a statement.

In the hospital-room interview with Kerry, we find that Kerry's obnoxious behavior (which provoked Bill's observation that "she's got a mouth on her") led to Bill's terminating the interview by saying in disgust to Pepper, "You wanna get me out of here?" The question itself and the consequent action in which they do leave the room suggest that the question was really an imperative, in illocutionary force, and was taken by Pepper as such. On the other hand, Pepper's "what do you think?" locution, although grammatically ordered as a question, actually served, as we have seen, to cede authority to Bill by inviting his opinion, even though the situation was one in which Pepper's expertise should have made her the pronouncing maker of statements. These two examples show us that in the study of empowered and powerless language, we need to do more than simply classify locutions by grammatical form.

These problems lead us into the terrain of the indirect speech act. Fishman's grammatical categories create problems in this analysis because they assume Grice's Cooperative Principle.

One of Grice's maxims is that of Quantity, which includes, as its second maxim, "do not say more than is necessary." When Grice explores the dangers of saying more than is necessary, he expresses three concerns: that this may be a waste of time, that the speaker may be damaged more than the listener, or that misleading perceptions may be generated by the excess of information. None of these concerns addresses the possibility that an empowered speaker may speak at unnecessary length as a means of domination, while an unempowered speaker may listen patiently to unnecessary prolixity because she knows it is her expected role to do so.

Searle's ground-breaking rules for illocution similarly apply inadequately to cross-sex conversation because illocutionary successes and failures, as they relate to power, are fundamentally different than the kinds of power and authority relationships that Searle builds into his rules. Searle, for example, can explain how warning is successfully executed by building into the rules the necessary authority relationship that allows it to be executed, for example, teacher/student, manager/employee, policeman/citizen. These relations can be easily discussed because they function in society not only on the level of actuality, but also on the level of rightful authority that is culturally acceptable to the state. The dominant role of the man over the woman in cross-sex conversations, however, exists in reality but cannot be talked about in speech-act rules because it is no longer acceptable in educated circles to speak of man's rightful authority over woman.

Accordingly, the linguistic situations that still characterize conversation between the empowered and the powerless, as with the empowered/powerless, exist outside the domain of authority relationships that can be acceptably talked about in speech-act rules. When Searle refines his position to address the problem of indirect speech acts, he continues to invoke the Cooperative Principle: "The apparatus necessary to explain the indirect speech act includes a theory of speech acts, certain principles of cooperative conversation and mutually shared factual background information of the speaker and the hearer, together with an ability on the part of the hearer to make inferences" (1975).

We see this problem again in grammatical explanations of conversational constraints such as rules for question and answer pairs. J. L. Morgan, among others, sets up pairs of acceptably grammatical responses to certain grammatically worded questions: that is, for example, certain questions are so worded that only a yes-no answer will be grammatically well formed. Consider, however, what happens in this scene, which takes place in the police station immediately after the murder has been discovered:

> PEPPER: Couldn't I at least have finished my sandwich?
> BILL: No, I need your help.

Pepper's question is grammatically capable of a well-formed answer, and Bill's response is grammatically well formed. Implied in Pepper's question, however, is another: "Is timing so urgent that it can't wait until I have had something to eat?" Bill's response is thus in another sense ill formed, since neither here nor subsequently is any time urgency explained. Hence, though Bill's reply is in a limited sense grammatically satisfactory, the nature of the cross-sex power situation has not been approached by the constraints on question-and-answer pairing.

Here as elsewhere, we have found that most of the discourse or speech act models, rules and maxims do not apply to what is actually happening in cross-sex conversation. Caught in this dilemma between the need to refine Fishman's categories and the inadequacy of existing rules and models that follow the Cooperative Principle, we have fashioned our own categories. These still rely on the principle of illocutionary analysis but adapt it as well to the very different sort of politeness that occurs in cross-sex conversation.

Statements: As a way to count statements, we have established two categories: statements that are really assertions and statements that are supportive conversational maintenance, which really belong with locutions such as "uh-huh," "yes," "I agree," and others. Pepper's agreeable "So do I," will thus count not as a statement but as a supportive conversation maintainer. To count as a statement, a locution will have to assert propositional content that contradicts, adds to, or otherwise varies from the propositional content of the statement to which it is a response.

Questions: We have designated five different kinds of questions, in terms of whether they maintain or control conversation and are hence likely to characterize the language of the empowered or the unempowered. Two kinds of questions we have included in other categories. The first of these is the maintenance question, for example, "Do you *really* think so?" which points toward and encourages a further utterance of the other speaker. We think it is appropriate to classify this type of question with other kinds of maintenance utterances, like "uh-huh." A second type of question we have classified into a larger group of utterances is the question that disguises an imperative, sometimes called a "whimperative." Searle and others have pointed out that the question form for an imperative is a function of politeness, for example, "Pass the salt" versus "Can you pass the salt?" The last would of course make the question-type imperative a characteristic of a powerless speaker. If, however, the powerless speaker is less inclined than the empowered speaker to give commands in any form, direct or indirect, the whimperative may actually be more characteristic of the speech of the empowered. In the hospital scene discussed earlier, for example, Bill decides it is time to terminate the interview with Kerry and ends the scene by saying to Pepper "You wanna get me out of here?" This is more polite than his termination of a scene shortly later, where Bill simply takes Pepper's hand and yanks her out of the frame, but it is an imperative nevertheless, and we have classed this question with other imperatives.

The other three types of questions we have classified separately. The first of these is the question that either makes sure the channel is clear, as in "Are you listening?" or functions as a setup for initiating a topic. We would expect both of these types, like Fishman's "d'ya know?" to be characteristic of powerless language, since they suggest the speaker's uncertainty about whether the hearer is listening. Lakoff, similarly, remarks on the tendency of children to set up conversations with adults with "You know what?" in order to secure their attention.

The final two types are two versions of the question that requests information, differing according to whether or not the speaker assumes that the hearer wishes to give the information or whether or not the speaker cares whether the hearer wishes to give it. We would expect the powerless speaker to preface such questions either with diffidence markers or with explanations, the empowered speaker to be more likely to dispense with explanations and ask questions directly. Again, in the hospital scene we find that even though Pepper has been the one designated to ask the questions and is dealing with a child, she does a great deal of explaining while Bill asks most of the direct questions. We reflect here Esther Goody's thesis, in *Questions and Politeness*, that "social status — in the sense of both hierarchy and position in a role system — [has an effect] on the meaning assigned to the act of asking a question" (5).

Modification of Fishman's variables are shown in Table 1. Our five categories include utterances and diffidence markers, statements, maintenance utterances, imperatives, and questions of three types. We show counts for utterance types for each of eleven segments, with totals at the bottom of each column. M indicates Bill's utterances and F Pepper's; the counts include only those scenes in which primary interaction occurs between Bill and Pepper. (Copyright restrictions prohibit reproducing the scenes here.)

Table 1. Counts of Utterance Types

Segment	Utterances with diffidence markers		Statements		Maintenance utterances		Imperatives direct or indirect		A*		Questions B**		C***	
	M	F	M	F	M	F	M	F	M	F	M	F	M	F
1	1	0	7	1	0	2	0	0	1	0	0	0	0	0
2	0	3	5	0	0	1	1	0	0	0	1	0	2	0
3	1	2	4	3	0	0	1	0	0	0	0	1	3	1
4	0	1	2	1	0	2	0	0	0	0	0	0	0	0
5	2	0	1	5	0	0	1	0	0	0	1	0	2	2
6	1	1	4	2	0	0	1	0	0	0	0	0	2	1
7	1	0	3	4	0	0	0	2	0	1	0	1	3	1
8	0	0	3	2	0	0	2	0	0	0	0	0	0	1
9	1	0	1	2	1	0	0	0	0	0	0	0	0	0
10	0	2	0	3	0	0	0	0	0	0	0	0	2	0
11	0	1	2	1	0	0	2	0	0	0	0	0	0	1
Total	7	10	32	24	1	5	8	2	1	1	2	2	14	7

*Channel/Set-up-topic questions
**Questions seeking information — with explanation
***Questions seeking information — without explanation

We can see from Table 1 that, although "Policewoman" was clearly intended to appeal to a feminist audience, the discourse world dramatized therein has much in common with the traditional and asymmetrical "real" world, where men dominate and women do the work of conversation maintenance. Here we find an interactional disparity not identical to but reminiscent of the disparity found in Fishman's work. In the first column, we see that Pepper uses more diffidence markers than does Bill, though the difference — seven as opposed to ten — is not as great as might be expected from Fishman's work. The second column shows that Bill makes 33 percent more statements than does Pepper, although the difference might not be so clear if we had not revised Fishman's "statement" category to exclude utterances like "I think so too." The third column counts maintenance utterances and shows Pepper making five times as many as Bill. Again, it is Pepper who does what Fishman calls the women's work of interaction. In the fourth column, Bill's domination of discourse is clear; he utters four times as many imperatives. The first two question columns tell us little, perhaps because there were so few occurrences in our data base. But in the category of questions without explanation, we see that once again the male partner is dominant, with twice the frequency as the female.

The application of natural discourse analysis techniques to interaction as dramatized on television can produce interesting results. Certainly as far as "Policewoman" is concerned, male dominance of discourse in this example of "feminist" programming is as great as in real life. But we hope we have also suggested that when men and women talk to each other, it is not just the Cooperative Principle that underlies whatever structure we might find.

References

Cole, Peter, and J. L. Morgan, eds. 1975. *Syntax and Semantics III: Speech Acts.* New York: Academic P.

Fishman, Pamela. 1978. "What Do Couples Talk About When They're Alone?" In *Women's Language and Style,* ed. Douglas Butturff and Edward L. Epstein, 11–22. Akron, Ohio: Studies in Contemporary Language, vol. 1, Dept. of English, U of Akron.

Goody, Esther N. 1978. *Questions and Politeness.* New York: Cambridge UP.

Grice, H. Paul. 1975. "Logic and Conversation." In Cole and Morgan, eds.

Lakoff, Robin. 1975. *Language and Woman's Place.* New York: Harper.

Morgan, J. L. 1975. "Some Interactions of Syntax and Pragmatics." In Cole and Morgan, eds.

Searle, John R. 1975. "Indirect Speech Acts." In Cole and Morgan, eds.

Zimmerman, Don H., and Candace West. 1982. "Sex Roles, Interruptions, and Silences in Conversation." In *Language, Gender, and Society,* ed. Barrie Thorne, Cheris Kramarae, and Nancy Henley. Rowley, Mass.: Newbury House.

PART 6

Language and Power

Gender is one determinant of discourse style, but it is not the only one. The way language is used is influenced by the social positions of those engaged in conversation; further, language can be manipulated so as to alter social positioning toward solidarity, submissiveness, or dominance. The chapters in this section examine how power affects language use. For an overview of the topic, the reader might want to look at Robin Lakoff's *Talking Power: The Politics of Language in Our Lives* (New York: Basic Books, 1990) or Norman Fairclough's *Language and Power* (New York: Longman, 1989). The chapters that follow are concerned with the representation of power relations in dramatic and narrative texts.

Nancy O. Wilhelmi examines the language of the powerful and the powerless in Tennessee Williams's plays, in which characters frequently engage in wars of words. Women who are subservient to men in a physical way can use language to exercise power. Blanche, in *A Streetcar Named Desire*, and Big Mama, in *Cat on a Hot Tin Roof*, control conversational exchanges by making careful linguistic choices. This chapter examines what constitutes the language of the dominant and the submissive, the extent to which sex dictates power roles, and how conscious change from powerless to powerful language can dictate a shift in actual power.

The chapter by Karen A. Hohne relates power to official and

unofficial languages. Expanding on Bakhtin's categories of literary and extraliterary languages, Hohne points out that official language adheres to the grammar of those who serve the entrenched power, whereas unofficial language violates that grammar. Unofficial language borrows from "unofficial culture — slang, obscenities, advertising, popular music, yellow journalism, the speech of children, peasants, workers, the illiterate." Hohne shows that in the science fiction stories of Stephen King and in other noncanonical works, unofficial language frequently proves official language inadequate in glossing the (heteroglossic) world. For discussion related to official and unofficial voices, see the chapter by Bernstein and Campbell in part 3 and the chapters that follow in part 7.

The Language of Power and Powerlessness
Verbal Combat in the Plays of Tennessee Williams

Often in the plays of Tennessee Williams, the men and women are at war, and the weapons are words. The battles, fought for power, are between those who are dominant and those who desire increased control. Though men may dominate physically, Williams demonstrates that the language of power is not restricted to men. Frequently, the more aggressive combatant in the war of words is female. Feeling powerless, she struggles for more control within her own life as well as within her relationships. Mostly waged in single combat, her battles are verbal duels of manipulation and control.

Although, in a physical sense, powerlessness is usually associated with women and power with men, powerful language is available to both men and women. Most of those writing about the language of power agree that the determinant need not be sex. Robin Lakoff in *Language and Woman's Place* (1976) discusses the semantics and syntax of feminine speech that, she states, is used not just by women but also by men who are "'uninvolved' or 'out of power'" (14). William M. O'Barr and Bowman Atkins in "'Women's Language' or 'Powerless Language'?" (1980) report that "speakers using a high frequency of powerless features, whether they be male or female, tend to be judged as less convincing, less truthful, less competent, less intelligent, and less trustworthy" (110). Even though linguists agree that powerful language is available to both sexes, they usually refer to the male as the user of dominant language and the female as the user of subservient language. Williams's plays, though, depict women as seizers of powerful language.

When Stella and Stanley confront each other in *A Streetcar Named Desire*, she fights with words whereas he resorts to physical force. One power play emerges during a card game. When Blanche and Stella return to the apartment after midnight, the men are engaged in playing poker. At first, Stanley's language is fairly inoffensive. He asks, "Why don't you women go up and sit with Eunice?" (48). Wanting to continue the all-male game, Stanley suggests "you women" leave but does not order them to go. Though Stanley's wishes are perfectly clear, putting them into the form of a question leaves the addressee a choice. The choice is not a real one, however, and Stanley is expecting no excuses. Powerful male language, according to Key (1975), does not invite explanation: "It is rare that a male will have the patience or desire to listen to explanations from females. Males are the givers of information, not the receivers. The male who uses *explanation* is not really interested in the female's acquiring more knowledge. . . . Rather, he is showing his superiority" (Key, 37). Stella, though, takes advantage of the opening left by the interrogative form of Stanley's request to express her own desires. She responds, "Because it is nearly two-thirty." Then she asks considerately, "Couldn't you call it quits after one more hand?" (48). Again the addressee has a choice. This is not an order or a command; it, too, is a request. Both speakers, up to this point, have maintained polite conversation; neither has given any ground in the verbal combat. Stanley, though, is quick to become frustrated in his failure to exert verbal dominance. Making up in physical actions for his lack of verbal power, *"Stanley gives a loud whack of his hand on her thigh."* It makes Stella angry, "That's not fun, Stanley" (48). Stanley wins by violence what he has failed to gain by language; the poker game continues. Although Stella does not win the linguistic battle, she does demonstrate that powerful language is available to women.

Unsuccessful with requests, Stanley escalates their power struggle. Continuing their conflict, Stanley commands, "You hens cut out the conversation in there!" (50). Not only does Stanley demand that

Blanche and Stella submit to his desires, but also his name-calling changes from "you women" to "hens." It is typical for the dominant speaker to use such put-downs. As Key (1975) asserts, "Labels and descriptors imply unequal status" (129). Stanley's use of them is part of his effort to claim talk as only his prerogative, not the women's. To this command, Stella does not submit verbally: "This is my house and I'll talk as much as I want to" (51). Nevertheless, Stella goes into the bathroom, terminating the conversation and the noise that Stanley had objected to. When Blanche turns on the radio, Stanley yells, "Turn it off!" Not waiting for his words to have their intended effect, he *jumps up and, crossing to the radio, turns it off* (51), physically compelling obedience.

Stanley first issues verbal commands, then resorts to physical force. Stella responds by confronting him verbally. When Stanley tosses the radio out of the window in order to silence it, Stella yells, "*Drunk — drunk — animal thing,* you! . . . All of you — please go home! If any of you have any spark of decency in you — " (57). Still not willing to submit, Stella tries to control the situation. Even when Stanley threatens her, Stella stands up to him: "'You lay your hands on me and I'll —' [*There is the sound of a blow. Stella cries out.*]" (57). Failing to dominate verbally, Stanley once again resorts to violence. Stella is strong in her verbal response to Stanley, but he wins the battle by physical force.

Demonstrating that females can take control of the conversation by their use of powerful language, Blanche assumes dominance in relating to Mitch. Unlike the power play between Stella and Stanley that is overt and often physical, the power struggle between Blanche and Mitch is subtle and verbal:

> MITCH: How old are you?
> BLANCHE: Why do you want to know?
> MITCH: I talked to my mother about you and she said, "How old is Blanche?" And I wasn't able to tell her.
> BLANCHE: You talked to your mother about me?
> MITCH: Yes.
> BLANCHE: Why?

MITCH: I told my mother how nice you were, and I liked
          you.
BLANCHE: Were you sincere about that?
MITCH: You know I was.

(98–99)

Wanting information, Mitch directly asks Blanche her age — a fact
that Blanche wants to hide from him. Asking a question is one way of
dominating a conversation. The questioner manages "the flow and
exchange of messages" (Folger 1980, 203). Blanche refuses to relin-
quish such control to Mitch. Avoiding the question while gaining
subtle control of the conversation, Blanche answers a question with
a question — changing the direction of the exchange. She controls
the dialogue by shifting the topic of conversation (see Eisen 1984,
100). In fact, she maintains this pattern throughout this dialogue —
asking questions, directing the conversation, giving no information. Her strategy of avoiding direct response is one usually
assigned to men (Zimmerman and West 1975, 124). Here, though,
the strategy has allowed Blanche to dominate the conversation. At
the end of this dialogue, Blanche discovers very important information: that Mitch likes her and that he has told his mother that he
likes her. She, in turn, has revealed nothing. Unknowingly, he has
been controlled. What has emerged is a power struggle that,
through her control of language, Blanche has won. Through her
manipulation, she has, at least temporarily, seized the more powerful position in the relationship. In her dialogue, Blanche reflects
conscious language choices — language choices that are available
to female as well as male.

Conversation is typically an interplay between dominant and
subservient speech patterns. Summing up the language choices that
correspond to dominance and subservience, Barbara and Gene
Eakins (1978) indicate how power positions are reinforced by interaction:

Superior	Subordinate
Orders or commands	Complies
Asks or requests	Acquiesces

Interrogates	Replies
Declares	Agrees
Interrupts	Allows interruption; stops talking (24)

Society's expectations and training frequently lead men to follow the conversational pattern of the *superior* and women that of the *subordinate*. Williams's characters, however, violate such stereotypes. In the exchange between Stanley and Stella during the poker scene, both participants attempt to maintain the superior position; the conflict is resolved by Stanley's superior physical force. In the case of Blanche and Mitch, Blanche assumes the superior role and Mitch the subordinate one.

Big Mama and Big Daddy in *Cat on a Hot Tin Roof* illustrate yet another type of challenge to stereotypical patterns of conversation. At the beginning of the play, the dialogue of the two characters illustrates traditional gender-based speech patterns, but by the last act Big Mama acquires the language of the powerful. The early speeches of Big Daddy reflect his masculinity and the superiority that he feels toward Big Mama. Big Mama's speeches mirror the submissive, powerless position that she holds in their relationship. By the end of the play, though, Big Mama shows that those roles can change.

At first, Big Mama is the butt of Big Daddy's jokes and the object of his cruelty: "I put up with a whole lot of crap around here because I thought I was dying. And you thought I was dying and you started taking over, well, you can stop taking over now, Ida, because I'm not . . . dying of cancer which you thought I was dying of. Ain't that so? . . . Your loud voice everywhere, your fat old body butting in here and there!" (57). Big Daddy's language is cruel, his name-calling reminiscent of Stanley's disregard for Stella and Blanche when he calls them "hens."

In an attempt to survive within this relationship, Big Mama fruitlessly tries, if not to be loved, to be accepted as loving: "*And I did, I did so much, I did love you! —* I even loved your hate and your hardness, Big Daddy" (59). Her language, though, makes it even less likely that she will be taken seriously. Intensifiers such as *so* as in "I like him *so* much" (Lakoff 1976, 55) reduce the impact of her message. Big Mama's discourse is stereotypical of the woman's "indirect, repetitious, meandering, unclear, exaggerated" style, as opposed to a man's, which is "clear, direct, precise, and to the point" (Lakoff, 73). Big Mama's style does not even allow her the acceptance she strives to achieve.

Since she is powerless to stop Big Daddy's abuse, she ignores his cruelties or pretends to herself that he does not believe the things he says:

> BIG MAMA: You don't mean that! . . .
> BIG DADDY: You don't know a goddam thing and you never did!
> BIG MAMA: Big Daddy, you don't mean that.
>
> (57)

Within this relationship, Big Mama's language reflects her subordinate position and her dismay at Big Daddy's mistreatment of her.

In spite of her subordinate role, she is still Big Daddy's wife, and this position carries with it prestige as well as responsibilities. Among these responsibilities, as she sees it, is that a certain level of decorum must be maintained. Part of her job is to censor Big Daddy's use of taboo language. (According to Key [1975], "Men's use of taboo expressions among themselves may be restricted in the presence of women and children. In our culture, taboos involve most acutely the matters of sex, body elimination, and body parts" [56].) Big Daddy uses taboo words when he questions Brick as if no one else were present: "Was it jumping or humping that you were doing out there?" (55). Big Mama, acting as self-proclaimed censor, tries to ensure propriety:

> BIG MAMA: Big Daddy, you are off the sick list, now, and I'm not going to excuse you for talkin' so —
> BIG DADDY: Quiet!
> BIG MAMA: — *nasty* in front of Preacher and —
> BIG DADDY: QUIET!
>
> (56)

By being a censor, the female attempts to counterbalance male tyranny. Frequently, as censor, she "will focus on her delicacies and purities and not permit the male to express himself emotionally or with 'rough talk' around her or her children" (Key, 131). This attempt to control those in dominant positions is a ploy of the subservient. Relationships in which power is not equally shared invite manipulative behaviors by the powerless in an attempt to obtain some power.

Big Daddy uses the typical male language, but with unusual cruelty. He commands. Also he interrupts Big Mama's speech, a sign of his disregard for her and for what she is saying (Zimmerman and West, 116). For emphasis, Big Daddy uses curse words, perhaps, as two critics theorize, reflecting the superior position of men that makes them believe they "have a claim on stronger means of expressing feeling" (Eakins and Eakins 1978, 31). Also Big Daddy uses nonstandard English such as, "You was just nothing but *spyin'* an' you *know* it!" (62) and "Naw I ain't" (71). According to Peter Farb (1974): "The reason why men resist adopting the female's more 'refined' speech apparently has to do with a factor that men deny but which shows up in studies. Males in most American and British speech communities unconsciously regard the roughness of working-class speech as displaying desirable masculine attributes" (51). For propriety, Big Mama attempts to control Big Daddy's language while reflecting this same decorum in her own speech.

As representatives of the less powerful position, women are the bastion of politeness and manners. As such, women "are trained to be polite, to be 'nice,' to be tactful. They are trained *not* to be 'vulgar,' *not* to swear or use 'dirty' words, *not* to be confronting" (Hiatt 1977, 107). This training helps them survive in a world in which other people's feelings and comfort take precedence over their own. In social interactions "women are the repositories of tact and know the right things to say to other people" (Lakoff 1976, 55). While this training makes the female thrive in the social situation, it limits her by making it inappropriate for her to express certain feelings. For example, she is not supposed to be angry or display anger. Consequently, the powerful have greater license with language than the powerless.

In their dialogue, Big Mama and Big Daddy at first reflect traditional speech patterns of the American male and female. In the last act, though, Big Mama consciously rejects the powerless female language and adopts the language of the powerful. When the family, primarily Gooper, bickers over the inheritance of Big Daddy, Big Mama establishes her power. Like Big Daddy, she orders, "Now you listen to me, all of you, you listen here!" She tells the family directly what she wants of them: "They's not goin' to be no more catty talk in my house! And Gooper, you put that away before I grab it out of your hand and tear it right up!" (146–47). She, who before had censored the use of curse words, now uses them, "I don't know what the hell's in it." And she tells the family that she is conscious of the language that she is using: "I'm talkin' in Big Daddy's language now, I'm his *wife*, not his *widow*, I'm still his *wife*! And I'm talkin' to you in his language an' — " (147). Gooper interrupts her, not believing that she has really taken on the role of the powerful.

The interruption is one way that the dominant control conversation. Zimmerman and West (1975) argue that men frequently interrupt women in conversations, disruptions that can be "viewed as a violation of a speaker's rights" while "continual or frequent interruptions might be viewed as disregard for the speaker, or for what the speaker has to say" (116). Gooper's interruption of Big Mama compels her to become even more forceful: "I say — what is that Big Daddy always says when he's disgusted? . . . I say CRAP too, like Big Daddy!" (147). Since Gooper and his family have always kowtowed when Big Daddy speaks, she seeks a similar response when she mimics Big Daddy. And she gets it, merely by changing her language.

Woman's language, then, serves only to reinforce her being out of power. She is caught in a double bind:

> Allowing men stronger means of expression than are open to women further reinforces men's position of strength in the real world: for surely we listen with more attention the more strongly and forcefully someone expresses opinions, and a speaker unable — for whatever reason — to be forceful in stating his views is much less likely to be taken seriously. . . .

Further, if someone is allowed to show emotions, and consequently does, others may well be able to view him as a real
individual in his own right, as they could not if he never
showed emotion. Here again, then, the behavior a woman
learns as "correct" prevents her from being taken seriously as an
individual. (Lakoff, 10–11)

Only when Big Mama ignores social expectations of politeness is
she taken seriously.

While Big Daddy is often cruel when using powerful language,
Big Mama uses it lovingly. She is trying to protect Big Daddy's right
to will his estate to the heir he chooses. Actually, by taking a
powerful stance, she is ensuring that Big Daddy will remain in
charge until his death or even after his death: *"Nobody's goin' to do
nothin'! till Big Daddy lets go of it, and maybe just possibly not — not
even then!"* (147). Big Mama proves her devotion by taking on his
power to protect the land he loves.

These examples from Tennessee Williams's plays demonstrate
how language choices mirror power relations between women and
men. The language of the powerful is not reserved for men alone.
Although Stella does not win her linguistic battle with Stanley, she
shows that women have access to powerful language. As this language is available to Stella, so it may be chosen by any person. By
selecting dominant words and phrases, by avoiding florid phrases,
by embracing a fuller range of emotions, people can shift from
powerlessness to power. Exemplifying this shift are both Blanche
and Big Mama, who consciously adopt dominant speech to control
their conversations and the persons in those interactions. In the
battle for dominance, each precisely chooses her ammunition: the
language of the powerful.

References

Eakins, Barbara, and Gene Eakins. 1978. *Sex Differences in Human Communication.* New York: Houghton.

Eisen, Jeffrey, with Pat Farley. 1984. *Powertalk! How to Speak It, Think It, and Use It.* New York: Cornerstone Library.
Farb, Peter. 1974. *Word Play: What Happens When People Talk.* New York: Knopf.
Folger, Joseph. 1980. "The Effects of Vocal Participation and Questioning Behavior on Perceptions of Dominance." *Social Behavior and Personality* 8(2): 203–7.
Hiatt, Mary. 1977. *The Way Women Write.* New York: Teachers College.
Key, Mary Ritchie. 1975. *Male/Female Language.* Metuchen, N.J.: Scarecrow.
Lakoff, Robin. 1976. *Language and Woman's Place.* New York: Octagon.
O'Barr, William M., and Bowman K. Atkins. 1980. "'Women's Language' or 'Powerless Language'?" In *Women and Language in Literature and Society,* ed. Sally McConnell-Ginet, Ruth Borker, and Nelly Furman, 93–110. New York: Praeger.
Williams, Tennessee. 1955. *Cat on a Hot Tin Roof.* New York: Signet.
———. 1947. *A Streetcar Named Desire.* New York: Signet.
Zimmerman, Don H., and Candace West. 1975. "Sex Roles, Interruptions, and Silences in Conversation." In *Language and Sex: Difference and Dominance,* ed. Barrie Thorne and Nancy Henley, 105–29. Rowley, Mass.: Newbury House.

Dialects of Power
The Two-Faced Narrative

Bakhtin is plainly useful in working with the novel, but it is perhaps less well known how productive is his theory when applied to shorter prose works. One of the most helpful concepts he developed in this respect was that of double accentuation, which when expanded and modified becomes quite effective in the analysis of writing other than the novel and which provides particularly efficacious tools to deal with power struggles as they appear in verbal texts.

In order to explicate double-accentuation in a way that will be useful for the present, we begin where Bakhtin begins, with double-voicedness — the Russian dialect story *(skaz)*. He first develops the category of double-voiced discourse, of which the double-accented is a subcategory, to deal with stylization, parody, dialogue, and the Russian dialect story. Double-voiced discourse is torn in two directions at once: toward the object of speech and toward someone else's speech. The dialect story, whose name indicates the language used by the narrator, is based partly on "oral everyday narration," but it is a stylization of that narration (1981, 262). The author of such stories speaks in another person's language, but he does not act simply as a tape recorder (no walking mirror here); the other's speech is refracted through the author. Thus the dialect story contains "two semantic intentions, two voices" in one utterance

(1984, 189). Further, the dialect story recognizes someone else's way of speaking as representing a particular point of view. In fact, according to Bakhtin, when such a narrative mode occurs it is generally "introduced precisely for the sake of *someone else's voice*, a voice socially distinct, carrying with it precisely those points of view and evaluations necessary to the author" (1984, 192).

Double-voiced discourse in the dialect story is then clearly not merely a question of rubbing two languages against each other — after all, parody can do that, and there is nothing truly interactive about parody's two languages, for there the other's speech is simply forced to bear witness against itself.[1] In parody, the point is to devoice others through their own words; it is a battle rigged from the beginning. Bakhtin's definition of parody is almost identical to his consideration that the monologic author uses other languages in order to further his own ideology, so that "[a]ny intensification of others' intonations in a certain discourse or certain sections of the work is only a game, which the author permits so that his own direct or refracted word might ring out all the more energetically" (1984, 203–4).

What is different about the dialect story is that there the other's speech acts on and influences the author's intention, a key concept, since in this relationship of author/other, the author is the one with the power. Therefore, one of the primary differences between language interaction in the dialect story (and, we will see, in other texts that utilize the self/other dichotomy in terms of the languages incorporated) and in parody is that in the former the other's language (which would for instance be the parodied in a parody) does not function as a helpless victim in the struggle between the two languages; indeed, the other's speech, although divested of power in society, in the work is capable of profoundly affecting the language of power, able almost to put it on the run. The other's speech thus has more vitality in the dialect story than in other types of double-directed discourse. The other's speech is in the vernacular and extraliterary, opposed to literary language; when literary and extra-literary languages interact, they are deformed, and it is then that "discourse loses its composure and confidence, becomes agitated, internally undecided and two-faced. Such discourse is not only double-voiced but double-accented; it is difficult to speak it aloud, for loud and living intonation excessively monologizes discourse and cannot do justice to the other person's voice present in it" (1984, 198). It is thus clear that the dialect story, so other directed, has more in common with the dialogic novel than with the monologic poetry to which it is usually connected on account of what is called its language play and the estrangement it generally uses. For Bakhtin, the difference between the dialogic novel and the double-accented dialect story seems to be that the latter is binary (literary/extraliterary) in terms of the languages at work, whereas the dialogic novel involves multiple language sets that apparently do not fall into these neat categories.

These two language sets in the dialect story are usually designated as written (literary) and oral (extraliterary), but in actually working with double-accented texts and developing the concepts associated with double accentuation, I found that these language categories were oriented incorrectly, revolving as they do around either literature or the written word. The real pole around which the two languages turn is power, in relationship to which they fall into the categories of languages of social power and disenfranchisement, or, as I called them, official and unofficial. Looking at the two categories from this slant allowed me to take the concept of double-accentuation out of the *skaz*'s narrow sphere and apply it to, for instance, general works of literature and popular culture, which application greatly enriched and developed the idea.

Official language is not singular in any society; it is a set that includes any language (even nonverbal languages) that attains value in that society based on its association with entrenched power — the language of the State (the political rhetoric of an in-power entity), of legal documents, of "distinguished" journalism, of high literature, or in a society with a high illiteracy rate, the written word. Although there is clearly some sort of hierarchy of language in society, these dialects of power may be nearly interchangeable in a given work, for they all buy into the system of power and thus in the final instance serve the same master; one may watch them scramble over each other's backs in an attempt to be first and best at giving voice to those who rule. It is notable that whatever particular language is most the language of power in any society, its energy is not wasted attacking other official languages; for instance, political rhetoric generally coexists peacefully with various literary languages in these texts. Officiality knows that other official languages all recognize authority, even if that authority is other than itself; should those other official languages attempt to garner for themselves monologic power, officiality understands and can even forgive, since monologism and the urge to it is the only value in its world. In these texts, official languages feel relatively free to cadge expressions from each other but do not demystify each other. Indeed, since there is so little difference between them in essence, they would then be in effect demystifying themselves, an impossible situation for ideologies that consider monologic power the only kind worth having. Official languages rarely dip into the murky waters of unofficiality to snatch a word or two. A word torn free of its language/world context must experience a change in meaning, but what is more, since unofficial language is always aimed against monologism, monologic forces cannot co-opt its expressions without disarming them, without replacing their meanings entirely, in other words, without obliterating their worlds.

Official language usually embodies its adherence to the ruling forces by its adherence to the rules for language set up by that power; it is grammatically correct according to the grammars penned by those who (consciously or not) serve entrenched power. In contrast, unofficial language as a category is composed of languages that are not valued (or, further, underground or illegal languages) in a particular society and that usually are furthermore rule-breaking in their form as well as their spirit, being ungrammatical, slangful, bastardized, and generally nonlinear. In the case of the dialect story, unofficiality may appear as the speech of peasants or uneducated urban workers; in other works, it may be the speech of children, criminals, and similarly marginalized people.

Whatever the instantial language, it is clear that what is official and unofficial depends on the society and is subject to historical change. At the same time, the power/not-power dichotomy that gives rise to these two language sets may not exist in all societies; thus this essential organizing force is not ahistorical. However, wherever there is official language, there must be unofficial language. We may refer to Bakhtin — monologism is never complete, for even in silence is response.

In the world, officiality either completely erases otherness or attempts to render it voiceless by reporting its speech incorrectly (lying, with which officiality is preoccupied). It smears unofficiality by attributing to it its own crimes and killing off, either literally or figuratively, its speakers. In texts, official ideology does not simply ignore the other (figuratively killing the other by making the other absent) but aggressively seeks others out, weighs their loyalty, and grants its benediction or places them under its interdict. The greatest sin against officiality is unofficiality (the greatest offense to power is powerlessness). It is not so much an act that offends, but existence itself, although one may say that officiality views existence as action. Any manifestation of unofficiality is a crime against nature — in other words, against officiality's scheme of things — and thus is considered (even if not intended as such) a blow directed against its rule. In texts (and, unfortunately, even in life), unofficial others are first deprived of their own voices as officiality reads their lines for them. Unofficiality in a masquerade version may be made to stream from others' mouths in a sort of divine manifestation as they are forced to accuse and condemn themselves of the great crime of unofficiality. Finally, they may be executed.

Just as it is often necessary to learn the language of a country in order to get along in it, one may find oneself taking on official language as one's own, in a text or otherwise. Officiality's most damaging effect on those who try to learn it as a second language is the loathing and fear towards the unofficial other it produces, be that other another person or within the speaker's own psyche. Within the individual, officiality's general attitude towards the unofficial other in the world is reproduced in miniature. The war between official and unofficial raging in society is duplicated within the individual in some of these texts.

Unofficial ideology, on the other hand, is distinguished not merely by its vocabulary but by how it behaves. It constantly tries to enter into dialogue and is apparently incapable of exiling others to absence or stripping them of their rightful voices.[2] It embraces otherness, with which it must sense the kinship of all outcasts and disenfranchised. It is eclectic, borrowing from various aspects of unofficial culture — slang, obscenities, advertising, popular music, yellow journalism, the speech of children, peasants, workers, the illiterate, etc. When the mongrel of unofficiality meets prim officiality in the contest of literature, the general result is that unofficial language/ideology sticks out its tongue and reveals official language/ideology as a lie. Yet as aggressive as unofficiality is in its demystification of officiality, it does not usually attempt to gain the position of power, to officialize itself by obliterating officiality and clambering onto the vacated throne. It seeks only to unseat, not to be coronated.

The kind of narrative that showcases double-accentuation takes monologism as its topic, revealing its negative effects. But these texts are no one-sided depictions of the horrors of some version of fascism, real as those horrors are. They speak not only monologism's deadly effects, but its slithery attractions. They duplicate the only two categories that monologism allows — self/good/true and other/bad/lie — but turn them on their heads. And if official language is usually the language of the author/reader, then taking monologism as a subject means monologism not just out there somewhere in the world, but in the internal world; in other words, writing (and reading, if one reads dialogically) this kind of text means attempting to demystify not only the world but the self.

I have observed double-accentuation in the short fiction of writers as diverse as Isaak Babel, H. P. Lovecraft, Raymond Chandler, and Stephen King. All have a relationship with the canon that is at least troubled. Babel flickers in and out of the world of officiality; during his lifetime, he was considered literature and thus official by most but was more or less erased from Soviet literature for a good twenty years after his execution. He is still not a dependable soldier in canon's ranks; even in the West he has never enjoyed the popularity he deserves — not monologic enough, perhaps, especially in his relationship to the Soviet State. Lovecraft has endured (totally unmerited) criticism for years, even from his fans, and although he has occasionally been taught in universities, one may rest assured that it was always off in the suburbs of a science fiction (SF) course. Raymond Chandler as a popular and therefore devalued author has fairly recently undergone a rehabilitation as the most literary and thus worthwhile of the hard-boiled detective writers. He is discovered to have been speaking official language all along, if in guttural accents, and is permitted in the hallowed halls as long as he behaves. But Stephen King has not even attained the status of Lovecraft, who at least can be passed off as Golden Age SF; although scholars of popular culture have begun to turn their attention to King, he is completely unofficial, with no place in the canon. It is plain that double-accentuation can occur in High Literature and popular lit, in Russian and English, in the twenties, thirties, seventies, and eighties, but I wonder if when it does occur it has a tendency to keep the author's works out of the canon. I would enjoy hearing from other scholars who may find examples for or against this. Because he is probably more familiar to more readers than any of the other authors, I will use Stephen King as my exemplar.

Since King's rough-cut narrators generally employ no literary language at all (although there are frequent exceptions), it might seem impossible to find officiality in his writings, but we will see that he has a great deal at his command, and when that loses its impact, he invents his own. He draws attention to language and acts as a mediator, providing a network for various languages to interact (reinventing the heteroglossic world and thus affirming that heteroglossia). King's narrators' speech is highly oral (sentences strung together with "and" or phrases repeated in the redundant stutter of conversation, for instance) and is full of highly unofficial slang, obscenities, and even snips of unofficial culture — bits of rock songs, advertising jingles, and set phrases born on TV. But it would be wrong to believe that this narrative is purely unofficial, lacking any elevated (and thus official) language; it is instead first of all an off-center version of slang, an interpretation that refracts it through a literary lens: "The bulbs couldn't banish the twelve-year darkness; it could only push it back a little and cast a sickly yellow glow over the whole mess" (*Night Shift*, 39). Here, the literary and almost biblical "banish the darkness" is proven inadequate by the conversational "a little" and "the whole mess." This passage is a good example of how in King (and others) official and unofficial languages rub shoulders and in the process may shatter into fragments smaller than a sentence.

In our society, the nonwritten has never had the power of the written word; it is highly unofficial. But in these writings it seems as if unofficial language becomes contaminated with officiality because it is elevated to the position normally occupied by literary language — it is indeed difficult to speak it aloud without excessively monologizing. Oral speech begins to need demystifying, and this comes in the intrusion of thoughts. These generally utilize typeface to signify and often lack punctuation. It is on the plane of external versus internal dialogue or narration versus the narrator's "authorial" comment that some of the greatest tension between official and unofficial is created. Rather than seconding or ratifying speech, thought may contradict speech and thus take on the role of the unofficial, revealing the narrator's speech as inadequate to the situation:

> 'As I said, there was a slight problem . . .
> *Yes. Horror, lunacy, and death. How's that for a slight problems, kids?*
> (*Skeleton Crew*, 242)

Here the narrator's blandly official "slight problem" (almost military in its flare for understatement/lying) is undercut by his own internal other rejoining with the slangy "kids." An even more powerful example is supplied by "The Mist," where the internal unofficial other speaks more like itself — not linearly, not in sentences, but in fragments, in whispers:

> [Mrs. Carmody was] [n]othing but an old woman with a few stuffed animals in the back room and a reputation for
> (*that witch . . . that cunt*)
> folk medicine.   (*Skeleton Crew*, 141)

For a somewhat more subtle usage, where one insists on one's own internal, unofficial word over the official word imposed from without, there is the story of a boy who finds a tiger in

> The bathroom
> (*!basement!*)   (*Skeleton Crew*, 156)

Of course, the internal, unofficial other who insists on "basement" is proven correct — there really IS a tiger in the boy's room.[3]

These examples illustrate more or less unofficial speech (that is, oral speech occurring either in dialogue, as it does here, or elsewhere as the narrator's voice) becoming official when used constantly for literary purposes such as narration. To deflate this now-tainted orality, then, requires another type of "spoken" speech — thought — so that thought is to spoken as spoken is to written. It is as if King cannot get enough of unofficiality and must increase it exponentially.

In King, not only the unofficial language is used for the sake of incorporating someone else's voice; officiality serves the same purpose. It gets the treatment usually reserved in our culture for the unofficial: it is depicted as monstrous, literally or figuratively. In the story of the tiger in the boy's room, official language is used by the authority figure (the teacher) to humiliate one who by virtue of being a child is powerless and who speaks an unofficial language. She demonstrates the violence of which officiality is capable when in front of the entire class she remarks to the boy, "Very well, Charles. You may go to the bathroom and urinate. Is that what you need to do? Urinate?" (*Skeleton Crew*, 156). Later on, the boys use among themselves the unofficial word, "piss," with, of course, no embarrassment.

Official language is also the peddler of dangerously false knowledge that pretends, as usual, to know everything. A version of official language I have elsewhere called Scientific because of its use of science-peculiar buzz-words and syntax occurs in King and normally has lethal consequences, but official language is not limited to this. Religious language proves to be a particularly virulent strain of officiality. It powers "Children of the Corn," where the children adept at religio-speak sacrifice passers-by and their own to a murderous god.

These official languages may easily coexist in the same text. They are well combined in "The Mist," where science, our present religious authority, overwhelms and destroys the world, and old-time religion kills off those who remain. The deadly Mrs. Carmody, who demands human sacrifice to appease the angry gods of scientific blunder, does it in a Revelations version of monologism:

> " — *expiation! It's expiation we want to think about now! We have been scourged with whips and scorpions! We have been punished for delving into secrets forbidden by God of old! We have seen the lips of the earth open! We have seen the obscenities of nightmare! The rock will not hide them, the dead tree gives no shelter! And how will it end? What will stop it?*"
> "*Expiation!*" shouted good old Myron LaFleur.
> (*Skeleton Crew*, 141)

Science and religion, which we would normally see as completely opposed, are revealed as quite similar in terms of their relationship to otherness: if it is not-I, kill it.

In King unofficiality takes over the narrative, dominating the narrator's language and manifesting itself in his truth-telling thought, but unofficiality here is never as impenetrable as it can be elsewhere (for an example in another horror/SF writer, see H. P. Lovecraft's rendering of alien speech as a stream of consonants or the illiterate peasant Russian of Isaak Babel's cossacks). There are no languages so other as to refuse to yield to our understanding, and King's characters are almost never of the "forbidden" sort that populate the worlds of other writers using this method — a college-educated Jew pretending to be an illiterate cossack, a homosexual avenging his lover's murder, and bad women galore. It seems to me that King does not use these social transgressors because his narrators' speech is already much more *in* unofficiality than most others'; popular culture is celebrated and accepted as a vital aspect of the narrative of our lives. It is unlikely that an untranslatable unofficiality could exist in a world so unofficial, but what is more, King's readers *live* in this particular unofficiality, which cannot be said of the other writers' works. I believe this accounts for a great deal of King's popularity; he is the native son who speaks the speech never before spoken so proudly or so out loud.

In short fiction (and in general in cultural products) that has an ear for heteroglossia, ideologies in power (official) and those which are disenfranchised (unofficial) interact as particular languages (usually levels within one language, but interactions between two languages such as Russian and French are also possible). The struggle between the two sets of languages bursts apart the narrative of officiality, overtaking the characters' or even the narrator's speech. In this way, the situation of lived reality, which in fact so deviates from its official version, is told or described. The overthrow of a dominant, prestigious language by a subordinate, devalued language is presented in order to demonstrate official ideology's actual inability to gloss the universe, despite its claims to the contrary.

Unofficiality is characterized by its constant attempts to engage in dialogism, to interact, and is generally associated with real knowledge — the truth of the story itself, of narrativity, while official language means bafflement (false knowledge), an inability to listen that results in the inability to create a story that makes sense of the situation. A language combining these two, as does the narrative language of King and other writers, foregrounds the very interaction that occurs in our daily lives but is somehow never given voice.

Notes

1. Notice that Bakhtin does not consider in parody, for instance, that the parodied need not necessarily be unofficial, need not occupy a lesser position in society in terms of power, although that might tend to be the case (think how often in our society, for instance, "black speech" or "women's logic" has been parodied). Yet even in the case of parody, where monologism has a far more important role to play than in the dialect story, it can be said that the speech of the other acts upon the speech of the self, since the self is deliberately responding to it.

2. It is not clear whether this situation exists simply because unofficiality has no power to commit monologism or whether it is inherently antimonologic. It would seem to depend on the particular language involved and its position relative to power, but it is important that most unofficial languages bask in heteroglossia, while official languages attempt to hold themselves aloof from the mongrelized world. There do seem to be times when unofficial languages practice monologism, but there are those who would argue that this tendency is simply a result of the ideology's pollution by official language.

3. I suspect that contemporary horror literature's specific social task is to validate unofficiality. Older horror literature simply pointed out that there existed entities and lives beyond the pale of the official (vampires, for example) but allowed officiality the last word (a stake through the heart). Contemporary horror does not let officiality off so easily; in fact, frequently that officiality is proved to lack any way of dealing with unofficiality (the accouterments of the Church do not work against vampires), and, more recently, that unofficiality is desirable (vampires are sexy and have a lot of fun living forever).

References

Bakhtin, M. M. 1981. *The Dialogic Imagination: Four Essays.* Ed. Michael Holquist. Trans. Caryl Emerson and Michael Holquist. Austin: U of Texas P.

———. 1984. *Problems of Dostoevsky's Poetics.* Ed. and trans. Caryl Emerson. Minneapolis: U of Minnesota P.

King, Stephen. 1978. *Night Shift.* New York: NAL.

———. 1986. *Skeleton Crew.* New York: NAL.

PART 7

Language and Culture

A literary work can be neither produced nor received apart from the cultural contexts of authors and readers. That statement is not as controversial today as it would have been a decade ago. Although some literary theorists might still see linguists as privileging the text to the exclusion of context, the trend in literary linguists has been to see a work of literature as no more isolated than any other form of communication from the circumstances that surround its production and reception. Linguists, who at one time were reluctant to accept literary studies into their domain, have begun to see the relevance of imaginative texts to the broader picture of language use. The essays in this chapter consider, among other things, how the language of the text encodes national, regional, social, and ethnic identity. They illustrate that the literary text is a legitimate source of linguistic data and, at the same time, that adequate linguistic analysis of literature does, indeed, go beyond the text.

In her chapter on German Immigrant Worker literature, B. A. Fennell demonstrates the interdependence of literary and linguistic studies. She explains how psycholinguistics and sociolinguistics can inform the reading of *Gastarbeiterliteratur:* she detects sequences of language acquisition in its poetry and expressions of power and solidarity relations in its prose. At the same time, she argues persuasively that "literature is linguistic data" and explores the contribution of *Gastarbeiterliteratur* to linguistic research, particularly to pidgin and creole theory.

Mashey Bernstein explores the role of language in the cultural self-definition of Anglo-Irish writers. Through language, people express their hopes, idiosyncrasies, and identities. Mueller (1973) sees language as a "repository of cultural tradition"; "What, then," asks Bernstein, "of the Irish who were forced to use a language whose 'culture' of religious persecution and 'tradition' of imperialism and political domination were anathema to them?" In their resistance to the "cultural tradition" of the British, Irish writers rebelled against the language, "desecrating" that which, as artists, they wished to "sanctify." Overall, they show a consistency of abandonment and freedom that marks their use of English as "defiantly heretical." Like Rosario Castellanos (see Parham's essay in this volume), Irish writers employ humor as a weapon in ideological warfare.

In the final chapter of this volume, Barbara Johnstone examines regional and social linguistic features within a literary text. Going beyond the usual topics of phonology, vocabulary, and syntax, her study of Harry Crews's novel *Body* emphasizes discourse features. She illustrates the effectiveness of the novel in representing the speech of lower-class Southerners through the terms of address they use and their strategies for hedging (indirect conditionals and evidential predicates). This chapter calls attention to a need to broaden the study of literary dialect to include discourse features.

Literary Data and Linguistic Analysis
The Example of Modern German
Immigrant Worker Literature

Elsewhere (Fennell 1988) I have talked about the "how" of linguistic analysis of literature. In this chapter I should also like to address the "why," since in my teaching and research I sense an immediate need for an explicit statement of why a linguist should care about litera- ture and why a literary analyst needs to know about linguistic theory and method. Since theoretical discussion benefits greatly from illustration with concrete examples, I will concentrate on an analysis of German Immigrant Worker literature. This body of literature has language and voice as two of its central themes and thus is the perfect vehicle to demonstrate the reciprocal enrichment of literature and linguistic analysis. By linguistic analysis, I do not mean simply the consideration of surface linguistic phenomena such as word order or morphological form, although these are clearly basic to a good linguistic analysis. Nor do I mean linguistic stylistics alone. Rather, I mean a broad-based knowledge of general linguistics and its applications, in particular socio- and psycho- linguistics. Under psycholinguistics I include knowledge of lan- guage acquisition and its universal characteristics. Sociolinguistics encompasses for me such topics as the ethnography of speaking and code-switching and discourse analysis, activities that have a very strong anthropological basis. As we shall see with the analysis of Immigrant Worker literature below, awareness of the larger linguistic context can significantly enhance our reading of a text (or genre), by giving us insight into the role that the language itself plays for an author. Language choice can express power and solidarity relations among the protagonists in a text and thus reflect the author's interpretation of the social situation. It can also reflect ethnic identification, feelings of power(lessness), and isolation and disenfranchisement. Since Immigrant Worker German is believed by many (including many of the immigrant workers themselves) to be substandard, arbitrary, and provisional or fleeting, its use can effect all of these qualities in a text or character. In short, since language choice is such an intensely personal matter, awareness of the larger linguistic issues provides the reader or interpreter with another tool for analyzing the many voices of the author.

We shall also see in this paper, however, that consideration of literary text can have a significant impact on our interpretation of the larger linguistic issues themselves. Tannen (1989) demonstrates that awareness of literary devices and conventions such as imagery and repetition has led her to conclude that everyday nonliterary conversation makes heavy use of the same strategies in order to promote involvement. This is a good example of how linguistic knowledge is enriched by the linguist's involvement in literary research. In this paper we shall see that consideration of Immigrant Worker literature has significance for pidgin and creole linguistic theory (cf. Fennell 1989) as well as for consideration of linguistic awareness and linguistic attitudes.

A major point I would like to emphasize is that literature is linguistic data. An individual work can provide us with a discrete microcosmic representation of a society, and insofar as authors generally manipulate linguistic structures without conscious knowledge of what they are doing, the literary analysis can extrapolate linguistic conventions from the data in the text.

German Immigrant Worker literature, or *Gastarbeiterliteratur*,[1] is a relatively recent genre of literature, one that has developed in the foreign worker population.[2] Knowledge of the specific structural characteristics of Immigrant Worker German as well as of its larger political, socio- and psycholinguistic context brings a fuller appreciation of the skills of the writers involved. That immigrant groups influence the literature of the host country is evidenced by the Southeast European immigrants to the United States at the turn of the century, who became themselves subject matter of realism and naturalism and whose children became the authors of the next generation. Noted immigrant worker authors in what had been West Germany include Jusuf Naoum, Aras Oren, Franco Biondi, and Rafik Schami. The language choice of these writers is particularly interesting, since it demonstrates in a creative fashion how language can be used as an expression of ethnic identity and of social and political solidarity. By analyzing this literature sociolinguistically (looking at the author's choice of standard German, Immigrant Worker German, or other nonstandard varieties in different social settings within a novel or play, for example), one is able to discern what social values a writer is trying to express through language. This approach links back to the work of Brown and Gilman (1960), who analyze linguistic expressions of power and solidarity relations, and forward to the work of Fairclough (1989), who carefully maps the interconnection between linguistic form and political opinion. While studies do exist that exploit such theories in the sociohistorical analysis of literature (e.g., Lahusen's work on forms of address in Russian literature), very little work of this nature has been done on the whole.

Awareness of the psycholinguistic background of the immigrant workers in Germany brings to light yet other important information about the literature they produce. The immigrant workers who have made Germany their home have had to develop a means to communicate with the Germans with whom they live and with other immigrant workers from different language backgrounds. Well over half of them have learned what German they can speak in the workplace (Klein and Dittmar 1979, 200), and most of them speak it less than proficiently. Those who have not learned German in the workplace probably have not learned German anywhere, though of course some have learned it in school. Very few states have an adult education program in German as a Second Language and even fewer companies (there are exceptions — e.g., Fordwerke

Köln), and even the classes for immigrant children are not very widespread and are of varying quality. This situation has led to the development of a provisional form of German that has been variously described as a pidgin, a creole, foreigner talk, and a fossilized learner dialect.

Michael Clyne (1968) first introduced the notion Pidgin German, or *Pidgindeutsch*[3] and soon projects developed at major universities (e.g., Heidelberg) to research the bilingual behavior of the immigrant workers. Later research suggested that this pidginization process is just one of the phases of development of learner varieties of a second language (Klein 1986, 51) and that the majority of immigrant worker language forms are the same as those of any other foreigner learning German as a second or foreign language. The two major differences are that (a) immigrant worker forms are in general stigmatized (whether they are the same as or different from those of other learner groups) and (b) because of the lack of formal training, immigrant worker forms tend to fossilize earlier — that is to say, speakers stick at a stage of development that does not equal native speaker norms, when other learners continue to progress toward native-like competence.[4]

In a study of foreign workers' speech, Jurgen Meisel (1976, 90–91) presents a list of typical features, after which the following listing is closely modeled:

Typical Features of Immigrant Worker German

1. Use of foreign words, not necessarily of the speakers' native language:

   amigo, capito, compris

2. Overgeneralization of Standard German words:

   a. *viel dumm* (much stupid)

   b. *ich nix mit kopf arbeit* (I no work with head)

   c. *Niks gut wetter* (No good weather)

   d. *Zwei monat nix arbeit!* (Two month no work!)

3. *Du* for *Sie* (i.e., the familiar form of "you" instead of the polite form):

Du viel arbeit! (You much work!)

Du verstehen was Frau sagt? (You understand what woman says?)

4. Semantically unmarked forms:

machen ("do," used instead of other, lexically more specific verbs)

5. Analytical paraphrase of "complex" expressions:

nix arbeit (not *arbeitlos*) ("no work" for "unemployed")

mehr geld (not *Lohnerhohung*) ("more money" for "[pay] raise")

andere platz (not *anderswo*) ("other place" for "elsewhere")

diese hand (not *links/rechts*) ("this hand" for "left" or "right")

nix gut (not *schlecht*) ("not good" for "bad")

tot machen (not *toten*) ("make dead" for "kill"; cf. also #4 above)

6. Decomposed predicates:

ganze mafioso, mach kaputt drei mensche (total mafioso, make dead three people)

7. Missing elements:

a. articles, especially definite articles, preferably within prepositional phrases and in subject noun phrases: *Leuten gut, Geld gut, aber was machen mit Fuss?* (Peoples good, money good, but what do with foot?)

Wir kommen aus Türkei ("We come from [missing article] Turkey," where German requires the definite article)

b. Prepositions: *Ampel stehen bleiben* ("Stand stoplight," i.e., no "at")

c. Copula, auxiliaries and main verbs, most frequently the copula:

Nachher Griechenland (Later Greece)

Kind alles in der Türkei geboren (Child all born in Turkey)

d. Personal pronouns, preferably in subject position:

Zwei monat nix arbeit (Two month no work)

8. Inflectional endings on verbs, adjectives, and nouns are omitted:

    Ich nix mit Kopf arbeit. Ich hier arbeit. (I no work with head. Work here.)

9. Pronouns in imperative:

    Du bitte sprechen! (You speak please!)

10. Word order:

    Milan hat gesagt sein Name (cf. "Milan has his name said")

    Und dann hat gesehen E. Feuer auf Dach (And then saw E. fire on roof)

    Im Moment ich mochte bleiben hier (At the moment would I like to here stay)

11. Complex sentences are rare. If they do appear, conjunctions and pronouns may be missing.

A large number of immigrant worker texts, particularly poems, where the idiosyncratic forms can be used most creatively, incorporate these features:

Franco Biondi[5]	
NICHT NUR	(NOT ONLY
GASTARBEITERDEUTSCH	GASTARBEITERDEUTSCH)
isch viile jaar hiir	(i many years here)
	[No verb or preposition]
isch kennen jetzz	(i knowing now)
	[Agreement]
viile doitsche loite	(many German peeple)
	[Eye dialect][6]
	(In Ackermann 1983, 85)

Tryphon Papastamatelos
WARUM WATER

warum water	(why father) [Word order
du mich holen	(you me bring) /Inflection]
in dieses land	(into this country)
wo ich nicht	(where I not)
auf strassen	(on streets)
spielen kann die	(can play that)
du so schon	(you so nicely)
putzen hast	(have clean) [Inflection]
	(Cited in Hamm 1988, 70)

The following piece pivots structurally about point (7c) above, in that it omits all verbs, particularly the copula *be*:

Franco Biondi
AUFSTIEGE
Klar, Deutscher: größte Kapo. Italiener: größe Kapo. Türke: kleine Kapo. Du [= Pakistani] noch kleinere Kapo. Afrikaner: Dreckarbeit und so. Wo arm und reich gibt, immer so.
(In Schaffernicht 1981, 57)

(PROMOTIONS
Sure, German: biggest Capi[talist]. Italian: big Capi[talist]. Turk: small Capi[talist]. You: even smaller Capi[talist]. African: shitwork and that. Where is poor and rich, always so.)

Here the writer leaves out the verb to underscore the absolute equivalence, the universality of these relations. At one and the same time he presents the immigrant worker language and with it the immigrant worker view and shows it to be a fact of life (*Klar*, "sure"). The title, "Promotions," reinforces this view.

The following poem by Marino also has as its theme the natural "pecking order" within the immigrant worker community. It is remarkable on the linguistic level for the fact that it replicates the universal order of acquisition of negatives and other function words (as researched by, e.g., Wode [1976]; cf. Dulay et al. [1982] for discussion of acquisition sequences). The linguistic progression reinforces the irony that with increased facility with the German language comes decreased ability to understand, culminating in the native German speaker, who is unable or unwilling to understand anybody:

>Pasquale Marino
>VERSTEHEN
>(UNDERSTAND)
>Ich Turke. Nix verstehen!
>(I Turk. No understand!)
>Ich Grieche. Deutsch nix verstehen!
>(I Greek. German no understand!)
>Ich Jugoslawe. Nicht Deutsch verstehen!
>(I Yugoslav. Not German understand!)
>Ich bin Spanier. Ich nicht verstehe Deutsch!
>(I'm a Spaniard. I not understand German!)
>Ich bin Italiener. Ich verstehe nicht gut Deutsch!
>(I'm an Italian. I don't understand German well!)
>Ich bin Deutscher. Ich verstehe euch alle nicht!
>(I'm a German. I don't understand any of you!)
>(In Taufiq 1983, cited in Hamm 1988, 116)

This work brings us to a discussion of what linguists know about developing facility in German among the immigrant workers. Like all languages, Immigrant Worker German is variable. The Heidelberg Research Project (1975) proposed four stages along a continuum of the migrants' development of German:

>Phase 1: Deficient knowledge of German, better comprehension than production.

>Phase 2: Contact with Germans and other guest workers, but they are not part of the main communication network and the subjects' German is insufficient for their communication needs.

Phase 3: Relatively stable; pidgin is integrated with their social and communicative needs; no motivation for
further language acquisition. (These are the most
frequently encountered categories.)

Phase 4: Completely integrated; speech gravitates towards
regional dialect. (Clyne 1968, 91)

Researchers (e.g., Klein and Dittmar 1979) in general agree that it
is the opportunity to socialize with Germans outside the workplace
that determines the level of language attained. Length of stay in
Germany is an insignificant factor in this development, especially
after the first six years. One poem in particular is remarkable in that
it traces the above pattern in its development, namely, Franco
Biondi's "Nicht nur Gastarbeiterdeutsch" ("Not only Guestworker
German"). The first section is written in the most basic (in terms
of pidgin and creole linguistics, 'basilectal') Guestworker German, displaying a large number of the features given in the list
above. It also uses unorthodox spelling to denote pronunciation
difficulties — such as *nix* [nɪks] for *nicht* [nɪçt] ("not") and *isch* for *ich*
("I"), denoting the pronunciation of standard German [ɪç] as [ɪš].[7]
Furthermore, the author employs eye dialect occasionally, such as
doitsch for deutsch (both presumably pronounced [dɔɪtš] and close
enough to the standard pronunciation to make no real difference in
speech). The point of using this device here is to promote the
stereotype of the Guestworker — undesirable and uneducated.

I. die anfange	(I. the beginnings)
maine nix gut doitsch.	(mine no good german.)
isch waiss —	(i know —)
isch sprech ja	(i speak)
nur gastarbaiterdoitsch	(only gastarbaiterdoitsch)
und immer problema	(and always problems)
iberall	(everywhere)
doitsch loite nix verstee	(german people no understand)
was isch sagen	(what i saying)
was isch wollen	(what i wanting)

Also in this first section, the poet stresses that he comprehends better:

aber	(but)
langsam langsam	(slowly slowly)
geets:	(it goes)
isch jetzz meer verstee	(i now more understand)

In the second section ("es geht den gastarbeiterdeutschen gang," [Guestworker German goes its (normal) course]), Biondi refers to the situation described in phase two above, in which contact is limited and the speaker's German is consequently also limited:

doitsche kollega	(german colleague)
warum du immer weggucken	(why you always look away)
warum du mir nix akzeptieren	(why you not accepting me)
isch nix schaiss	(i not shit)
isch mensch	(i human being)
zusammen	(together)
isch arbait du arbait fabrik	(i work you work factory)
isch leben du leben hiir	(i live you live here)
. . . .	
aber du immer zusammen	(but you always together
mit doitschen loite	with german people)
isch immer zusammen	(i always together
mit auslendischen[8] loite	with foreign people)
. . . .	
isch schon viil doitsch	(i already much
denken	german thinking)
in fabrik und zuhaus	(in factory and at home)
allein meine sprache	(only my language)
noch gastarbaiterdoitsch	(still gastarbaiterdoitsch)

The third section illustrates what happens between phases three and four above, where the immigrants speak much better German, enough to be able to discuss their problems with other immigrants. Since they feel the Germans don't want to hear, they are forced, and anxious, to use the nonstandard German voice they have as the voice that represents them as a group; they simply will not wait until they command "better" German. The third section is entitled "ich warte nicht auf besseres deutsch" ("I'm not waiting for better German"):

> ich gehe nun in deutsche schule
> (i'm going now to german school)
> in volkshochschule
> (to secondary school)
> deutsche sprache lernen.
> (learn german language.)
> nun diskutieren wir viel
> (now we discuss much)
> und sehen immer mehr
> (and see more and more)
> die viele diskriminierungen
> (the many discriminations)
> gegen uns gastarbeiter
> (against us *gastarbeiter*)
> oder besser
> (or better)
> arbeitsemigranten
> (immigrant workers)
> und merken immer mehr
> (and notice more and more)
> wir haben viele rechte nicht —
> (we have not many rights —)
> aber alle pflichten.
> (but all obligations.)
> . . . .
> und ganz wenige deutsche kollegen
> (and very few german colleagues)
> helfen uns oder hören an unsere problemen.
> (help us or listen to our problems.)
> doch: unsere sprach in deutsche gesellschaft
> (but our language in german society)
> ist eine sprach die sprechen will
> (is a language that wants to speak)

aber nicht nur —
   (but not only —)
wir warten nicht auf besseres deutsch.
   (we're not waiting for better german.)

The final section mirrors phase four to some extent. The German is much less idiosyncratic, approaching the standard (to a pidgin/creolist it would be almost acrolectal). But the twist is that, rather than signaling integration, what is left of the *Gastarbeiterdeutsch* still acts as a stigma, a marker of the special status the immigrant worker has in Germany. Knowing more about the language, he now knows so much more about the society and his designated place in it as neither insider nor complete foreigner. Trapped inside his shell there are other languages and other cultural values — there is more than *Gastarbeiterdeutsch*:

IV. was mir bleibet
      (what is left to me)
   mein gastarbeiterdeutsch ist eng
      (my gastarbeiterdeutsch is narrow)
         wie das ausländergesetz
            (as the immigration law)
   und tief
      (and deep)
         wie die ausbeutung
            (as the exploitation)
. . . .
   mein gastarbeiterdeutsch ist
      (my gastarbeiterdeutsch has become)
         ein stempel geworden
            (a stamp)
   darauf steht:
      (on which it says)
         Made in Westgermany
            (Made in Westgermany)
   mein gastarbeiterdeutsch hat sein nest
      (my gastarbeiterdeutsch has built its nest)

in den furchen meines gehirns aufgebaut
(in the branches of my brain)
hat als wiege meine träume gewogen
(as a cradle has rocked my dreams)
hat wie eine schmiede hoffnungen geformt
(as a smithy has formed my hopes)
mein gastarbeiterdeutsch ist eine hülse —
(my gastarbeiterdeutsch is a shell —)
innendrin
(within)
nicht nur gastarbeiterdeutsch
(not only gastarbeiterdeutsch)
(In Ackermann 1983, 84–87)

The major contribution linguistic knowledge can bring to the analysis of the above poem is the awareness that the experiences the author is writing about are endemic in the immigrant worker population; that is, they are universal experiences. Of course it also reinforces the incredible astuteness of Franco Biondi, the author, as an observer of the immigrant group to which he belongs. What the linguist gets out of all this is exactly that microcosmic illustration of the macrolinguistic situation alluded to above in the claim that literature is data.

At this point one should pause to consider other implications of the existence of this kind of literature for linguistic theory. As I mentioned above, there has been considerable discussion about the "varietal status" of Guestworker German, particularly in the German literature but also in works on pidgin and creole linguistics generally (cf. Romaine 1988). The question is, is it a pidgin (and if so, is it stable in character?), is it a creole, or is it neither of these, but merely an idiosyncratic learner dialect like any other (cf. schoolroom German)? While there is no real agreement on exactly how to define any of these varieties of language, three main criteria for creolization can be discerned. The first is largely demographic: unlike a pidgin, a creole must become the major language of a group of speakers (i.e., it must "acquire native speakers"). The second is structural: it must possess a number of specific structural characteristics (cf. Romaine 1988). The third criterion is functional, and this is the most important in this context: it must be used as the primary means of expression of its speakers and in all communicative contexts, in particular, in affective as well as instrumental functions.[9]

The examples given so far in this chapter might at first raise the objection that they are merely sophisticated manipulations of Immigrant Worker German that have been altered by native speaker editors before publication. Irmgard Ackermann (personal communication) points out that in hardly any of the literature discussed here does the author himself really use *Gastarbeiterdeutsch* as his own form of expression in the German language, but rather uses it "second hand." She goes on to say that this usage therefore means that the linguistic examples are less than authentic (and presumably present less than reliable data for linguistic analysis). The fact is, however, that there are enough common features in these texts, and enough features that hold up to close linguistic scrutiny in comparison with "authentic" data from "real" linguistic projects, to make Immigrant Worker German literature a very valid source of inquiry. They represent an author's interpretation of how this variety of German is used in context, and as such are extremely important to sociolinguistic analysis (though my point in this whole chapter is, of course, that such an analysis is heavily dependent on prior knowledge of the more "purely linguistic" literature on the subject).

Another potential concern with the materials chosen might be that they all have as their theme the status and importance of *Gastarbeiterdeutsch* itself. However, the writers in question are not bound to use Immigrant Worker German to talk about Immigrant Worker German but rather *choose* to do so, and therefore they must consider this nonstandard dialect to be recognized by their potential readership so that there is no vicious circularity involved here. By the very act of their using Immigrant Worker German, they are making a statement about its status. However, it would certainly indicate stronger acceptance of the dialect if one were to find *Gastarbeiterdeutsch* in works where it accompanied other themes, and this idea will certainly be a focus of future research.

Other observers might even object to these extracts being called literature in the first place! The fact is that many immigrants have published a considerable body of work in poetry, prose, and drama. While very little critical work exists on the topic of Immigrant Worker literature, it is indeed considered a very important genre. Hamm (1988) provides an excellent literary and sociohistorical introduction to the genre. Ackermann (personal communication) points out that, as with all other genres, Immigrant Worker literature cannot be given a blanket value (good or bad), but must be judged on the merits of the individual works.

If we reconsider the three factors mentioned above involved in classifying a variety of language as a creole, two are uncontroversially present — the formal and the functional. While it would be premature (and possibly irrelevant) to make a definitive statement about the nature of Immigrant Worker German in the context of this chapter, it is important to point out that ultimately the literary information will play a significant role in judging its status.

Whatever one chooses to call it, reduced German is not always in the mouths of the immigrant workers. Sometimes it is the native German speakers themselves who speak in this way, and when they do, it is often referred to as Foreigner Talk ("You Tarzan, me Jane"). New immigrants with no prior formal German training have no idea that this language they are hearing is not German, but with their increasing knowledge of the language, Foreigner Talk quickly becomes a symbol of oppression and appears recurrently as a theme in Immigrant Worker German:

Michel Boiron
GOETHE — EIN FREMDWORT
Seitdem ich ein bißchen mehr Deutsch kann, habe ich bemerkt, daß viele Deutsche kein Deutsch können. Gestern, da sagte mir die Frau am Kiosk, sie ist blondhaarig, fett und hat eine Raucherstimme: "Sie, Ausländer? Nicht wahr? . . . Aus welchem Land kommen?" Ich fragte: "Sind Sie auch Ausländerin?" Sie sagte: "NEIN! Ich Deutsche!" Und 'putzte' mir Rauch ins Gesicht. Ich bin Nichtraucher.
(In Ackermann 1983, 235)

(GOETHE — A LOAN WORD
Since I can speak a little more German I have noticed that many Germans cannot speak German. Yesterday the woman at the stand, she's blonde, fat, and has the voice of a smoker, said to me: "You foreigner? No? What country you come from?" I asked: "Are you also a foreigner?" She said: "NO! I'm German." And 'blew' smoke in my face. I'm a nonsmoker.)

Rafik Schami
DIE GEPANZERTE HAUT
. . . Der bärtige [deutsche] Mann setzte sich nun aufrecht und schob seine Begleiterin zur Seite.
"Die Türkei viel schön, ich Deutschland, nix Sonne . . . viel Arbeit. Arbeit nix gut — nicht wahr?"
Ich musterte ihn, dann seine Begleiterin, die kopfnickend lächelte.
"Reden sie immer so miserables Deutsch?" fragte ich.
Beide schauten einander verlegen an und schüttelten die Köpfe.
"Können Sie nicht Deutsch sprechen?"
Beide sprachen kein Wort mehr mit mir, sie wußten aber auch nicht, daß ich mir diese zwei Sätze von einem Gewerkschaftskollegen beibringen ließ und sie so oft wiederholt hatte, bis ich sie akzentfrei sprechen konnte, um sie solchen Typen vor die Nase knallen zu können. Die zwei Fragen hatten Wunder gewirkt, diese arroganten Typen stotterten, erröteten und wurden sprachlos.
(Cited in Hamm 1988, 117)

(ARMORED SKIN
The bearded [Ger]man sat up straight and pushed his companion aside.
"Turkey very nice, i Germany, not sun . . . plenty work. Work no good — yes?"
I eyed first him, then his girlfriend, who smiled and nodded. "Do you always speak such appalling German?" I asked. Embarrassed, they looked at each other and shook their heads. "Can't you speak German?"
They both said not another word to me, but they didn't

know that I had a union colleague teach me these two sentences, and that I had practiced them until I could say them without [a trace of] accent, so that I could hurl them at such types. The two questions had worked miracles; these arrogant types stuttered, reddened and became speechless.)

The word "speechless" (in German also "without language") is very important here. A stereotypical remark about the immigrant workers, and particularly their children, is that, speaking neither the home language nor German perfectly, they have no language. What this Immigrant Worker literature shows above all, however, is that, rather than having no voice, the immigrant workers often have several voices from which to choose, each of them representing some sort of ethnic, social, or political compromise. Nowhere is this choice of voices more obvious than in the consideration of texts in which the author switches codes (for a linguistic discussion of code switching see Cook-Gumperz and Gumperz, 1976). The linguistics literature on code switching has often pointed out that, rather than being a marker of incomplete mastery of a code, which is what is often concluded by the uninitiated, code switching is usually a marker of familiarity and facility with more than one code (and its attendant sociocultural values). This final extract is a glorious example of linguistic and personal triumph that illustrates the misunderstood prowess of the immigrant worker. By switching from one standard language to another in this text and refusing to acknowledge the Foreigner Talk with which his main character is addressed, the author here is able to embody in her the social and linguistic plight of the immigrant worker in Germany. While one does not have to be a linguist to appreciate the poignancy of this text, as a linguist one has a unique framework for its interpretation:

Jiri Kral
SUPERMARKT
    "Nix lesen, putzen, putzen!"
Es ist der Leiter des Geschäfts, ein unbeliebter Mann, der allen hier das Leben schwer macht. Besonders uns [Ausländern]. Er

benutzt nur Infinitive, wenn er mit uns spricht — es beleidigt mich jedesmal, genau so wie sein Benehmen uns gegenüber. Bis heute habe ich mich immer beherrscht, aber jetzt weiß ich, daß es zu einem Krach kommt. Ich frage ihn höflich: "Bitte?", als ob ich ihn nicht gehört hätte.

"Du nix lesen, du arbeiten, putzen, putzen," wiederholt er. Ich fühle, wie mein Blut tobt, beiße die Zähne zusammen und suche in meinem Gedächtnis nach den besten Worten. Gleichzeitig sehe ich in seinem Gesicht Triumph, man kann seine Gedanken fast lesen: "Jetzt habe ich euch erwischt." Es vergeht ein kleiner Moment, und ich sage voll konzentriert und so deutlich wie ich es kann: "Entschuldigen Sie, aber wie Sie selbst sehen können, sind wir mit allem außer der Wurst — und Obstabteilung fertig. Jetzt warten wir, bis das Geschäft zugeschlossen wird. Früher können wir dort nicht putzen!"

Überraschung in seinem Gesicht.

Dann fällt mir noch etwas ein, und ich sage ohne nachzudenken: "By the way, if you don't speak German, you can speak English. I understand English."

Schock!

"Was?" fragt er mit gefrorenem Gesicht. Ich lache innerlich: "Er spricht also nicht Englisch," und ich sage langsam: "Ich habe nur gesagt, wenn Sie nicht Deutsch sprechen können, können Sie mit uns Englisch sprechen. Oder," füge ich hinzu, "mit ihr," ich zeige auf Hedwiga, "auch Französisch. Und wenn es Ihnen nicht genügt, verstehen wir beide Russisch, ganz zu schweigen von unseren Muttersprachen, also Polnisch und Tschechisch." Seine Überlegenheit verschwindet, es ist, als ob er sich verkleinerte. "Aber ich spreche doch Deutsch," antwortet er zuletzt ganz verwirrt. "Habe ich nicht bemerkt," antworte ich. "Sie benutzen nur Infinitive, wenn Sie sich mit uns unterhalten. Wie kann ich dann erkennen, daß sie Deutschsprechender sind?" Jetzt sehe ich, daß er wirklich nicht weiß, was er antworten soll. Er hat keinen Widerstand erwartet, und jetzt fühlt er, daß er in eine Falle geraten ist.

(In Ackermann 1983, 90)

(SUPERMARKET

"No read, cleaning, cleaning!"

He is the manager of the shop, an unpopular man, who

makes life difficult for everyone. Especially for us foreigners. He only uses infinitives when he speaks to us — it insults me every time, just like his behavior towards us. Up until today I've kept control of myself, but I know now that there's going to be trouble. I ask politely: "Pardon me?", as if I hadn't heard.

"You no read, you working, cleaning, cleaning," he repeats. I can feel my blood boiling, clench my teeth and search in my memory for the best words. At the same time I see triumph in his face; you can almost read his thoughts: "I've got you this time." A short pause, and I say with complete concentration and as clearly as I can: "Excuse me, but as you can see, we have finished all but the delicatessen. Now we're waiting until the store is closed. We can't clean there any sooner!"

Surprise in his face.

Then something else comes to me, and I say without reflection: [in English] "By the way, if you don't speak German, you can speak English. I understand English."

Shock!

"What?", he asks, his face frozen. I laugh inwardly. "So, he doesn't speak English," and I say slowly [in German]: "I merely said, if you can't speak German, you can speak English to us. Or," I add, "with her," I point to Hedwiga, "you can even speak French. And if that's not enough for you, we both understand Russian, let alone our native languages, Polish and Czech." His superiority vanishes; it was as if he was shrinking. "But I do speak German," he finally answers, quite confused. "I hadn't noticed," I answer. "You only use infinitives when you converse with us. How am I supposed to recognize that you speak German?" Now I see that he really doesn't know what he should say. He hadn't expected resistance, and now he feels as if he has fallen into a trap.)

Notes

1. The terms *Gastarbeiter* (Guestworker), *Gastarbeiterdeutsch* (Guestworker German), and *Gastarbeiterliteratur* (Guestworker literature), while still commonly used in Germany, are disputed on a number of grounds.

Primarily, the reason is that *Guestworker* (rather like the term *Negro* or *black* in the United States of America) has unpleasant, often racist associations. Other terms have been suggested, such as *(Arbeits)immigranten* (Immigrant [Workers]), to try to alleviate this problem. In this chapter, I have chosen to use the terms *Immigrant Workers*, *Immigrant Worker German*, and *Immigrant Worker literature* but to use the *Gastarbeiter* terms wherever they were used by the original authors.

2. Foreign workers now constitute what the latest edition of *Facts About Germany* describes as the largest "social minority," the largest "under-privileged sector," and a "fringe group" of (West) German society made up of about 4.5 million people out of a total population of 57 million. In other words, Guestworkers make up 7.5 percent of the population and 10 percent of the work force of the FRG. Guestworkers were originally imported into Germany according to the *Rotationsprinzip* (the Rotation Principle), which denied the worker the right to stay home. There was for a long time no provision for workers to bring their families with them, or to learn German in a formal setting, or to be integrated in any way into mainstream society. For a number of reasons, not all the Guestworkers returned home. The result is that half the workers have now lived in Germany over fifteen years and two-thirds of the rest over ten years, while more than 25 percent of the immigrant population is under sixteen years of age; their number is increasing rapidly, despite the fact that in the early seventies first a restriction and then a stop were placed on the importing of labor.

3. The term *Pidgindeutsch* has been contested on a number of grounds, ranging from the question of how stable a pidgin should be before it is called a *pidgin*, to criticisms of linguists' preoccupation with theory in the face of urgent social and political needs.

4. Those readers familiar with the history of African-American English might hear an echo here.

5. The original German is reproduced in plain text, and rough translations that aim at not only glossing but also interpreting the effect of the original follow in parentheses. Commentary on grammatical features is given in brackets.

6. See below for further discussion of eye dialect.

7. Irmgard Ackermann points out (personal communication) that this pronunciation is probably indicative of regional (Rheinland?) pronunciation of *ich* rather than a feature of Immigrant Worker German per se. The

fact is, however, that this is a nonstandard feature. In my experience, immigrant workers do tend to adopt regional pronunciations of this word in particular (e.g., *isch* in Swabia and *ik* in Berlin). What is interesting from the linguistic point of view is that such features might be relatively neutral or even (locally) prestigious in the mouths of native Germans but that they are frequently stigmatized in the mouths of immigrants (cf. the lack of nonprevocalic "r" in African-American English).

8. Note the gradual acquisition of umlauts reflected in this poem. Lack of umlauts is frequently found in renditions of Immigrant Worker German.

9. Since German Guestworkers are now in their third generation and since they show few signs of returning to their homeland (despite financial incentive from the federal government to do so), the situation is theoretically ripe for creolization. One sign of this process is the fact that Guestworker children have very poor education — graduation levels stand as low as *officially* 40 percent in parts of Berlin. There are continued restrictions on contact with native German speakers, largely due to ghettoization, and there are few if any viable special education programs for children in place. It is frequently said by educators and others that these children have *no* language, since they learn neither standard German nor the first language of their parents.

References

Ackermann, I. 1983. *In zwei Sprachen leben.* Munich: Deutschen Taschenbuch Verlag.

Bondi, F. "Nicht nur Gastarbeiterdeutsch." In Ackermann, 84–87.

Brown, R. and A. Gilman. 1960. "The Pronouns of Power and Solidarity." In *Style in Language,* ed. T. A. Sebeok, 253–76. New York: John Wiley.

Clyne, M. 1968. "Zum Pidgindeutsch der Gastarbeiter." *Zeitschrift für Mundartforschung* 35: 130–39.

Cook-Gumperz, J., and J. Gumperz. 1976. "Context in Children's Speech." *Papers on Language and Context.* Working Papers 46. Language Behavior Research Laboratory, U of California, Berkeley.

Dulay, H., M. Burt, and S. Krashen. 1982. *Language Two.* New York: Oxford UP.

Fairclough, N. 1989. *Language and Power.* London: Longman.

Fennell, B. A. 1988. "Sociolinguistic Theory and Literary Analysis." Paper presented at the 20th Anniversary Conference of the Southeastern Conference on Linguistics, Norfolk, Va., October 1988.

————. 1989. "Now You See It, Now You Don't: Pidgin and Creole Characteristics of Immigrant Worker German in the Federal Republic." Paper presented at NWAVE 18, Duke University, October 1989.

Hamm, H. 1988. *Fremdgegangen-freigeschrieben: Einführung in die deutschsprachige Gastarbeiterliteratur.* Würzburg: Königshausen und Neumann.

Klein, W. 1986. *Second Language Acquisition.* Cambridge: Cambridge UP.

Klein, W., and Dittmar, N. 1979. *Developing Grammars: The Acquisition of German Syntax by Foreign Workers.* Berlin: Springer-Verlag.

Meisel, J. 1976. "Linguistic Simplification: A Study of Immigrant Workers' Speech and Foreigner Talk." In *The Notions of Simplification, Interlanguages and Pidgins and Their Relation to Second Language Typology,* ed. S. P. Corder and E. Roulet. Actes du 5ème Colloque de Linguistique Appliquée à Neuchâtel, 20–22 May 1976. Liebefeld, Bern: Langdruck.

Romaine, S. 1988. *Pidgin and Creole Languages.* London: Longman.

Schaffernicht, C., ed. 1981. *Zu Hause in der Fremde.* Discherhude.

Tannen, D. 1989. *Talking Voices.* Cambridge: Cambridge UP.

Taufiq, S., ed. 1983. *Dies ist nicht die Welt die wir suchen.* Essen, Germany: Klartext/PRO.

Wode, H. 1976. "Developmental Sequences in Naturalistic L2 Acquisition." In *Second Language Acquisition,* ed. E. Hatch. (1978), 102–17. Rowley, Mass.: Newbury House.

"What a Parrot Talks"
The Janus Nature of
Anglo-Irish Writing

Of all the injustices the British have heaped upon Ireland, Ireland has had the lasting revenge of producing masterpieces of English literature.
— Lord Derwent, British Minister to Bern,
at the funeral of James Joyce

A number of years ago, as undergraduates in English at Trinity College Dublin, we were asked on our final exam to select one element as the major contribution of the Irish to English literature. Having feasted on Joyce, O'Casey, Synge, Behan, Flann O'Brien, Frank O'Connor, and others, I responded that humor was the great gift of the Irish. I wrote what I considered an appropriately witty paper on the subject that was, in turn, duly praised by the examiners. Over the years, however, I have often thought about that question and now consider my initial response insufficient. Certainly, Irish writers use wit and humor effectively, but their penchant for the comic emerges from a more fundamental impulse, one that finds its roots in their idiosyncratic use of English. While it is true that writers from diverse nationalities and backgrounds will inevitably bring their own colorizations to a language, Irish writers indulge in a peculiar looseness with English that speaks volumes, not only in purely aesthetic terms but also and more significantly as a nationalistic and revolutionary reaction to the actions of the British and development of their language in Ireland.

It cannot be considered a coincidence that many Irish writers use identical literary devices when writing in English. While drawn to the comic, they reveal themselves as so adept at word-crafting and punning that their use of English emerges as defiantly heretical. Critics have tended, on the one hand, to view this tendency as simply an example of the creative genius of a writer adapting local speech — Synge going to the Aran Islands, for example — or, on the other hand, as a result of the Irish having "imperfectly" learned English from "inadequate teachers." Six of the nine lectures, for example, in a 1977 series of Thomas Davis lectures on Radio Eireann on the use of English in Ireland, considered one of the most important recent examinations of this subject, use the term "dialect" to define Anglo-Irish.

These "imperfections" that differentiate it from other forms of English and also give it a richness are a direct result of the way the language emerged in Ireland. Until 1800, the majority of the population spoke Gaelic. As they switched to English, they created a peculiar hybrid: the words were English, but the syntax and grammar remained rooted in Irish. The accents, too, sometimes altered the sound of the word. These elements gave birth to the tendency to malapropism that has been the mainstay of many an Irish writer, not to mention the trademark of the stage-Irish character.

While these twists and turns in the language may have given writers grist for the mill and amused audiences and readers, in reality their genesis was the result of dire causes, mainly political. Primarily the (Catholic) lower and peasant classes were isolated from schools and institutions where their English could have been more carefully regulated. They picked up their English in a garbled form, and even when they did have the opportunity to learn more formal English, their teachers may have been one-eared kings in a land of the deaf. As Alan J. Bliss argues in one of the aforementioned Thomas Davis lectures, their incorrect usage may have been due to "an erroneous interpretation by [the teacher] a hedge schoolmaster" (1977, 61). Leaving aside the question of why these usages would continue beyond the initial stage of the conversion of Gaelic speakers into English speakers, or, more important, what defines "standard" English, one cannot escape the implication that lies behind this approach: that the Irish form of English is somehow degenerate.

Further, P. L. Henry (1977) argues that as a rule language serves to strengthen nationalism when it enjoys a high social status, but that was not the case in Ireland: "A normal development would have been to adopt the new language at the appropriate level for all other spheres of activity outside Ireland, . . . [but] there was no scope for the rise of Anglo-Irish as a national speech norm fashioned by the people and therefore adapted to their own needs, educational, social and political" (25).

But, I would argue, this view of the Irish as simply victims of bad educational or social deprivation ignores the strong role that language played in their cultural self-definition. More to the point, the way the language developed in Ireland *did* serve "their own needs," socially and politically. Their consistent use of erroneous words, it can be argued, goes beyond being a mere idiosyncrasy in Irish literature but forms the core of its "Great Tradition." Behind it lies a strong anti-British bias, and that approach — whatever the Irish writers' feelings for the land of Ireland itself — remains part of their ethos. When Stephen Dedalus explains why, if he was disgruntled with Roman Catholicism, he never became a Protestant, he may well be talking of why he never became an Anglophile: "I haven't lost my self-respect."

Anglo-Irish, therefore, according to this definition and as used by the writers in this chapter, is primarily the language of the lower classes, the poor of Dublin, the peasants in the farms, or those who emerged from those backgrounds. In more contemporary terms, we would call these the marginalized, the disenfranchised, and the radical. (The upper class, "The Ascendancy" as it was called, had access to schools in Britain and were more prone to imitate "proper" English and even to look down on the way the lower classes used and spoke English. In fact, their spoken and written English is generally devoid of the "trademarks" of Anglo-Irish literature.[1])

For this reason, to look at the development of Anglo-Irish in purely "academic" terms, i.e., as the result of syntax, phonology, and lexicon emerging in some sort of rarefied atmosphere, would be to ignore a fundamental aspect of how a language evolves. The political isolation of the Catholic Irish, their lack of civil rights, and their lack of religious freedoms during the years when they began to speak English must also have affected their attitude toward not only the English people but also their language.

Claus Mueller, in *The Politics of Communication* (1973), sees language as a "repository of cultural tradition." When people speak in a certain language, they echo its vision, its peculiarities, its sense of importance, and even its sense of separateness. The author Cynthia Ozick senses this "limitation" when she notes, "A language, like a people, has a history of ideas; but not *all* ideas; only those known to its experience" (1977, 9).[2] What, then, of the Irish who were forced to use a language whose "culture" of religious persecution and "tradition" of imperialism and political domination were anathema to them?[3]

When the Irish came to learn English, they would naturally try to duplicate their own philosophical and psychological insights as well as the freedom that their language had given them. Yet this attempt to unite culture and language would not be easy. They would be aware of the cultural and traditional implications of English; and in their resistance to losing their national identity, unconsciously or consciously, they showed that to impose a language on another people and try to make it fit was to invite linguistic chaos. With this inheritance, Anglo-Irish, therefore, emerges as more than a dialect or a variant of "standard" English. For the Irish speaker of English it has also served symbolically as a response to a history of oppression and exclusion.

The Irish did not come to English easily. It is no simple thing to switch from Gaelic to English, to leave one's language and all that it contains of history, myth, religion, ethos, symbol, and metaphor. It is no easy thing to adopt a language that in the words of Henry (1977) reinforced the impression of the Irish as so low in self-esteem that they would even desert their language to be accepted by the rest of the world and that made them seem, "inferior, unfashionable and gross" (25).

Brian Friel takes up this point in his play "Translations." Here,

Friel belies the notion of a people benignly switching over from one tongue to the other without devastating effects, as if they were changing clothes. While the play is written in English, Friel uses a double technique to get his point across. When the Irish characters use their own language, they speak in a mellifluous, poetic, and imaginative manner, but when they speak in an English that they have only begun to learn, they mangle it beyond comprehension. At the same time, Friel goes way beyond a simple lesson in language skills, and his device shows that no simple "translation" from one "repository of cultural tradition" to another can work without devastating effects.

In the opening scene of act 2, George, a British officer, and Owen, whom the British call "Roland" as they think his Gaelic name is pronounced, a native of Donegal where the action takes place, are redoing the maps of the area. As Friel himself explains in a stage note that fairly bristles with anger, they were to take "every hill, stream, rock, even every patch of ground which possessed its own distinctive Irish name — and Anglicize it, either by changing it into its approximate English sound or by translating it into English words" (1968, 14). It is an act of imperialism that will alienate the Irish from their own land just as Owen/Roland has become a man lost between two worlds.

As Owen and George discuss the name of a seemingly insignificant place, Friel makes it clear what is lost of tradition, of placement and belonging. They earnestly strive to find an English equivalent for the Irish name "Bun na hAbhann," which literally means "river bottom." In their attempt, they explore a number of options. Initially, they consider using the name "Banowen," but it only duplicates the sound and not the meaning of the original. Each subsequent variation becomes more meaningless than the last as they come up with names that are, as Owen puts it, "neither fish nor flesh."

Ultimately, they decided on "Burnfoot," a name that while a stab at both the sound and meaning of the original ("burn" for "Bun," the British once again as they did with Owen's name adding an "r" to the sound, and "foot" for "bottom"), bears only the most tangential relationship to the Gaelic, besides sounding ludicrous. It reverses what a great Englishman suggested was the task of the poet. Here the "local habitation" has been denied a name and turned to "airy nothing."

Obviously, Friel rejects the myth so lovingly created by Yeats and Synge of a people blithely making a new hybrid form of language. Instead, Friel shows us a moment in time that is paradigmatic of the loss that Ireland itself suffered on the larger scale. If I may pun here, they no longer have their "ow[e]n" names. The English word imposed on the Irish locale bears no relation to time or place, people or history.

Friel also raises another and perhaps far more crucial issue: if language is indicative of culture, then the writer who grows up in an environment in which the English are despised and their language is viewed with ambiguity will certainly inherit some of that same attitude. What then are the tools of the Irish writer? In a sense the Irish were in danger of having no language of their own. They had no positive linguistic mode. They were estranged from Gaelic, the repository of their traditions, culture, and history, and forced to wander in the English language looking for a home among the "alien words."

This sense of distance from one's mode of expression is shared to some extent by the sons and daughters of immigrant parents. The American-Jewish writer Delmore Schwartz notes, for example, that such children hear two languages, both forms of English but one "spoken with ease in the streets and school and the other spoken poorly at home." This leads, he suggested, to both positive and negative results: "It gives the author . . . a heightened sensitivity to language, a sense of idiom, and a sense of how much expresses itself through colloquialism. But it also produces in some a fear of mispronunciation [and] a hesitation in speech" (quoted in Atlas 1977, 258).[4]

Schwartz's comments bring to mind Stephen Dedalus's outburst in *Portrait* when he is arguing with his tutor over the word "tundish": "The language in which we are speaking is his before it is mine. . . . I cannot speak or write these words without unrest of spirit. His language, so familiar and so foreign, will always be for me an acquired speech. . . . My soul frets in the shadow of his language" (1976, 189).

As a result of this dislocation, English for the Irish becomes Janus-like, with two distinct and contradictory natures working at the same time: the writer seeks to "desecrate" the word that he also, as artist, wishes to "sanctify." Luckily, this dilemma has fallen into the hands and mouths of a people who with centuries of underhanded fighting against British rule were well capable of rising to the challenge. Their use of language becomes a revolutionary act.

The Irish critic David Norris gets at the root of this issue when he suggests that the "joyful experimentation" of *Finnegan's Wake* is Joyce's way of revenging himself for "the taking away of the Irish language by the English" (McCrum 1986, 188). Leaving aside the fact that Joyce's work obviously demands a broader examination of its virtues, one can extend Norris's approach to nearly every writer born and bred in Ireland who writes in English — and even some who came there later in their career — for they seem to share Joyce's ambivalent attitude toward English. In typical Irish fashion, these "corrupters," these Christy Mahons of language who attempt to kill the parent tongue, are admired as models for discourse and writing.

In a more positive vein, perhaps this Janus-like nature is also the root of the greatness of Irish writers: they do not hold English in awe or with the esteem an English writer might but instead view it as something with which to play. They break up the word, alter its sound, garble its intention; they do everything they can to smash British domination over their language and thought. They philoso-phize on it, analyze it, take it apart, dress it up, stick pins in it, turn it upside down, but they do not respect it, for it is the repository of the enemy, and one way to show the enemy disrespect is to mangle and distort its most prized possession: its language.

The Irish person in the street and the Irish writer grasp innately that there is nothing wrong in "mangling" the English language and not because there is no one around to tell them that they are not speaking English properly! For them, there is something "right" in speaking English this way. Indeed, perhaps Norris is correct in reading *Finnegan's Wake* as the ultimate revenge of an Irishman on the English language! Whatever the beauty of the result, the wonderful cunning that holds the piece together, visually what one sees and orally what one hears are a "desecration," a ripping apart of the word: "Sir Tirstram, violer d'amores, fr'over the short sea, had passencore rearrived from North America on this side the scraggy isthmus of Europe Minor to wielderfigth his penisolate war: nor had topsawyer's rock rocks by the stream Oconee exaggerated them-selse to Lauren's County's gorgios while they went doublin their mumper all the time: nor avoice from afire bellowsed mishe mishe to tauftauf thuartpeatrick . . ." (Joyce 1968, 27).

In *Finnegan's Wake*, Joyce does imaginatively what Friel suggested the British had first done carelessly and with the malice that comes from ignorance. Just as Bun na hAbhann became "Burnfoot," names here go through a multitude of transformations and permutations, some of them having as little relation to their originals as they do in Friel's play but more often than not with a deeper implication. In this case, the voice is the voice of Esau. Not only does Joyce pun, but he also plays around with words including non-English and nonsense words, syllables, rhymes, half-rhymes, inventions, ana-grams, "quashed quotatoes, messes of mottage," and every kind of associative device. English is only used as a starting point and leads, like the Liffey itself, into an endless ocean of words, some of which, like the events in the book, are real and others imagined. What is this language? Is it English? In attempting to answer this question, Flann O'Brien, himself a master of the form, perhaps hit on the truth; it was "merely an example of silence, and punning" (Stories, 207). Joyce in a famous remark stated that if the city of Dublin was destroyed it could be rebuilt from his novel *Ulysses*. One doubts, however, that if the English language would vanish, it could be reconstructed from a reading of his *Finnegan's Wake*. One may add that it seems fitting that Joyce who through his alter-ego Stephen Dedalus had shouted the cry of the devil, "non-serviam," was able to play the desecrator Satan and the creator God at one and the same time.

Joyce was not the only writer to see the value in taking liberties with the sounds and meanings of the English language. Sean O'Casey's great early plays are about the struggles of the Irish under British domination, and they deal with this theme not only in terms of action but also in terms of the language that the characters use to describe their own lives. Language and culture once again run along parallel lines. One finds that the chaos of the language echoes the chaotic world of the characters. There is more than simple word play in the epigrammatic motif of his masterpiece, *Juno and the Paycock,* which puns on the word "chaos": "The world is in a state of chasis."

In his first great success, *The Shadow of a Gunman,* O'Casey presents a scene that captures the ambivalent approach of the Anglo-Irish writer. Two residents of a Dublin tenement, Mr. Gallogher and Mrs. Henderson, are arguing over the merits of another resident, Mr. Shields:

MR. GALLOGHER:	Mr. Shields is a man of exceptional mental capacity, and is worthy of a more dignified position.
MRS. HENDERSON:	Them words is true, Mr. Gallicker, and they aren't. For to be wise is to be a fool, an' to be a fool is to be wise.
MR. GALLOGHER	(with deprecating tolerance): Oh, Mrs. Henderson, that's a parratox.
MRS. HENDERSON:	It may be what a parrot talks, or a blackbird, or, for that matter, a lark — but it's what Julia Henderson thinks.

(Plays, 100)

The scene can serve as a paradigm for an approach to use of English in Anglo-Irish literature.

Mr. Gallogher is a Dublin type that would have been well known to O'Casey's original audience and was often a figure of ridicule and ripe for lampooning. Although not as egregious an example as Mrs. Malaprop, he speaks with all the pretension of a lower-class man trying to imitate the language and sound of the upper class. While he tries to avoid the linguistic mayhem associated with his peers, he nonetheless cannot escape the unintended irony that ensues from his speech patterns, so neatly undermined by the equally lower class but less pretentious Mrs. Henderson.

The key word is "parratox," which is in itself a paradox. It is both symbol and synonym, pun and parody. As we move from "parrots" to "a lark" (both an avian metaphor and a pun on the words), we have the movement of the Irish themselves. Not only do they view the language as a "lark," but they are and are not "parrots" of the English language. Like a parrot they repeat the words and have no sense or, in this case, no respect for the value of the words. Sometimes, they appear to live in a sort of existential dislocation from the words they utter. Anglo-Irish is itself a paradox: a strange hybrid, a mixture of seeming disparate elements that shouldn't make sense and yet do.

Not only does O'Casey share a common approach with Joyce, while also looking forward to the nihilism of Beckett, but he also calls to mind the work of another "desecrator" of the English language, one who delighted in use of "parratoxes," the son of a raving patriot and poet, who mocked and jeered the mores of the British and who never hesitated to proclaim his Irish nationalism: Oscar Fingal O'Flahertie Wills Wilde.

> LADY BRACKNELL: . . . Is this Miss Prism a female of repellent aspect, remotely connected with education?
>
> CANON CHASUBLE (*somewhat indignantly*): She is the most cultivated of ladies, and the very picture of respectability.
>
> LADY B.: It is obviously the same person. . . .
>
> (Wilde, 501)

Do Canon Chasuble and Lady Bracknell even speak the same language? This concept of the dubious value of English as a means of proper communication, as a seesaw of sense and nonsense, haunts the Anglo-Irish writer. It is hardly surprising that an Anglo-Irish writer would mock the English use of their native tongue as George Bernard Shaw does in *Pygmalion* or that yet another Irishman would invent a character like Mrs. Malaprop, who in her social aspirations and linguistic desecrations is the progenitor of both Lady Bracknell and Mr. Gallogher. One can perhaps take Wilde's famous aphorism about the Americans and the English being separated by a common language and apply it to the Irish and the English as well.

All in all, this decidedly ambivalent attitude toward English may indeed lead to "joyful experimentation," but it also carries with it less positive elements. To the extent that language influences one's perceptions of self and environment, the Anglo-Irish language — with its twists and turns, with its sense of distrust — has drawn the Irish writer into self-hatred and a sense of failure.

Thematically and linguistically, there is in Anglo-Irish literature a tendency to negativism, to loss and to irony, to disintegration, and to nihilism. Humor may cloud these themes, but looking at Irish literature as a whole, one is drawn time and again to its themes of loss, of vacuity and malaise. One finds it in the cry of Pegeen Mike that concludes Synge's *Playboy:* "I've lost him, the only Playboy of the Western World" and in the dying cry of Bessie in O'Casey's *The Plough and the Stars:* "This is what's afther comin' on me for nursin' you day an' night. . . . I was a fool, a fool, a fool!"

These elements also dominate the works of Beckett and Joyce, in the sense of paralysis that seems to overtake so many of their characters, from the dust that covers Eveline to the sand that almost swallows up Winnie. Even in the *oeuvre* of a single author, there is a sense of entropy, from the unequivocal "yes" of Molly Bloom that concludes *Ulysses* to definite but less positive "the" of *Finnegan's Wake*, from the positive search for meaning in early Beckett to a form of silence and brevity that dominates his later work. Friel, in *Dancing at Lughnasa*, goes so far as to dismiss language in favor of music.

For some, Irish literature is just a literature of words, and while I do not subscribe to that view, there is no doubt that the Irish writer is obsessed with the value of words. The Irish cannot shut up. Language is the last refuge of the scoundrels, Christy Mahon and

Joxer; it is also the last refuge of their creators. But it brings with it strangely discolored clouds. Yeats mourned that he had no "speech but symbol," and Beckett in a sentence with deeper implications and yet Irish at its core remarked, "all words are lies." In the light of this argument, Beckett may be the most Irish of writers, so Irish that he gave up the use of English altogether! He acted as one who inherited a language that came with values that he could not accommodate philosophically or psychologically. In attempting to deal with this issue, he has Watt, the protagonist of the novel of the same name and the last novel he wrote in English, strip words of their inherited value. Unfortunately, Watt takes the argument to its absurd(ist) conclusion and is driven insane by the search for a pure language free of imperialist and traditional connotations. Even a simple pot, much like the "tundish" for Stephen, becomes a source of anxiety: "It was in vain that Watt said, Pot, pot. Well, perhaps not quite in vain but very nearly. For it was not a pot, the more he looked, the more he reflected, the more he felt sure of that, that it was not a pot at all. It resembled a pot, but it was not a pot of which one could say, Pot, pot and be comforted" (81). If "all words are lies," how can one define oneself, since one can only know oneself through language? The solution cludes Watt. Ultimately, he reduces language to gibberish. He inverts and twists it so that it possesses only a passing resemblance to the "mother tongue": "Deen did taw? Tonk. Tog da taw? Tonk. Luf puk saw? Hap! Deen did tub? Ton sparp. Tog da tub? Ton wonk" (166). What sounds like gibberish is actually a play with words. Only when placed against a "mirror-glass darkly" does the meaning become clear: "Wat did need? Knot. Wat ad got? Knot. Was kup ful? Pah! But did need? Praps not. But ad got? Know not." Words are reduced to sounds, stripped of their inherited value, as if starting all over again in the creation of language. This desire to reach beyond the cultural limitations of English into a Platonic kind of language may simply not be possible. It leads Watt to become meaningless and devalued, which is not the most desirable of ends.

Thus Irish writers wear the mask of Janus, pulled between creation and desecration at one and the same time. On the one hand, they react negatively to English, but on the other, as artists, they want to express the integrity of their vision in a language that has value and meaning. It posits a unique dilemma. Usually for the writer, when all else fails, language offers a refuge. The very creation of a piece of writing acts as a bulwark against the despair of a time or a feeling. How can they do this with the tools that have been given them? They realize that they must use English for other purposes, and so their literature pivots on a delicate seesaw of mixed messages.

What then is Irish literature about? It creates a world narrowly escaping from imprisonment, a world poised constantly on the brink of disaster and yet sustained by a comic impulse, the ability to take serious matters and see the humor in them, to undermine their potentially devastating effects through a sense of humor that distances the immediacy and the impact. Indeed, to return to my original argument of many years ago: there is a sheer joy in Irish literature that is unmatched for consistency in other world literatures. From Frank O'Connor to Flann O'Brien, from Brendan Behan to Roddy Doyle, and from Molly Keane to Maeve Binchy, there is a zest and energy that make all the pinings for sense a wonderful trip into no man's land. If there is a skull beneath this mask of Janus, it has the "risus sardonicus," the grim smile of the death mask.

The greatness of Anglo-Irish literature is also in triumphantly claiming English as its own language, free of English imperialism and English doctrines. The Irish revolution gives the English back their language transformed in such a way that they cannot claim it as their own.

And it is a commentary on Anglo-Irish life that this "desecration" continues. A few years back when Ron Hutchinson's play *Rat in the Skull*, an unrelenting examination of the conflict in Northern Ireland, was presented at the Royal Court in London, the audience found in the playbill a glossary of terms that explained the new words and phrases that had arisen over the twenty years since the "troubles" began. The struggle continues, and possibly our only solace for this current Irish agony is that once again it gives the impetus to a new flourishing in this strange and strong language we call "Anglo-Irish."

Notes

1. For this reason, a number of important Anglo-Irish writers, including Yeats, who came from a different social class, do not fit into what I have termed the Irish Great Tradition.

2. She continues: "English is a Christian language. When I write English, I live in Christendom." This comment of the distinctive flavor of a language and its nuances further illustrates our problem here.

3. A similar question could arise as to whether an Arab living in Israel could write effectively in Hebrew, given the modern history of Arab and Jew. Could the Arab writer use a language replete with historical and religious assumptions and beliefs that would most probably not mesh with his or her own self-definition or national and religious history?

4. Katherine Anne Porter's response to this use of language is worth noting in this context. She suggests that these writers "hate English and are trying to destroy it" (quoted in Irving Howe's *World of Our Fathers*, New York: Harcourt, 1976, 588).

References

Atlas, James. 1977. *Delmore Schwartz: The Life of an American Poet*. New York: Avon.

Beckett, Samuel. 1970. *Watt*. New York: Grove.

Bliss, Alan J. 1977. "The Emergence of Modern English Dialects in Ireland." In *The English Language in Ireland*, ed. Diarmaid O'Muirithe. Dublin: Mercer.

Friel, Brian. 1968. *Three Plays*. New York: St. Martin's.

Henry, P. L. 1977. "Anglo-Irish and Its Irish Background." In *The English Language in Ireland*, ed. Diarmaid O'Muirithe. Dublin: Mercer.

Howe, Irving. 1976. *World of Our Fathers*. New York: Harcourt.

Joyce, James. 1968. *A Shorter Finnegan's Wake*. Anthony Burgess, ed. London: Faber & Faber.

———. 1976. *Portrait of the Artist as a Young Man*. New York: Penguin.

McCrum, Robert, William Cran, and Robert MacNeil. 1986. *The Story of English*. New York: Elizabeth Sifton Books, Viking.

Mueller, Claus. 1973. *The Politics of Communication*. New York: Oxford UP.

O'Brien, Flann. 1973. *Stories and Plays*. London: Hart-Davis, MacGibbon.

O'Casey, Sean. 1968. *Three Plays*. New York: St. Martin's.

Ozick, Cynthia. 1977. *Bloodshed and Three Novellas*. New York: New American Library.

Synge, J. M. 1911. *Playboy of the Western World: A Comedy in Three Acts*. Boston: J. W. Luce.

Wilde, Oscar. 1981. "The Importance of Being Earnest." In *The Portable Oscar Wilde*, ed. Richard Aldington and Stanley Weintraub, 430–507. New York: Penguin Books, Viking.

"You gone have to learn to talk right" Linguistic Deference and Regional Dialect in Harry Crews's *Body*

In a survey of uses of nonstandard language in English literature, N. F. Blake (1981) suggests that dialect can be represented by manipulating spelling, vocabulary, or syntax, of which, Blake says, "the former is the most important" (15). The assumption that regional and social variation has primarily to do with differences in pronunciation, and secondarily with differences in lexicon and grammar, underlies most scholarship on literary representations of regionally and socially marked speech. Literary dialectologists have focused almost exclusively on phonological, lexical, morphological, and syntactic features of nonstandard varieties, with by far the most emphasis on the spelling strategies by which dialect pronunciation is indicated. Raymond Chapman (1989), for example, echoes many students of dialect in literature in saying that "once a system of orthography has been established in a language, it is not difficult to give some impression of dialect in writing" (165), suggesting that literary dialect consists primarily of respellings that represent marked phonology. Chapman also approvingly cites Stubbs's description of dialect as "an amalgam of syntax and lexis" (Stubbs 1980, 125) — a somewhat different way of defining the field, but a common one, too. Leech and Short's (1981) textbook focuses on pronunciation, syntax, and lexis; and Burkett's (1978) bibliography,

American English Dialects in Literature, lists works dealing with only these aspects of nonstandardness. To give one recent example of such a study, Toolan's (1990) list of features of "low-prestige non-standard speech" in Faulkner's *Go Down, Moses* includes five grammatical items and two respellings.

But literary fiction also often represents features of dialect that have to do with discourse structure and style. To mark narrators and characters as speaking in dialect, writers may, in addition to or instead of respellings or nonstandard lexis or syntax, use such things as nonstandard or regionally marked patterns of cohesion, forms of reference and address, strategies of politeness, and discourse markers. Features such as these are often more responsible for the regional and social speech stereotypes on which writers draw than are differences in pronunciation or grammar, and their representation in fiction may convey as much about character, setting, and culture as do traditionally studied dialect respellings and nonstandard grammatical usages. Yet despite much work by literary theorists on the pragmatics of literature (e.g., Booth's [1961] *Rhetoric of Fiction*) and by stylisticians on linguistic pragmatics as represented in literature (e.g., Hickey's [1989] collection, *The Pragmatics of Style*), we have not yet paid much attention to the pragmatic aspects of dialect.

In this chapter I want to show how attention to discourse-level aspects of regional variation can enrich the analysis of literary uses of dialect.[1] I will do so by examining the representation of the speech of lower-class, rural white Southern Americans in Harry Crews's 1990 novel *Body.* I will show that Crews represents class and region in his characters' speech with elements on all levels. He manipulates spelling to represent nonstandardness both in conventional ways and in ways that capture specifically regional pronunciations, and his characters employ nonstandard and specifically Southern morphology and syntax. Most interesting, though, are the representations of discourse-level aspects of Southern white folk speech in Crews's novel. Whether or not *Body* turns out to be a work of lasting literary merit, describing the range of strategies its author uses to represent regional speech patterns will, I hope, encourage other literary dialectologists to broaden their focus from the traditional concern with nonstandard spelling and grammar to a wider conception of literary dialect.

I begin with a passage that exemplifies some of the features I will discuss. *Body*'s central character is Shereel, a young woman from Waycross, Georgia, who is a contender for the Ms. Cosmos title at a bodybuilding competition in Miami. Members of her family — parents, sister, two brothers, and fiancé — travel to Miami for the occasion, where, provincial and uneducated, they are pathetically, hilariously, and menacingly out of place. The day before the contest, they meet Billy Bat, a bodybuilder from Tennessee who shares their Cracker values and ways of talking and becomes smitten with sister Earline. From Billy, they learn how the competition will proceed.

> "I know more'n you think I know, and I can at least tell you how the Cosmos works," said Billy Bat, "if you'll just slow down with that bottle. Ain't no use me talking to a drunk."
>
> Nail passed the bottle carefully to Fonse, looked off for a moment at the horizon, and then back to Billy Bat. "You gone marry into the Turnipseed family, you gone have to learn not to be a asshole. You gone have to learn to talk right for starters."
>
> "I come from the same part of the country you do, old son," said Billy Bat, shifting on his heels. "I'll talk any damn way I please."
>
> "We may have to go into that another time," said Nail.
>
> "We can talk about it any time you want," Billy Bat said.
>
> "Didn't say nothing about talking, said we'd go into it."
>
> "Any time, any place," Billy Bat said.
>
> Alphonse, who had been following the talk with his good ear, put his elbow into Nail's ribs hard, and wheezed a laugh before he slapped his own knees with both hands. "Damn if I don't believe I like this boy." (209–10)

Apart from the conventional eye-dialect spelling "more'n" (which represents the sound of casual speech in any variety of English and thus indicates nonstandardness but not region), there is only one respelling in this passage, "gone" representing the Southern /gɔn/ future-tense marker. There is a characteristically Southern form of negative concord in "Ain't no use me talking to a drunk." Subject pronouns are deleted in "Didn't say nothing about talking, said we'd go into it," and "a asshole" employs nonstandard article morphology.

It is not just these features that give these characters' speech its regional flavor, though. A large part of what makes the dialogue seem Southern is its elaborate indirect formality. The conversation is a series of careful, hedged, ritualistic suggestions and threats, phrased in conditional structures ("if you'll just slow down with that bottle"; "[If] You gone marry into the Turnipseed family you gone have to learn not to be a asshole") and evidential constructions such as *I don't believe* ("Damn if I don't believe I like this boy"). Nail's indirect "We may have to go into that another time" and "Didn't say nothing about talking" and Bat's tactical use of the address form "old son" to remind Nail of their relative status also contribute to the ritually menacing tone of the exchange. Though none of these features is exclusively Southern, their juxtaposition and frequency in talk like this are typical of the speech of people like these characters. In one way or another — though never systematically — elaborate displays of linguistic civility, sometimes double-edged as in the passage above, have often been noted among rural Southern men and women.

Perhaps one reason for the lack of attention to literary representations of discourse-level features of dialect is that research about regional, ethnic, or social-class variation in discourse structure and style is fairly recent and still, for most groups, fairly sparse. By "discourse structure" I mean the grammar of units larger than sentences and the closely related issue of cohesion (Halliday and Hasan 1976), as well as discourse-marking strategies (Schiffrin 1987) by which speakers show, as they produce talk or writing, how it is to be interpreted. "Discourse style" consists of typical choices for expressing linguistic politeness (Brown and Levinson 1987) in general and for performing specific speech acts: requesting, persuading, narrating, and so on. Scholarship about the discourse style of African Americans has the longest tradition, beginning with work by Abrahams (1962; 1976) and Kochman (1972) on such speech events as signifying, hoorawing, and styling out. Kochman (1981) describes African Americans' speech styles in aggressive talk, boasting, flirting, and handling accusations and personal information; Labov (1972a) compares lower- and middle-class blacks' expository style and (1972b) discusses teenage boys' personal narratives; Erikson (1984) describes the structure of boys' conversations; and Gumperz (1982, 187–203) analyzes African-American political oratory. Tannen (1981; 1984) shows how the interactional style of New York Jews is characterized in such features as the tendency to tolerate only very brief pauses in conversation and to ask rapid-fire personal questions to demonstrate friendly solidarity. Reissman (1988) talks about Puerto Rican women's narratives, and Johnstone (1990a; 1990b) describes how white Midwesterners construct and use stories, contrasting this population with the urban Northeasterners studied by Polanyi (1985) and others. Bernstein's (1970) work has to do with discourse "elaboration" and "restriction" as correlated with social class in Britain, and Dines (1980) uses the quantitative research methodology developed by students of phonological variation in her analysis of the discourse marker *and stuff like that* in Australian working-class speech. About discourse-level features of Southern white Americans' speech, almost nothing has been written, with the exception of some studies of Southern oratory (Braden 1983; Ross 1989, 138–233) and Heath's (1983) work on language socialization in a working-class Carolina community. This omission occurs despite the fact that longstanding stereotypes about "Southern charm," the "soft" quality of Southern talk, and the indirectness and slowness of Southern speech suggest that Southerners do use speech in ways others find marked, and despite decades of descriptions of Southern phonology, vocabulary, and grammar far too numerous to catalogue. (McMillan and Montgomery [1989] list many of these.)

I turn now to a discussion of how Harry Crews represents the speech of the lower-class white Southerners he depicts in *Body*. Crews has written fifteen published novels and collections of essays, most set in the South. His novels are often peopled with characters from rural Bacon County, Georgia, Crews's own childhood home. The worlds Crews creates can be bizarre or grotesque (the New Orleans sexual underworld in *The Knockout Artist*, for example, or the world of professional bodybuilding in *Body*), but the characters who inhabit them are not caricatures. They speak with real voices, the rural Southerners among them with the same voices Crews depicts in his autobiography (*A Childhood*). To capture these voices, Crews uses all the resources of written English.

Although, as suggested by the excerpt quoted above, Crews manipulates standard spelling less frequently than do some other "dialect" writers, he does so in the same ways. Crews's nonstandard spelling represents several things. Some is "eye-dialect," or partly phonetic spelling of standard speech, as in items like "celbrate," "fambly," "forgit," "I should of known," "innerduced," "innersted," "likker," "ruther," or "TeeVee." Other nonstandard spellings are "allegro forms" (Preston 1985) that represent casual speech forms common to all American dialects. These include contractions such as "told'm," "how's 'at?," "Mr. Bill'n me," and "a lotta." Allegro forms can also represent deletion of unstressed syllables, as in "'bout," "'cause," "'fraid," "prechate," or "zactly," or consonant cluster simplification: "a course," "lemme," or "les" (let's), as well as the common pronunciation of "ing" as /ɪn/ in spellings like "blowin'," "cuttin'," "stayin'," or "wantin'." Other nonstandard spellings actually do represent nonstandard pronunciation. These include a number of individual words — "agin," "Ay-rab," "bidness" (for business), "ceegret," "Cuber/Cuburns," "ever" (every), "everbody," "everday/ever day," "everone," "fee*and*say," "git/gitting," "Jane Fonder," "looka here," "neked," "oncet," "purty/purtiest," "ruint," "shore" (sure), "sumbitch," "summers" (somewhere[s]), "surp" (syrup), "swaller," "this-away," "tobacker," "twicet," and "Veet Nam" — as well as several nonstandard contracted forms: "it'as" or "ittas" for "it was," "cain't," and "that'n" for "that one." Most of these respellings represent Southern pronunciations.[2]

Despite the fact that the novel's rural characters are just educated enough to sound uneducated, Crews employs only one malapropism, *cataronic* for *catatonic*. The dialect vocabulary in the novel includes words and phrases that are nonexistent or infrequent in standard English, as well as standard words with different semantic ranges, different phonological structure, different subcategorization patterns, or different register usage than in other varieties. Southern lexical items include *to ail* (as in "what ails them"), *to light on* (to land on), *menfolk*, *to misdoubt*, *sight* (in "a sight better"), *yonder*, and *youngun*. *If you a mind to*, *cash money*, *to show manners*, *to keep a civil tongue*, *a God's wonder*, *just to be doing* (just for the fun of it), *this day and time* (this day and age), and *x and them* (for a group of associated people) represent nonstandard collocations. Some of these can be attested as Southern forms; others are attested in Southern as well as other varieties of English. Others are not attested in the literature of Southern dialectology and may be Crews's creations.

Standard English words with different phonological structure are *amongst*, *fitting* (fit, as in "fitting to eat"), *hereabouts*, *howsomever*, *near 'bouts*, *somewheres*, *where 'bouts*, and *yeller* (yellow); words with different semantic ranges are *behind* (after), *figure* (seem), *look for* (expect), *old* (familiar; also an intensifier), *rank* (unsophisticated), *sorry* (despicable, pathetic), *study* (be concerned with), and *visit* (chat); and words that take different complementation structures than in standard American English include *to come by* + p.p. ("Come by up here"), *to hush* + v-ing ("Hush talking like that"), *to talk* and *to be wrong* + *on* ("We'll talk more on it later"; "You wrong on that"), *on account of* with a sentential complement ("on account of I ain't had nothing to eat"), and *to set* as an intransitive verb ("a place to set down"). Finally, lexical items that appear in standard English only in elevated, somewhat archaic-sounding registers of speech appear in *Body* in casual talk, as with *at times* (sometimes), *as you will* (as you like, want), *commence* (start), *mean* (intend, plan), or *one day*. Conversely, *daddy* and *mama* or *ma*, which in other varieties of American English are intimate terms used only by children, are used here for address and for reference by adults, in public as well as private situations.

Almost all the nonstandard word-forms in Crews's novel are attested in nonstandard speech. Two have been described as characteristically Southern: the use of *you-all* as the second-person plural pronoun (subject and object), and indefinite article *a* with vowel-initial nouns, as in "a air hose," "a asshole," or "a old man." Other nonstandard morphology includes various function shifts. Standard English adjective forms are used adverbially as in "You always did put things *nice*," a prepositional phrase is used adverbially ("I'm *by God* in control"), and standard adjectives are used nominally as in "*Strange* is just something I think we gone have to get used to hereabouts." Crews's Southern characters usually use singular noun forms after numbers, as in "a girl who can still blush when she's twenty *year* old" or "Well, I did think to lose ten *pound*." Marked pronoun forms include the nonstandard second-person possessive form *you* ("in front of me and you sister") and the reflexive forms *youself, hisself, ourself,* and *theirselves;* the nonstandard demonstrative forms *them* and *this* [*right*] *here;* and the use of the relative pronoun *that* with human antecedents.

Nonstandard verbal morphology includes the use of *ain't* for the negation of *be,* in the first and third person singular ("I ain't in no crisis"; "It ain't something you fall into or out of just to be doing"; "He ain't our kind of people is he?") and in the third person plural ("Ain't none of us wantin' to catch flies"), and for the negation of *have* in the first, second, and third person singular ("I ain't told you"; "You ain't got a degree in Problems of Living, either"; "She ain't forgot us") and in the first person plural ("Well, we ain't see her, have we?"). There are also many nonstandard participial forms ("we ain't *see* her"; "She ain't *forgot* us"; "Everybody here is so *eat* up with the desire to win") and nonstandard preterit forms (all of which are standard past participle forms) as in "I *known* this'd happen," "ever tree I *seen* had a light in it," or "with the name his mama *given* him." *Be* and *do* have nonstandard inflections in the third person: "People *is* a whole lot funnier than you think"; "My family *don't* mess with anyone *don't* mess with them first"; and "But I pointed out to him it *weren't* necessary."

Crews's representations of nonstandard syntax include several features that are sometimes described as exclusively Southern, as well as features characteristic of many nonstandard varieties and features that occur even in standard casual speech. The Southern forms are negative concord with preposed auxiliary verbs, as in "Ain't none of us wantin' to catch flies, Ma," negative concord across clauses, as in "I ain't told you you had to do nothing," deletion of the copula form *are* in equational sentences ("They all some knotty, ain't they?"), and existential *it* as in "It was a time when you known that" or "it ain't nobody making a move to help."

Two kinds of verbal meaning expressed in *Body* that are characteristically Southern are completive *done* ("Me and my knife done give up on need a long time ago"; "I believe this trip is done ruint you disposition") and *a-* prefixed verbs, as in "can we go in a bathing then?" or "light as the wind a blowin'." Other nonstandard syntactic and semantic patterns are found in other varieties of American English as well as Southern speech, but they are also forms that people like Crews's characters would be likely to use.

Having shown that Crews's Southern characters produce words and sentences that rural white Southerners might in fact produce, I turn to an aspect of the literary representation of dialect that has not systematically been examined before. In what follows, I suggest that Crews's characters also *use* words and sentences the way Southerners like them do. The aspects of language use on which I focus have to do with expressing social distinctions and avoiding social imposition. I first discuss the use of terms of address that reflect and define social status in discourse. I then describe strategies for indirectness — for suggesting meanings without fully claiming responsibility for them. I focus in particular on two strategies that seem characteristically Southern: elaborate uses of conditional syntax and frequent expressions of hedging evidentiality.

Terms of address. Crews's Southern characters frequently use terms of address that identify the intended addressee while at the same time expressing the speaker's social relationship to the addressee. The address forms used in the novel are *son, old son, boy, bud, girl, child, Sister Woman, honey, you old honey, you old thing, sir, ma'am,* and expressions formed of *Mr., Miss,* or *Mizz* with a person's first name. The men in the novel use address terms more often than do the women, and they use a wider range of them. Terms used by men can suggest that the speaker has higher status, either in general or in the interaction at hand, as when the father uses *son* in talk to his sons and other young men or when a motel guest says *son* to the bellhop. Social superiority of the addressee is indicated with *sir* and title plus first name; in the book's most extreme example of social rank marking, a young man says, "*Mr. Alphonse, sir,* I have come to ask for your daughter's hand in marriage." Crews is also faithful to Southern tradition in having younger people invariably answer older people's yes/no questions with "Yes, sir, I did," "No sir, I'm not," or "No, ma'am."

Parity in social rank seems not to exist among these men; interaction among potential equals involves constant negotiation for status. Forms of address can serve as provocations, as when a man addresses a rival as *bud;* or they can be more subtle assertions of equal footing, as when an outsider trying to become part of the family addresses the young men in the family as *old son. Girl, child,* and *Sister Woman* are used by men to sisters and girlfriends. By identifying individuals with categories, these terms label women as social inferiors, though they are also terms of endearment.

Just as the men's *son* picks out a social inferior and *old son* makes a claim to equality, so the women use *honey* for inferiors (such as the bellhop), and *old honey* or *old thing* to create parity — though in the women's case parity is tinged with endearment, and in the men's case parity is tinged with animosity. The women do not use *boy, child,* or *brother* for men. Like the men, the women use *sir* and *ma'am* to elders.

For terms of address as for the grammatical markings of Southernness discussed above, Crews's ear seems to be good, at least according to the anecdotal evidence about Southern discourse style, all that is currently available. Their constant awareness of social rank and the linguistic forms by which they express this awareness are an important part of what makes Crews's characters seem Southern.

Conditional indirectness. Crews's characters almost never express a proposition in such a way as to take full responsibility for it. So, for example, when a mother tells her husband to stand behind their daughter in a crisis, the father responds with "I never let a youngun of mine down yet," a general assertion rather than a specific commitment to help. People asking personal questions point out that they "don't mean to pry"; a young man requests dessert by saying to his father, "Wisht you'd thought to tell [the bellboy] to bring back a little chocolate ice cream."

Indirectness like this has two effects. First, it mitigates speech acts. Indirectness hedges the speaker's bet; if it turns out that a claim was wrong, a request denied, or a commitment not met, the speaker is not automatically embarrassed. Thus indirectness helps protect one's own social position. Second, indirectness expresses deference to one's addressee. It allows the addressee to save face if forced to contradict or refuse. Indirectness is part of a "politeness strategy" (Brown and Levinson 1987) based on acknowledgment of one's own and one's addressee's need for independence, distance, and respect. It is the obviously appropriate strategy in the world of the Southern characters in *Body*, who are acutely or, as one reviewer of the novel put it, "murderously" aware of their own and others' social status at every moment (Weldon 1990).

Crews's characters are indirect in a variety of ways, but one of the most striking, because of its frequency, is the use of conditional syntax. Assertions can be phrased in *if-then* form ("And if he's breathing, I shore cain't tell it"; "If I ever seen a ruint gene, I'm lookin' at it right now"; "I'd think that whiskey'd be a trifle hot"), as can suggestions ("There'll be trouble if you can't learn to keep a civil tongue about my family"; "You gone marry into the Turnipseed family, you gone have to learn not to be a asshole"). The *if I were you* format, sometimes with the *if* clause elided, is especially favored for orders and threats,[3] as when a man remarks to a rival, "Now if I was you and I was standing in front of a man holding a ten-inch blade I'd shut the fuck up while he was trying to talk about blood," or in this conversation between a man and his fiancée, who is threatening to castrate him:

> "*If you don't look out, you gone shake me dickless,* tremble us right on into a trick of shit we neither one'll ever git out of. That ain't the sort of knife you can hold and tremble."
>
> "It's something to think about then, isn't it? You thinking, Nail? You thinking about it? Because *if I was you, I'd think.*"
>
> "*That's what you would do if you was me, is it?*"
>
> "*That's what I'd do. I'd rethink the whole thing.*" (113)

Formulaic conditional structures such as *if you a mind to, if you could be good enough,* or *I'd take it as a personal kindness if* often mitigate requests; and *if you don't mind my saying so* or *damned if I don't think* can hedge potentially threatening observations.

Conditional syntax is deferential. Conditional sentences create distance between the speaker and the meaning, and they give the hearer the option, in theory, of denying the proposition expressed in the *if* clause and hence denying the rest. In this way, conditional syntax can mitigate potential social impositions. Its use reflects a heightened awareness of social distinctions and is appropriate in a situation in which threat and imposition are always immanent, and always socially dangerous.

Evidentials. The characters' utterances often include predicates such as *believe, reckon, think, guess, have the feeling,* and so on: "evidential" predicates that express the speaker's mode of knowledge (Chafe and Nichols 1986). These occur in the first person in assertions ("You already said that once *I believe*"; "*I don't think* they our kind of people"; "Might be catching *for all I know*"; "*I wouldn't want to guess,* but *I have the feeling* we'll know soon enough"), and in the second person in questions ("*You reckon* we ought to get help?" "What *do you think* made them grow them knots?"). *Reckon* is the most common evidential predicate in questions, *don't believe* in assertions.

Evidentials are required in many genres of discourse, and they are not, of course, exclusively Southern (although the verb *reckon* is nonstandard in American English, and the expression *I don't believe* with a sentential complement is uncommon). What is striking is their frequency and their specific function in these Southern characters' speech.

In only two of the hundreds of utterances in the novel that include evidential predicates do the evidentials express speakers' complete security in their knowledge: *"One thing's for sure,* he cain't last much longer like he is," and "Now *I know* that is right for a dead solid fact." Evidentials are overwhelmingly in the negative (*I don't believe, I don't misdoubt, I don't guess, I can't say as, I don't know as*), and/or conditional (*I wouldn't know about, I'd say*), and when they are not, the semantics of the predicates expresses uncertainty (*think, believe, have the feeling, strike someone as, expect, seem, make x to be, look to be*). In other words, with the two exceptions mentioned above, the evidential predicates invariably have the effect of hedging assertions and allowing respondents to hedge theirs. Characters say what they believe to be true and describe how things seem to be rather than telling what they know and how things are.

Like conditionals, evidentials leave space between speakers and the meaning of their utterances. By hedging assertions, evidentials protect speakers from the social embarrassment that would result if the assertion turned out to be false. They are also deferential. Speakers who hedge assertions avoid imposing their version of the world on others. Hedged assertions are not, literally, claims about how the world is, but only claims about how the speaker sees it.

Hedging has long been seen as a linguistic correlate of powerless-ness (Lakoff 1975; O'Barr and Atkins 1980): speakers who fail to assert authority of knowledge put themselves, it is thought, in an inferior position. Crews's characters certainly appear powerless when they converse, in their conditional- and evidential-laden way, with characters from elsewhere. When the Southerners talk among themselves, though, their hedging may be deferential, but it is certainly not powerless. Evidentials protect speakers' and hearers' social personas.

Harry Crews gets Southern speech right on all levels. This accuracy is crucial to how his novel works. If Crews's Southern characters' speech were marked only by nonstandard vocabulary, word-formation patterns, syntax, and semantics, the characters would seem Southern only in an unauthentic, parodic way. Crews uses these characters to portray the grotesque results of rural isolation and ignorance. But they are not just caricatures; they come across as thinking, feeling, endearing people, strongly rooted in place. This is in large measure because they *use* talk in a believable way.

The sociolinguistic stereotypes that novelists strive to evoke by having characters speak in dialect have as much to do with how people in different social groups use language as with the sounds and structures they produce. Nonlinguists speak vaguely about regional "drawls" or "twangs" and are only rarely aware of grammatical differences among regional dialects (and then their knowledge is often faulty: Northerners in the United States, for example, might be able to identify *y'all* as a Southern speech feature, but they are likely to think it has exclusively singular reference). Stereotypes of regional discourse styles, on the other hand, though not much more factual, are much more readily available. Northeasterners, to others, "talk fast" and seem pushy, aggressive, overly direct, or even rude; Midwesterners seem matter-of-fact in speech; Southerners seem slow, quiet, indirect, and genteel. (One such description of just the group of Southerners Crews depicts is that of novelist Marjorie Kinnan Rawlings: "The Cracker speech is soft as velvet, low as the rush of running branch water" [quoted in Burkett 1978, 60].) It should not be surprising to find that novelists with good ears for dialect make use of discourse-level aspects of regional speech; one might in fact suppose that a novelist would have more to gain by doing so than by getting the sounds and sentence structures right.

A regional or social dialect is not simply a set of nonstandard words and rules for pronunciation and grammar. It is also a set of strategies and norms for language use, rooted in local culture. The study of dialect in literature could be enriched by more systematic work on the dialectology of discourse.

Notes

1. Students in my fall 1990 seminar in linguistics and literature got me started thinking about this issue, and a helpful audience at the Southeastern Conference on Linguistics Spring 1991 meeting encouraged me to continue with it. Kathleen Ferrara and Judith Bean commented on an earlier draft, and Jeutonne Brewer provided bibliographic help. I am grateful to all.

2. Sources for claims about Southern speech, here and elsewhere, are Feagin (1979), Wolfram (1981), Wolfram and Christian (1976), Wolfram and Fasold (1974), and Pederson et al. (1972). Some of the features I identify as Southern are of course found elsewhere in the United States, in the speech of African Americans. With respect to phonology, morphology, and syntax, African American Vernacular English is very similar to Southern white varieties. Crews's characters in *Body* are "Crackers" from southern Georgia, members of a group that moved to the Lower South from the mountains farther north and west (McWhiney 1988). Their speech — if it is an accurate representation of the speech of nonfictional Crackers — can be expected to include linguistic features from the South Midland area as well as Lower Southern features. I use "Southern" broadly, to include both.

3. I examine the mechanism by which indirectness can be threatening, with reference to the male characters in *Body*, in a 1992 *SECOL Review* article. Parts of the current study are adapted from that essay.

References

Abrahams, Roger D. 1962. "Playing the Dozens." *Journal of American Folklore* 75:209–18.

———. *Talking Black.* 1976. Rowley, Mass.: Newbury.

Bernstein, Basil. 1970. *Class, Codes and Control Vol. 1: Theoretical Studies towards a Sociology of Language.* New York: Routledge.

Blake, N. F. 1981. *Non-Standard Language in English Literature.* London: Deutsch.

Booth, Wayne C. 1961. *The Rhetoric of Fiction.* Chicago: U of Chicago P.

Braden, Waldo W. 1983. *The Oral Tradition in the South.* Baton Rouge: Louisiana State UP.

Brown, Penelope, and Stephen C. Levinson. 1987. *Politeness: Some Universals in Language Usage*. Cambridge: Cambridge UP.

Burkett, Eva M. 1978. *American English Dialects in Literature*. Metuchen, N.J.: Scarecrow.

Chafe, Wallace, and Johanna Nichols. 1986. *Evidentiality: The Linguistic Coding of Epistemology*. Norwood, N.J.: Ablex.

Chapman, Raymond. 1989. "The Reader as Listener: Dialect and Relationships in *The Mayor of Casterbridge*." In *The Pragmatics of Style*, ed. Leo Hickey, 159–78. New York: Routledge.

Crews, Harry. 1978. *A Childhood: The Biography of a Place*. New York: Harper.

———. 1988. *The Knockout Artist*. New York: Harper.

———. 1990. *Body*. New York: Poseidon.

Dines, Elizabeth. 1980. "Variation in Discourse — 'And Stuff like That.'" *Language in Society* 9:13–31.

Erikson, Frederick. 1984. "Rhetoric, Anecdote, and Rhapsody: Coherence Strategies in a Conversation among Black American Adolescents." In *Coherence in Spoken and Written Discourse*, ed. Deborah Tannen, 81–154. Norwood, N.J.: Ablex.

Feagin, Crawford. 1979. *Variation and Change in Alabama English*. Washington, D.C.: Georgetown UP.

Gumperz, John J. 1982. *Discourse Strategies*. Cambridge: Cambridge UP.

Halliday, M. A. K., and Ruqaiya Hasan. 1976. *Cohesion in English*. London: Longman.

Heath, Shirley Brice. 1983. *Ways with Words: Language, Life, and Work in Communities and Classrooms*. Cambridge: Cambridge UP.

Hickey, Leo, ed. 1989. *The Pragmatics of Style*. New York: Routledge.

Johnstone, Barbara. 1990a. *Stories, Community, and Place: Narratives from Middle America*. Bloomington: Indiana UP.

———. 1990b. "Variation in Discourse: Midwestern Narrative Style." *American Speech* 63:195–214.

———. 1992. "Violence and Civility in Discourse: Uses of Mitigation by Rural Southern Men." *The SECOL Review* 16:1–19.

Kochman, Thomas, ed. 1972. *Rappin' and Stylin' Out*. Urbana: U of Illinois P.

———. 1981. *Black and White Styles in Conflict*. Chicago: U of Chicago P.

Labov, William. 1972a. "The Logic of Nonstandard English." In *Language in the Inner City*, 201–40. Philadelphia: U of Pennsylvania P.

————. 1972b. "The Transformation of Experience in Narrative Syntax." In *Language in the Inner City*, 354–96. Philadelphia: U of Pennsylvania P.

Lakoff, Robin. 1975. *Language and Woman's Place*. New York: Harper.

Leech, Geoffrey N., and Michael H. Short. 1981. *Style in Fiction: A Linguistic Introduction to English Fictional Prose*. London: Longman.

McMillan, James B., and Michael B. Montgomery. 1989. *Annotated Bibliography of Southern American English*. Tuscaloosa: U of Alabama P.

McWhiney, Grady. 1988. *Cracker Culture: Celtic Ways in the Old South*. University: U of Alabama P.

O'Barr, William M., and Bowman K. Atkins. 1980. "'Women's Language' or 'Powerless Language'?" In *Women and Language in Literature and Society*, ed. Sally McConnell-Ginet, Ruth Borker, and Nelly Furman, 93–110. New York: Praeger.

Pederson, Lee, Raven I. McDavid, Jr., Charles W. Foster, and Charles E. Billiard, eds. 1972. *A Manual for Dialect Research in the Southern States*. University: U of Alabama P.

Polanyi, Livia. 1985. *Telling the American Story: A Structural and Cultural Analysis of Conversational Storytelling*. Norwood, N.J.: Ablex.

Preston, Dennis R. 1985. "The Li'l Abner Syndrome: Written Representations of Speech." *American Speech* 60:328–37.

Reissman, Catherine Kohler. 1988. "Worlds of Difference: Contrasting Experience in Marriage and Narrative Style." In *Gender and Discourse: The Power of Talk*, ed. Alexandra Dundas Todd and Sue Fisher, 151–73. Norwood, N.J.: Ablex.

Ross, Stephen M. 1989. *Fiction's Inexhaustible Voice: Speech and Writing in Faulkner*. Athens: U of Georgia P.

Schiffrin, Deborah. 1987. *Discourse Markers*. Cambridge: Cambridge UP.

Stubbs, Michael. 1980. *Language and Literacy*. New York: Routledge.

Tannen, Deborah. 1981. "New York Jewish Conversational Style." *International Journal of the Sociology of Language* 30:133–49.

————. 1984. *Conversational Style: Analyzing Talk among Friends*. Norwood, N.J.: Ablex.

Toolan, Michael J. 1990. *The Stylistics of Fiction: A Literary-Linguistic Approach*. New York: Routledge.

Weldon, Fay. 1990. "A Single Shining Muscle of a Girl." Review of *Body*, by Harry Crews. *The New York Times Book Review* 9 Sept., 14.

Wolfram, Walt. 1981. "Varieties of American English." In *Language in the USA*, ed. Charles A. Ferguson and Shirley Brice Heath, 44–68. Cambridge: Cambridge UP.

Wolfram, Walt, and Donna Christian. 1976. *Appalachian English.* Washington, D.C.: Center for Applied Linguistics.

Wolfram, Walt, and Ralph W. Fasold. 1974. *The Study of Social Dialects in American English.* New York: Prentice-Hall.

Contributors

CYNTHIA GOLDIN BERNSTEIN is associate professor of English Linguistics at Auburn University. She edited the Summer 1990 special issue of *South Central Review* on linguistic approaches to literature and is currently researching social and regional causes of language variation.

MASHEY BERNSTEIN, a native of Ireland, graduated with honors in English from Trinity College, Dublin. He lectures in the Program in Composition at the University of California, Santa Barbara.

EWING CAMPBELL, associate professor of English at Texas A&M University, was the 1992 Ralph A. Johnston Creative Writing Fellow at the University of Texas at Austin. His research interests include modern literature and theory.

WILLIAM S. CHISHOLM, professor of English at Cleveland State University, has recently become editor of *Dictionaries*, the journal of the Dictionary Society of North America. His main research interest is cohesion.

MARY JANE CHILTON CURRY, a doctoral student at Auburn University, is writing a dissertation on Jane Austen's use of pastoral modes in politeness conventions, narrative voice, and setting. At the Sixth International Conference on English Historical Linguistics in

Helsinki, she presented a paper on periphrastic *do* in the writings of Jane Austen.

JANET M. ELLERBY is assistant professor of English at the University of North Carolina at Wilmington. She is interested in the links between authors and the narrators of their fictional autobiographies.

B. A. FENNELL, associate professor of English at North Carolina State University, has presented papers on the relationship between sociolinguistic theory and literary analysis. She is writing a book on the language of immigrant workers in Germany.

JUNE M. FRAZER is professor of English at Western Illinois University. She coedited a book with Roanald Walker on detective fiction and contemporary literary theory and has written articles and reviews on Jane Austen, Virginia Woolf, and Alison Lurie.

TIMOTHY C. FRAZER, professor of English at Western Illinois University, has published a monograph on dialect patterns of Midland Illinois, as well as articles and reviews on language variation in midwestern United States.

KAREN A. HOHNE is assistant professor at Moorhead State University. Her research involves the interaction of language and ideology in texts. She is presently coediting a collection of essays on feminism and Bakhtin.

BARBARA JOHNSTONE, associate professor of linguistics at Texas A&M University, has published numerous articles on discourse analysis. She has written books on narrative discourse and repetition in discourse. Currently she is researching Southern discourse features, especially in literature.

MELISSA MONROE is associate professor at the Berklee College of Music. She is working on a study of Kafka's "Der Bau" and translating the contemporary Austrian poet Ernst Herbeck.

REI R. NOGUCHI is professor of English at California State University, Northridge. He has published articles on fictional conversation and other aspects of literary linguistics. He is also the author of *Grammar and the Teaching of Writing: Limits and Possibilities*.

MARY GOMEZ PARHAM is associate professor of Spanish at the University of Houston–Downtown. She has published widely in Latin American literature and is especially interested in Central American literature.

JOYCE TOLLIVER teaches in the Department of Spanish, Italian, and Portuguese at the University of Illinois in Urbana. She has published in *Style, Hispania,* and *Revista de Estudios Hispánicos.* She is preparing a book-length manuscript on feminine double-voicing in Pardo Bazán, which draws heavily on linguistic discourse analysis.

NANCY O. WILHELMI is associate professor of English at Louisiana State University in Shreveport, where she is director of general studies. She has recently published an article on Tennessee Williams in the *Tennessee Williams Literary Journal* and is currently doing research using the Tennessee Williams manuscripts at the University of Texas at Austin.

Index